INTELLIGENCE AND
PRIVATE INVESTIGATION

INTELLIGENCE AND PRIVATE INVESTIGATION

Developing Sophisticated Methods
for Conducting Inquiries

Edited by

HANK PRUNCKUN, Ph.D.

Charles Sturt University

(With 10 Other Contributors)

CHARLES C THOMAS • PUBLISHER, LTD.
Springfield • Illinois • U.S.A.

Published and Distributed Throughout the World by

CHARLES C THOMAS • PUBLISHER, LTD.
2600 South First Street
Springfield, Illinois 62704

© 2013 by CHARLES C THOMAS • PUBLISHER, LTD.

ISBN 978-0-398-08888-0 (paper)
ISBN 978-0-398-08889-7 (ebook)

Library of Congress Catalog Card Number: 2013007335

With THOMAS BOOKS *careful attention is given to all details of manufacturing
and design. It is the Publisher's desire to present books that are satisfactory as to their
physical qualities and artistic possibilities and appropriate for their particular use.*
THOMAS BOOKS *will be true to those laws of quality that assure a good name
and good will.*

*Printed in the United States of America
SM-R-3*

Library of Congress Cataloging-in-Publication Data

Intelligence and private investigation : developing sophisticated methods for
conducting inquiries / edited by Hank Prunckun, Ph. D., Charles Sturt University (with 10 other contributors).
        pages cm
Includes bibliographical references and index.
ISBN 978-0-398-08888-0 (pbk.) -- ISBN 978-0-398-08889-7 (ebook)
    1. Private investigators. 2. Investigations. 3. Intelligence service. 4. Criminal
investigation. I. Prunckun, Henry W. editor of compilation.

HV8081.I53 2013
363.28'9--dc23
                                                                                    2013007335

ABOUT THE EDITOR AND CONTRIBUTORS

EDITOR

Dr. Hank Prunckun, BSc, MSocSc, PhD, is Associate Professor of Intelligence Analysis at the Australian Graduate School of Policing and Security, Charles Sturt University, Sydney. He specializes in the study of transnational crime – espionage, terrorism, drugs and arms trafficking, and cyber-crime. He is the author of numerous reviews, articles, chapters, and books, including: *Counterintelligence Theory and Practice* (Rowman & Littlefield, 2012); *Handbook of Scientific Methods of Inquiry for Intelligence Analysis* (Scarecrow Press, 2010); *Shadow of Death: An Analytic Bibliography on Political Violence, Terrorism, and Low-Intensity Conflict* (Scarecrow Press, 1995); *Special Access Required: A Practitioner's Guide to Law Enforcement Intelligence Literature* (Scarecrow Press, 1990); and *Information Security: A Practical Handbook on Business Counterintelligence* (Charles C Thomas, 1989). He is the winner of two literature awards and a professional service award from the International Association of Law Enforcement Intelligence Analysts, and is associate editor of the *Australian Institute of Professional Intelligence Officers Journal* and the *International Association of Law Enforcement Intelligence Analysts Journal.* Dr Prunckun has served in a number of strategic research and tactical intelligence capacities within the criminal justice system during his twenty-eight year operational career, including almost five years as a senior counterterrorism policy analyst during the Global War on Terror. In addition, he has held a number of operational postings in investigation and security. Dr Prunckun is also a licensed private investigator and a radio engineer.

CONTRIBUTORS

Tony Buffett, BSc, MJus, is a Lecturer of Intelligence at the Australian Graduate School of Policing and Security, Charles Sturt University, Sydney. His research specialization is in tactical and strategic intelligence. Mr. Buffett served in the Australian Defense Force for twenty-six years, predominantly in the fields of policing, security, and counterintelligence. He has also served in both Australian state and federal governments in such capacities as protective security advisor, security risk management consultant, and finally as the Manager of Intelligence Collection and Liaison with the Australian Customs Service. Mr. Buffett is currently completing his doctorate in policing and security.

Mark S. Bradley holds a BA (Hons) in Organizational Studies. He is a former British Police Officer who served for 32 years before retiring at the rank of Detective Chief Superintendent. During his operational career he served as chief of the Anti-Corruption and Professional Standards Command, a position he held for over eight years. He was in charge of corruption investigation and prevention as well as the gatekeeper for the ethical standards. He was also the Vice Chair of the United Kingdom Association of Chief Police Officers Counter-Corruption Advisory Group. He has over fifteen years' experience in the field of anti-corruption having held international posting in Australia, Azerbaijan, Cyprus, Germany, Greece, India, Kosovo, Latvia, Palestine, Poland, Serbia, Turkey, the United States, and Albania where he lived for over two years as anti-corruption advisor to the State Police and Ministry of Interior. Mr. Bradley is an accredited Senior Investigating Officer and has also completed the Senior Course in Criminology at Cambridge University England. As an accredited Senior Investigating Detective, he also had the responsibility for conducting national external police force inquiries, primarily into allegations of corruption, and deaths involving police. He has been Senior Investigating Officer on a number of United Kingdom national corruption inquiries and has acted as adviser to a number of United Kingdom government projects.

Michael Chesbro, BSc, MA, is a criminal intelligence specialist with the U.S. Department of the Army. His operational career spanned over twenty years, serving in the U.S. Army as a radio communications specialist as well as a counterintelligence special agent. He is the author of numerous books, including: *Save Your Identity: ID Theft Awareness, Prevention and Recovery* (Paladin Press, 2004), *Communications for Survival & Self-Reliance* (Paladin Press, 2003), *The Privacy Handbook* (Paladin Press, 2002), *Wilderness Evasion* (Paladin Press, 2002), *Don't Be A Victim: How to Protect Yourself from Hoaxes, Fraud, and Scams* (Loompanics, 2002), *Freeware Encryption & Security Programs* (Paladin Press, 2001), *The Complete Guide to E-Security* (Paladin Press, 2000), *Privacy for Sale* (Paladin Press, 1999). He holds certification as a crime and intelligence analyst (CCIA), and is a certified in homeland security (CHS-III) and intelligence analysis (IAC) with the American Board for Certification in Homeland Security. He is a radio engineer who holds an amateur radio licence, a general Mobile Radio Service license (GMRS), and a Military Amateur Radio Service (MARS) radio license from the U.S. Federal Communications Commission. He is also a licensed private investigator in the U.S. state of Washington. At present, Mr. Chesbro is a candidate for the degree of doctor of philosophy (PhD) at Northcentral University.

Jeff Corkill, MProfSt, is a lecturer at Edith Cowen University, Western Australia. He is a graduate of the Royal Military College and served in the Australian Army for twenty years as an officer in the Australian Intelligence Corps. His post-military career has included appointments as a security and intelligence consult in both, Australia and overseas. Mr. Corkill is a member of the Australian Institute of Professional Intelligence Officers, the International Association for Intelligence Education, and the International Studies Association. His research interests include information and source evaluation, security and risk, as well as security vetting. He is the author of numerous conference papers and journal articles.

Dr. Petrus "Beer" C. Duvenage, PhD, is employed with the State Security Agency, South Africa. Dr. Duvenage is a member of International Advisory Board for the Research Institute for European and American Studies. He completed his PhD in political science at the University of Pretoria, South Africa in 2010. His doctoral dissertation was entitled *Open-Source Environmental Scanning and Risk Assessment in the Statutory Counterespionage Milieu.* This study advanced a conceptual framework for the methodological structuring of open-source environmental scanning when it comes to the identification and assessment of national security espionage risks.

Dr. Rick Sarre, LLB, MA, SJD, is Professor of Law and Criminal Justice and teaches criminology, criminal law, and media law in the School of Law at the University of South Australia. He was educated in Adelaide, Iowa, Ontario, and Canberra. He currently serves as the President-elect of the Australian and New Zealand Society of Criminology and is on the Offenders Aid and Rehabilitation Services Board. In 1997, he taught criminal justice at Graceland University, Iowa, and in 2004 he spent a semester in the Law Department at Umeå University, Sweden as a Visiting Research Fellow. In 2005, he and Dr Tim Prenzler published *The Law of Private Security in Australia* (Thomson Reuters, now in its second edition, 2009).

Rebecca Vogel, BA, MPICT, and is a lecturer in intelligence at the Centre for Policing, Intelligence, and Counterterrorism (PICT) at Macquarie University, Sydney. She specializes in intelligence, national security, and intelligence theory. Prior to receiving her master's degree, she worked for Dun & Bradstreet as a senior business analyst and fraud investigator assessing high-risk businesses. Ms. Mitchell was also a government licensed private investigator in the U.S. state of Wisconsin. She is co-author of a chapter on Australia's emerging national security challenges that appeared in *Asian Transnational Security Challenges: Emerging Trends, Regional Visions* (Ziemke-Dickens and Droogan, Editors; The Council for Asian Transnational Threat Research, 2010). Ms. Mitchell is completing a postgraduate certificate in higher education and is about to start a PhD at Macquarie University. She is a member of the board of the Australian Institute of Professional Intelligence Officers and a member of the Institute's journal editorial board – the *Journal of the Australian Institute of Professional Intelligence Officers.*

Patrick F. Walsh, BA, MSocSc, is Senior Lecturer of Intelligence Analysis at the Australian Graduate School of Policing and Security, Charles Sturt University, Sydney. He is also the course coordinator and discipline head for intelligence studies at the university. He specializes in issues involving transnational security, intelligence reform, and intelligence management. He has written widely on strategic intelligence, intelligence and management including the watershed study entitled *Intelligence and Intelligence Analysis* (Routledge, 2011), which examines thematically intelligence reform across Australia, Canada, New Zealand, United Kingdom, and the United States. Prior to taking up his current academic post, Mr. Walsh was an intelligence analyst who worked in both national security and law enforcement intelligence. Mr. Walsh has been long-standing a board member of the Australian Institute of Professional Intelligence Officers as well as the managing editor of the Institute's journal – the *Australian Institute of Professional Intelligence Officers Journal.*

Levi J. West, BA, MIntSecStud, MPICT, GCNSP, is a lecturer in security and terrorism at the Australian Graduate School of Policing and Security, Charles Sturt University, Canberra, Australian Capital Territory. He has a background in national security research with a specialization in non-traditional security and terrorism problems. He teaches subjects on the social impacts of terrorism and counterterrorism as well as the history and motivators of terrorism. He was a Visiting Fellow teaching terrorism and counterterrorism at the Sardar Vallabhbhai Patel National Police Academy in Hyderabad, India, and has worked in Israel and the Palestinian territories, having been a 2011 Australia Israel Jewish Affairs Council Rambam Israel Fellow. Mr. West was a researcher at the Center for the Study of the Presidency and Congress in Washington, DC in 2006. He is a graduate of the Australian National University's National Security College and Macquarie University's Centre for

Policing, Intelligence, and Counter-Terrorism. He is currently completing a Graduate Diploma in International Law with Melbourne Law School, and a Masters of Letters (MLitt) through the Centre for the Study of Terrorism and Political Violence at St. Andrews University, Scotland. Mr. West plans to begin his PhD studies in 2013.

Dr. Troy Whitford, BA, GradDipEd, MA, PhD, lectures in history and politics in the School of Humanities and Social Sciences, Charles Sturt University, Wagga Wagga, New South Wales. He specializes in political and policy research with a focus on the political and operational tactics of radical nationalist groups in Australia. He is the author of a various reviews, articles, and book chapters that include *All in the Name of Human Rights: Australian Nationalism and Multiculturalism in Nationalism and Human Rights* (Palgrave Macmillan, 2012), *A Political History of National Action: Its fears, Ideas, Tactics and Conflicts* (Rural Society, 2011), "Bush Politics" in *Where the Crows Fly Backwards: Notions of Rural Identity* (Post Pressed, 2010), and *An Ideological Divide: the Nationals Parliamentary Representatives and its Grassroots Membership in The National Party: Prospects for the Great Survivors* (Allen Unwin, 2009). Dr. Whitford also holds a private investigator's licence.

To Isobel, a bright, talented young medical student and government licensed private investigator, who was the inspiration for this book.

PREFACE

Private investigation is the theme of countless novels. The genre is so popular that it has captured the imagination of millions worldwide. This is especially true when it comes to the portrayal of the so-called hard-boiled detectives that have been depicted in stories by legendary writers such as the late Dashiell Hammett. But the reality of private investigation work is often less glamorous than portrayed in novels as private investigators spending long hours poring over records in archives, making field observations, or simply sitting silently observing a location while they wait for their "target" to appear.

Hundreds of books have been written about private investigation work and these include manuals and training texts about how to acquire a private investigator's license, as well as the proliferation of fictional accounts that range from the classic stories by the likes of Raymond Chandler, Mickey Spillane, and James Cain; through to the modern writers including Marcia Muller, Sara Paretsky, and Sue Grafton.

However, this book is different – it does not deal with private investigation from these traditional perspectives. What makes this book different is that it examines how private investigation has grown into an exacting and sophisticated occupation that is an honourable career pursuit. In its totality, private investigation is a multi-billion dollars industry that spans the world. Certainly, its practitioners include some of the hard-boiled types characterized by Hammett, but in the post-9/11 world, private investigation demands sophisticated intelligence methods for conducting inquiries.

This book examines this issue and the way the private investigation industry has evolved over the decades, from what could be said was the watershed period of the 1930s to the present. The book looks at the key issues in what it describes as *private intelligence*. That is, intelligence activities which are practiced by operatives other than law enforcers and operatives employed in national security or the military. So, in the context of private investigation, private intelligence means the skills, ability, and knowledge that a private investigator needs in order to conduct the demanding tasks that have emerged since 9/11.

In order to do this, I have brought together a number of subject area experts who have turned their attention to these issues. Each contributor addresses a key practice issue with regard to private intelligence. More importantly, they do this by couching their discussions in the context of free societies, and in particular, those countries bound together in an intelligence alliance known as *the Five-Eyes* – Australia, Britain, Canada, New Zealand, and the United States.

The book begins with a look at private intelligence and why it is important to present-day private investigation. Chapter 2 is an overview of the topic and they set the scene for an examination of the specific various intelligence issues that follow. These include the skills that are now needed to perform in the post-9/11 world, which, as you will see in Chapter 3, are manifestly different to the skill-set displayed by Hammett's "Continental Op" in, say, *Red Harvest*.

The next eleven chapters take the reader progressively through a number of intelligence-related topics that have direct application to the current investigation environment – for instance, producing target profiles, using open-source intelligence, and conducting political intelligence operations. The post-9/11 private investigator may find him- or herself engaged in the pursuit of domestic terrorists or violent gang members; or tracing clandestine organizations with regard to their illicit financing.

Unlike the period prior to 9/11, private investigators now need to exercise the highest standards of security and hence the chapters on counterintelligence and clandestine communications are included. When the infamous Watergate burglars conducted their private intelligence operations in the early 1970s, their counterintelligence practices were rudimentary and their communications involved passing messages via a number of off-the-shelf Radio Shack TRC100B citizens' band (CB) radios that operated on 27MHz. This meant that anyone who had a radio receiver or radio scanner tuneable to those frequencies could eavesdrop on their conversations. This is not an acceptable practice in today's domestic intelligence environment where not only the operatives' lives would be at risk, but that of their clients, and arguably, the community's well-being.

Unlike Hammett's Continental Op who could conveniently weave his way through legal and ethical issues when pursuing "the truth," the events of 9/11 have left all intelligence practitioners, including private investigators that now practice the craft, with legal and ethical lessons to learn. So, there are chapters on each of these key issues.

Finally, the book contains several features that will appeal to students and instructors of private investigation courses, as well as intelligence subjects at college or university level. These features will also find appeal with the general reader or those who are interested in a self-development study. For instance, each chapter contains a set of key terms and phrases, a number of study questions, and a learning activity. These study aids help readers to consolidate their learning; they offer instructors and professors a way of using the text for classroom instruction, or assigning selective chapters for background readings.

I would like to thank all the contributors for the time and effort they put into thinking about their issue and the way it has impacted on the private investigation industry. They all wrote with passion and dedication in order to illustrate the most important points for the reader. Each contributor is academically well-qualified and a peer-recognized specialist in his or her area (in addition, four were government licensed private investigators). This expertize has added something special to this collection of writings and the reader will no doubt benefit from it. My gratitude goes out to you all – Tony Buffett, Mark Bradley, Mick Chesbro, Jeff Corkill, "Beer" Duvenage, Rick Sarre, Becky Vogel, Patrick Walsh, Levi West, and Troy Whitford.

Hank Prunckun, PhD
Sydney
2013

DISCLAIMER

The information provided in this book is for academic purposes and is not intended as legal advice. Readers need to consult an attorney over questions they may have about legal issues regarding the application of intelligence or investigation methods. Hence, the editor, authors, and publisher will not be held responsible for any loss suffered by any person, or body corporate that is directly, indirectly, or consequentially attributed to reliance on the information provided in this book.

CONTENTS

INTELLIGENCE AND
PRIVATE INVESTIGATION

Chapter 1

PRIVATE INTELLIGENCE
AND INVESTIGATION

Hank Prunckun

INTELLIGENCE-LED INVESTIGATIONS

Repeatedly, it has been argued that the world changed after 9/11. To catalogue all of the changes society has experienced – political, economy, technological, social, and psychological – is pointless as the changes are so numerous and they have become accepted, commonplace and pervasive. Suffice to say that these impacts are most noticeable in the area of security. Take as only one example the impact it has had on air travel – anyone who has flown pre- and post-9/11 knows first-hand the numerous changes to processes and procedures, as well as the techniques and technology now in everyday use to cater for the new risks posed. Inescapably, we live in a post-9/11 world.[1]

But what about private investigation? Has this specialized field of inquiry been impacted? The short answer is "yes" – security is related to private investigation as a complementary function (generally accepted under the concept of "public policing").[2] But how have the events of 9/11 and the subsequent attacks on London, Madrid, Bali, and Mumbai impacted on the practice of private investigation? It will be argued in this anthology that these events have brought about a number of challenges that now require private investigators to use structure thinking methods – intelligence – to meet these challenges. In law enforcement investigation, this is referred to as intelligence-led policing. Intelligence-led means a system where ". . . data analysis and . . . intelligence are pivotal to an objective, decision-making framework. . . ."[3] It is now imperative that private investigators adopt these sophisticated methods.

In order to discuss intelligence in relation to private investigation, we need to first step our way through a few scene-setting topics in the same way sands traverse an hourglass – from the general to the specific. We will first examine the question what is intelligence; we will then look at the types of intelligence that are practiced to understand where private intelligence fits in. From this point we will discuss what we mean by private intelligence before we start to look at private investigation. In this regard, we first describe the theory behind private investigation and how we define it in the context of this book. It is at this juncture that we look specifically at the traditional services offered by private investigators in order to outline the challenges we see for private investigation in an intelligence-led world post-9/11.

WHAT IS INTELLIGENCE

Simply put: intelligence is research conducted in secret. The term distinguishes research conducted as part of an undisclosed operation or project to understand some phenomenon. The reason one would conduct an intelligence operation – that is, a secret operation – as opposed to a research project is that it needs to be kept secret to protect safety of personnel, ensure surprise is not lost, not alert others to the goal being pursued, or any number of other related reasons.

The outcome of an intelligence operation is to be in a position to make decisions that are based on fact and reason, and as such, have some level of probability attached to choosing one option of dealing with a problem or issue over other options. Definitions of intelligence are many and varied, but there essentially four meanings:

1. Actions or processes used to produce knowledge;
2. The body of knowledge thereby produced;[4]
3. Organizations that deal in knowledge (e.g., an intelligence agency); and
4. The reports and briefings produced in the process or by such organizations.[5]

Knowledge in the context of intelligence equates to *insight,* or viewed another way, the ability to *reduce uncertainty.* Insight and certainty offer decision-makers the ability to choose options that enable them to take better control over the "unknown," or stated another way, to understand the subject of their inquiries.

TYPOLOGY OF INTELLIGENCE

There are several types of intelligence that are practiced today – national security intelligence, military intelligence, law enforcement intelligence, corporate or business intelligence, and private intelligence. An explanation of each of these types of intelligence is not necessary. Their names indicate adequately the focus of their interests and suggest the kinds of targets they seek.

However, it is important to note the environments in which these types of practitioners operate can overlap – for example, an investigation into the capability of a terrorist cell may be of interest to local law enforcement agencies as well as to agencies involved in national security, the military, and some private security firms. Moreover, with regard to military intelligence, it is in some cases intimately aligned with national security because it not only informs military commanders of the intent and capabilities of an adversary, but also political leaders who are responsible for authorizing the use of military force and directing strategic military policy.

Five-Eyes

This book will focus on private investigation in what has been termed the *Five-Eyes* countries of Australia, Britain,[6] Canada, New Zealand, and the United States. As these countries are members of an intelligence gathering and sharing allegiance,[7] it was considered appropriate that we discuss private intelligence within the scope of the member countries to this compact.

PRIVATE INTELLIGENCE

What may not be clear from the description of intelligence typologies is an account of what private intelligence might comprise. One could argue that private intelligence is a sub-set of corporate/business intelligence. Others might say that it forms a unique type of intelligence practice deserving of its own category. Regardless of how it may be viewed, private intelligence is the craft of conducting research in secret by individuals and businesses for fee or reward.

Although a cursory glance of private intelligence would lead one to conclude that the craft's practitioners would be private investigators, many, and perhaps most, are not. This is because *intelligence* is about structured thinking – devising research questions, formulating data collection plans, collecting and collating data, and finally analyzing these data items. So, many of those who practice the craft are other than private investigators. Some, for instance, come from backgrounds in policy; some are subject area experts; some might be methodologists; some are data analysts; and so on.

But this is not to say that all of these private intelligence partitioners have policy, analytical, or research backgrounds; some are private investigators. Private investigators have a history of being associated with intelligence work dating back to the beginnings of the industry. Even today, PIs are recruited as "operations officers"[8] in the clandestine services of the Central Intelligence Agency (CIA).[9]

Defined

Private intelligence can be defined as those principles, processes, practices, techniques, and materials used by non-government entities to gather information and analyze these data in secret.[10]

A Few Early Examples

From time to time, businesses and people have a need to conduct inquiries into matters that may fall outside the jurisdiction of law enforcement, or law enforcement does not have the manpower to assist – as in the case of private security augmenting law enforcement. In such cases, the role of the private investigator comes to the fore. The private investigator provides the means for facilitating an inquiry.

In Europe, the first acknowledged private investigation agency was that of *Le Bureau des Renseignements Universels pour le commerce et l'Industrie* (or in English, The Universal Intelligence Department for Trade and Industry).[11] Rather than use the term *investigation* or *detection,* the French company that began service in 1833 used the term *intelligence.* Like its military origin,[12] the term intelligence is used to refer to research that is conducted in secret.[13] And, arguably, secret research is a good description of what investigation involves.

Granted, intelligence involves far more than what investigation entails, but nonetheless, the fact that Europeans (well, at least the French) were thinking along the lines of private intelligence rather than private investigation is an interesting linguistic taxonomy. It is especially interesting in the post-9/11 period, as the expansion of private investigation services has branched into intelligence and counterintelligence.

Like the French who linked private detective work with intelligence, Britain's MI5, which was created in October 1909, began life in the rented offices of the Drew Detective Agency, London.[14] In the United States, the link between private intelligence and detective work was there, too. For instance, Allan Pinkerton was credited for foiling an assassination attempt on President-Elect Abraham Lincoln prior to the outbreak of the Civil War. This assassination attempt later led to him providing a close personal protection service to the President and during the American Civil War, Mr. Pinkerton was hired to provide intelligence to the Union Army.[15] Pinkerton's operatives ". . .were also hired to track western outlaws Jesse James, the Reno Brothers, the Wild Bunch, including Butch Cassidy and the Sundance Kid."[16]

The late-Dashiell Hammett,[17] private detective fiction writer, was himself a former Pinkerton operative and was known for his authenticity and realism in his writing because of this experience.[18] Hammett is said to have drawn on his familiarity of detective work and once proclaimed: "All my characters were based on people I've known personally, or known about."[19]

In the security environment that has been dominated by the events of 9/11, governments now recognize that law enforcement cannot manage to control every threat there is to national security. As such, governments have called for the support of private sector agencies and personnel in a variety of forms – from the concierge who maintains a watchful eye on a city's hotel, to the cadres of licensed security guards who patrol commercial and industrial sites of all descriptions, and all those personnel in between.[20] These security officers play a virtual observe-and-report roll in what is called the Global War on Terror. After all, it was not a Federal Air Marshal, but a group of passengers who exercised their common-law powers of citizen's arrest to subdue terrorists when they tried to take control of United Flight 93 over Pennsylvania on September 11, 2001. This underscores the rationale for this book – intelligence has risen to such a prominent position that the use of private intelligence requires coverage in greater depth.

PRIVATE INVESTIGATION'S THEORETICAL FOUNDATION

Society is a complex structure of people and the relationship between them. Sociologists explain that it is in these structures that social norms – folkways and mores – are developed and that these conventions are what govern human behavior.[21] However, when humans interact, there are competing needs, wants, and desires, and as a result, some of these social norms and mores are breached. In modern society, we have transformed these social norms into codified civil and criminal laws, which have religious equivalents (or moral imperatives, e.g., in Judeo-Christian holy books there are what is commonly referred to as the Ten Commandments).[22]

It then follows that if laws are created, these laws will be meaningless unless there is a way to enforce them. However, before the law can be enforced, the facts of the matter need to be collected, preserved, and presented before a body set up to adjudicate such matters (e.g., a court or tribunal). This is where investigation comes in. Investigation comprises the actions and processes, as well as the outcomes of making inquiries into an alleged matter.

Investigation is a system of inquiry, similar to academic research, that using fact and logic to answer a question – or more precisely, an allegation. This system is transparent and replicable (or reproducible) and hence it complies with the scientific method of inquire that is used in the physical and biological sciences as well as the social and behavioral sciences. It is transparent because the facts discovered and the conclusions drawn must be able to be presented in a court of law. These methods need to be replicable as the adversary, whether this is the prosecution/claimant in a defense case, or the defense/respondent in a prosecution case, will try and seek to reveal flaws in the methods used, or fault the quality of the information, or how it was collected, handled/stored, analyzed, and so on.

If the matter falls to the state to enforce, as it is with criminal matters, then an investigation function needs to exist. Usually, this is in the form of a police agency (or sheriff's department). But law enforcement does not reside solely with police – it could be argued that there are many more laws that are enforced by government regulatory and compliance agencies than statutes under the jurisdiction of a police force.

This also does not entail the area of civil law. The police, as well as other law enforcements agencies, have no jurisdiction over civil disputes. Yet the same rules of collecting, preserving, and presentation of evidence apply in civil courts. This is where the private investigator comes in. He or she fulfils the need left by the vacuum created by the absence of a police force overseeing civil law. The private investigator provides a service that is needed by individuals, groups, and organizations that have a legal grievance, but are unable to perform the tasks that a trained investigator can do.

"Ninety-nine percent of detective work is patient collecting of details – and your details must be got as nearly first-hand as possible, regardless of who else has worked the territory before you."[23]

This is not to say that private investigators perform civil investigation exclusively – this is not the case. Private investigators also perform inquires in relation to criminal matters on a routine basis. Consider who it is that performs inquires for a defendant charged with a criminal violation – it is not the police; they are the ones prosecuting the matter. It is a private investigator who acts on behalf of the defendant. Private investigators also perform inquires that do not end in a court trial or hearing – for instance, fining a missing person (in the case of recovering bad debts), locating a runaway teenager or spouse, tracing lost financial assets, conducting a background investigation or integrity checks for businesses; and the list goes on.

So, the theory on which private investigation is based could be summarized as follows: in matters of "social dispute," the facts of the matter are usually at issue. In order to ascertain these facts and provide evidence in support of a legal position in relation to the dispute, a person trained in the art and science of inquiry is required. As the state is not able to provide investigators for every form of inquiry, it falls to the private investigator to conduct these inquires.

PRIVATE INVESTIGATION DEFINED

At this stage of the discussion, it is important to clarify a few terms, particularly the terms *investigator* and *detective*. In contemporary practice, the term *detective* is usually reserved for sworn police officers, whereas the term *investigator* is used for those occupations other than police – for instance, private investigators and investigators who may be employed in government regulatory and compliance work. Examples of the latter include customs and immigration services, attorney-general's departments, and health, education, and environmental management. The list can be very long as there are many government agencies – from local to federal – that enforce laws and regulations through investigation.

This is not to say the terms investigator and detective are not used otherwise – they are,[24] but their use may have specific task connotations. Take for instance, within some police forces, there may be units that conduct internal investigations and these positions are designated as "investigators" (or, senior or chief investigators, or crime scene investigators, and so on). Doing so may help distinguish these roles from the detective branch that is tasked with conducting criminal investigations.

Likewise, there may be private investigators who have branded themselves as detectives as part of their business's marketing strategy. These may wish to try to leverage the image of those early-day private investigators in order to project the persona of a by-gone era into today's climate. There is no doubt that some people view the nostalgic image portrayed by the early private detectives with romantic longing and hence have adopted the term *private detective* in order to promote this image.

Today, one of many designations is that of *inquiry agent.* This is a term that has sprung from the legislation that governs the licensing of private investigators. For instance, in the Australian state of New South Wales, the law that governs private investigators uses the term *inquiry agents*[25] to define operatives who are hired to carry out inquiries for others; so they are *agents,* but more precisely, *inquiry agents.*

The other term that needs clarification is *operative.* In essence, an operative is someone who performs a task or carries out a job. In the context of private investigation, an operative is another term for the person tasked to conduct some aspect of an investigation – whether it is carrying out a physical surveillance, or the person tasked to gather information through a records research. In this book, the term *private investigator* (abbreviated as *PI*) will be the preferred term and *operative* is used as a convenient substitute when referring to the PI in action.[26]

Figure 1.1. An Australian private investigator's badge. Note the licensee holds the designation of "inquiry agent." The badge's central crown symbolizes the licensee is under the legislative control of the Queen (via Parliamentary-made laws and the government's licensing requirements) and the laurel wreath symbolizes the noble attributes of courage and valor (photograph courtesy of Hank Prunckun).

Readers will note the use of the term *private eye* is in common usage. General consensus is that the term originates from America's first formal private detective agency – The Pinkerton Detective Agency. The company's logo was that of an eye with the motto "We never sleep."[27] Some may mistake this term being derived from the abbreviation *PI* – the *I* sounding like *eye* – but this is not an accepted interpretation.

TRADITIONAL PRIVATE INVESTIGATOR SERVICES

The role of private investigators in contemporary society is as great as ever. Private investigators are hired by individuals, groups, and organizations, as well as small businesses and large corporations. They work locally, regionally, and nationally. Some even take-on assignments that have an international scope – for instance, helping a parent retrieve his or her child from their estranged or divorced partner who has, for all intents-and-purposes, kidnapped him or her.[28]

The main reason for the private investigator is that the state cannot perform these tasks through its police force. Contacting the police about an employee whom a business suspects of stealing is likely to be met with a sympathetic ear, but a firm reply that "we are unable to help." It is not feasible for the police to post an undercover operative within the business or to conduct a surveillance to gather evidence of the suspected offense. This is where the private investigator enters the equation.

The range of work that a private investigator engages in has expanded manifestly since those first agencies in the 1800s, and certainly since the work depicted in fictional accounts like *The Maltese Falcon*.[29] To list the range for services that today's private investigator can engage is extensive. A survey of any large city's *Yellow Pages* or a search of the Internet will demonstrate this wide variety of work. To illustrate the point, consider the following typology:

- background investigations (e.g., pre-employment screening and business due diligence inquiries);
- counterespionage/countersurveillance;
- employee theft investigations;
- finding lost financial assets;
- fraud investigation (including insurance fraud);
- infidelity investigations;
- locating missing persons;
- physical surveillance;
- legal process server or private bailiff;
- reconnaissance;

- political risk assessments;
- serving of legal processes;
- technical surveillance countermeasures (abbreviated as TSCM or collo-
  quially, *de-bugging*); and
- undercover investigation.

INTELLIGENCE-LED PRIVATE INVESTIGATION

One might argue that the types of services listed above are no different to those offered by Allan Pinkerton to President Abraham Lincoln,[30] or those of-fered by Anthony "Tony" Ulasewicz to President Richard Nixon.[31] So what makes today's private investigator different? In essence, it is the development of communications, travel, and information. In a nutshell, the factors have moved private investigation from the measured and paced group of affairs that might have existed in past decades to one where the events have been in-fluenced by modes of communications, the ability to move about the globe and access information that have increased every few years.

In the post-9/11 environment, today's PI must negotiate a far more com-plex set of conundrums that include the legal issues unheard of before as well as technological issues involving information and its analysis. Intelligence re-places judgments based on "gut feel," "a hunch," or "experience." It replaces vague and arbitrary judgments with decisions based on fact and reason. This is why the book's collection of essays is aimed more toward the practicing in-vestigator rather than the academic scholar, though it should find home on the library shelves of both groups of persons.

With this in mind, this book presents a collection of essays that address some key drivers for PIs in the post-9/11 world, and what these issues mean in terms of working differently. Terrorism is one driver, but private investiga-tors need to understand how these global-outlaws use technology differently and how this may impact on the public, but more importantly, the private sec-tor where most private investigators work.

So, how can private investigators work better with government security agencies? Well, let's reflect on the words of the English philosopher and sci-entist Francis Bacon, who is attributed with saying: "He that will not apply new remedies must expect new evils; for time is the greatest innovator." If pri-vate investigators are to avoid "new evils" presented by the passage of time since the events of 9/11, it follows then, that they must apply "new remedies." To understand these new remedies, this book discusses some of the challenges for private investigation – sophisticated intelligence methods.

CHALLENGES

Investigative Intelligence

The approaches needed by the post-9/11 private investigator could be referred to as *investigative intelligence.* Intelligence is a word used widely though what it is and how a PI can exploit its functionality is much less clear. Chapter 2 will canvass these issues by introducing the reader to the basic concepts of intelligence and then explain how intelligence can and should be used in private investigation work. It will discuss the *intelligence cycle,* what analysis is and how it is performed, and touch on the methods used to turn information into intelligence. It will also explain how intelligence is based on empirical research methods and how these methods can be applied by private investigators to help solve cases under investigation.

Skills for Intelligence-Led Private Investigators

Having established the principles of intelligence in the private investigation context, chapter three will lead the reader through an assessment of the key skill sets needed to perform today's inquiry work: these include, critical thinking skills, understanding structured analytical techniques, developing self-discipline, and an ethical mindset. It will look at how the private investigator can go about acquiring these skills – e.g., through formal training and education, self-study, and on-the-job experience. A template to help devise a learning plan is provided.

Open-Source Intelligence

The private investigation industry is often associated with clandestine operations. However, with the exponential increase in social media and other forms of on-line information, it is now possible for the private investigator to conduct his or her covert operations using open-source information. Chapter 4 looks at what comprises "information," the developments in acquiring it via the public domain, and how information can be used in private intelligence.

Target Profiling

Unlike the hard-nosed fictional PI of the past, or the glamorous detective driving his convertible sports car, the post-911 private investigator needs thinking skills. Chapter 5 discusses one of the most important analytic techniques for the practicing PI – the target profile. The chapter shows how these skills can form the foundation of an intelligence-led investigation. It looks at what constitutes a target profile and how it is developed. Step-by-step instructions are provided with an example of a completed profile of a notional criminal enterprise.

Fraud Intelligence

Traditionally, the role of a private investigator was one where they reacted to requests for assistance. In this regard, PIs have long been hired to solve cases involving frauds – workers compensation, welfare, tax, and insurance. However, since the attacks of 9/11 private investigation has undergone a transformation. Therefore, Chapter 6 examines identify theft and economic espionage – arguably, two of the more pressing issues concerning fraud today, and areas where the PI can expand his or her services.

Political Intelligence

Since 9/11, political intelligence has been an important method for ensuring national security. But increasingly, the gathering and analysis of domestic political intelligence has become a vital practice in the corporate sector and among private security firms. As Chapter 7 explains, political intelligence involves gathering information on governments, political groups, commercial enterprises, and issue-motivated groups (IMG).

The outcome of political intelligence is an understanding of the organization's structure, key personnel, tactics, and objectives. This kind of information is being used by corporate lobbyists, trade advisors, and business to effectively negotiate with the private and public sectors at home and abroad. Since the 9/11 attacks, environmental, religious, and social activism has increased and now represents a range of security issues for businesses, whether the business operates regionally, nationally, or internationally.

Private security firms are often contracted by businesses to deal with activists' protests or internet protest campaigns. Intelligence gathering on the activities and operations of these political groups can better inform security planning. The private investigator with an appreciation and knowledge of political intelligence gathering can play an important part in providing information to improve commercial and private security objectives.

Anti-Terrorist and Anti-Gang Intelligence

The danger of terrorism has driven the expansion of services offered by private investigators. Although missing persons, workers compensation claims, and character inquiries, still entail a large proportion of a PI's work, private investigators are now being called upon to investigate the threat posed by terrorists and other outlaw groups. Chapter 8 focuses specifically on how intelligence can be used by the private investigator in dealing with threats posed by potential terrorists as well as a range of domestic gangs. The chapter not only presents the theory behind this type of intelligence-led investigation, but takes the reader through the steps necessary to conduct such inquiries. The chapter provides examples of the different phases that comprise these inquiries, and explains how the private investigator conducts each phase.

Illicit Organizations and Financial Intelligence

The end of the Cold War brought with it changes to global political structures, in addition to the way businesses operate and trade. In this since, globalization has been hailed as a blessing. But along with the prosperous conditions that globalization has given birth to, came an increase in illicit trade.

But different to its predecessors, these illicit businesses have adapted sophisticated methods for financing their illicit enterprises. Chapter 9 examines what this new criminal landscape means for the private investigator. It discusses the complex financial manifestations so that PIs understand the new criminal environment. Although, this chapter does not hold out the promise that it will make private investigators economic crime specialists, it does expose the reader to the essential elements of financing intelligence so that he or she can apply intelligence-based approaches to investigating issues concerning illicit organizations.

Counterintelligence

Counterintelligence is usually the material that forms the basis for spy fiction with surveillance and countersurveillance, agents and double-agents, and cunning penetrations aimed at discovering the opposition's classified information. However, the discussion in this explores how the private investigator can work with clients to protect their secrets from hostile information gathering – that is, threat-agents. Commonly referred to as *defensive counterintelligence,* this chapter explains the underlying theory of protecting secrets and gives examples of how it can be done. It is a practical chapter, but one that goes beyond the simple locks, guards, and safes approach to explain the range of issues involved in counterintelligence. A template for developing a counterintelligence plan is also provided.

Clandestine Communication Methods

Two-way radio has long been a part of a private investigator's means of communicating. However, given the advances in digital communication and the widespread use of radio scanners by everyone from radio "hobbyists" to terrorists, the post-9/11 PI needs to understand these developments and how he or she can exploit this type of equipment to his or her advantage.

This chapter discusses commercial two-way radio equipment for PIs who may not have exposure to radio work before – e.g., what is easy to buy and service. The chapter includes discussion about radio procedures in the context of covert field operations. The chapter takes the reader through the key issues a private investigator needs to consider when using radios in covert operations (e.g., surveillance and undercover work) and what the strengths and weaknesses are of the various radios systems that are commercially available. This includes non-technical discussion about radios designed to operate on difference radio services.

The chapter provides private investigators with practical ideas about operational radio security by providing instruction on using a simple encryption technique, and in doing so, contrasts this method's effectiveness with the example of the failed Watergate operatives who used no operational security.[32]

Preparing a Prosecution Brief

As the outcome of any inquiry conducted by a private investigator could potentially end in a court case, this chapter looks at what is involved in preparing a matter for litigation. The chapter explains what is involved in compiling a prosecution brief and does so for both criminal matters and civil disputes.

The chapter discusses what a private investigator needs to do in order to compile a brief and in doing so, discusses what needs to be included in a brief, as well as what should excluded. This is important in regards to intelligence-led investigations as only facts should be presented in a brief of evidence. Intelligence-based information, inferences, and other conclusions drawn for data that does not comply with the rules of evidence should not be included. A template-like outline of a prosecution brief is included with general guidelines for the kinds of information that are required.

Legal Issues for Intelligence-Led Private Investigators

Every day, somewhere in the Five-Eyes intelligence alliance – Australia, Britain, Canada, New Zealand, and the United States – private investigators undertake hundreds, if not thousands, of inquiries into a kaleidoscope of personal and commercial issues. These investigations take place on private property and in public areas. But what laws apply to empower such private inquires? Moreover, what does the law say about intelligence gathering in areas such as the Internet, covert surveillance, telephone intercepts, and the use of listening devices? Not much has been written to inform the private investigator about these and other legal questions. So, Chapter 13 sets out to fill this legal void by summarizing some of the key challenges.

Ethical Issues for Intelligence-Led Private Investigators

In some circles, the private investigator is associated with the idea that he or she conducts his or her covert operations on the edge of the law. However, Chapter 14 discusses ethical issues that all private investigators need to be aware of post-9/11 – a world where intelligence is now a feature. Issues such as acting honestly with clients and demonstrating integrity in business dealings are discussed. The chapter also discusses the need for transparency, accountability, confidentiality, being objective and respectful, as well as operating within the law.

KEY TERMS AND PHRASES

The key words and phrases associated with this chapter are listed below. In one or two sentences, demonstrate your understanding of each by writing a short definition or explanation.

- Agent;
- Counterintelligence;
- Detective;
- Five-Eyes;
- Intelligence;
- Investigator;
- Operative;
- PI;
- Private intelligence; and
- Private-eye.

STUDY QUESTIONS

1. Provide a summary of the theory on which private investigation is based.
2. List the countries that comprise the Five-Eyes intelligence allegiance.
3. List three post-9/11 challenges for private investigators and explain why these are concerns.

LEARNING ACTIVITY

In addition to the typology of services offered by the traditional private investigator, research three additional services: use the *Yellow Pages* or an Internet search engine to assist your exploration.

Chapter 2

INVESTIGATIVE INTELLIGENCE

INTRODUCTION

Although private investigators will no doubt be aware of the craft of intelligence – television, cinema, and fictional novels are not only popular sources of entertainment, but they are also a means by which real-world operatives discuss their profession. Take for instance former-CIA operative E. Howard Hunt, who wrote two dozen "spy novels" under his own name and another seventeen under pseudonyms such as Robert Dietrich, P.S. Donoghue, David St. John,[33] Gordon Davis, and John Baxter. There are many other intelligence operatives who have done the same,[34] but suffice to say that because of the restrictions placed on these personnel – due to legislative secrecy provisions – they have channelled their discussion of intelligence work through these media.

These accounts, along with the numerous texts on the non-fictional side of intelligence work, address the categories of intelligence known as national security intelligence, military intelligence, and law enforcement intelligence. There are even books that address the secret work of the business community – *business intelligence.*[35] However, the subject literature on private intelligence is thin. Therefore, this chapter discusses what intelligence is and how the processes that underpin it can best support the work of private investigators, specifically post-9/11.

The focus of this chapter is not to provide an overview of all the duties, roles, and responsibilities of private investigators. There are a number of books that already provide this information.[36] Rather, this chapter will introduce private investigators to the fundamental concepts of intelligence, and explain how intelligence can, and should be, used in private investigation work.

But given the variety of work private investigators are engaged in, it is difficult to define how intelligence could be used in *all* cases. In some private investigations, perhaps simple straightforward matters, intelligence support may not be required, but in other cases, the intelligence process provides a "value added" component to the investigative outcome. So, let us examine what intelligence is in the context of its traditional practice of national security and law enforcement. By doing so, we establish the foundation for applying intelligence to private investigation.

WHAT IS INTELLIGENCE?

Debates go on unabated amongst intelligence scholars about what is intelligence, particularly in the post-9/11 era, where the security environment is more fluid than it was during the Cold War. It is an environment made up of "global outlaws" – that is, arms traders, terrorists, drug cartels, and war lords and a host of other transnational criminal organizations. Rather than the predictable stand-off that once existed between two super powers during the Cold War (i.e., between the former Soviet Union and the United States), this shift in the security environment has shed a new way of thinking on what the role of intelligence is, and therefore, how to define it. The best way to understand what intelligence is is to examine it from three perspectives: *context, process,* and the *level of decision making.*

Context

Intelligence in the National Security Context

The word *intelligence* conjures up many images and thoughts of James Bond-like heroes driving fast sports cars as does the image of an analyst poring over a large data-set using the latest in high-tech gadgetry to gain insight into a problem.[37] Intelligence needs to be first understood in the *context* in which it is practiced. Intelligence is practiced across a range of contexts; including national security, policing, businesses, and increasingly a number of other emerging practice areas. Understanding these different contexts will help the reader understand *how* it is used.

Historically, the key contextual focus for intelligence has been the kind practiced in national security agencies, such as Britain's Military Intelligence 5 (MI5), the Australian Security Intelligence Organization (ASIO), and India's Intelligence Bureau (IB).[38] Intelligence has been used in these agencies chiefly to promote "state security." In other words, intelligence in the national security context has played a core role in assessing the intentions of foreign states, and those that would interfere against the interests of states – such as those engaged in espionage on behalf of a foreign state.

During the Cold War period, national security intelligence was defined largely by the battle between the former Soviet Union and the United States. For other liberal democracies, too, such as Australia, Britain, Canada, New Zealand, and the United States, national security intelligence during this time was also defined fairly narrowly by how it could contribute to defeating the Soviet communist bloc.[39] It was not until the end of the Cold War that non-state threats, such as terrorists and global drug traffickers, became a greater priority and core business of what national security intelligence agencies do today. Although these threat-agents are now shaping the fluid security environment post-9/11, historically, it was the single threat – that of the Soviet Union. It was during the Cold War that intelligence agencies developed the current "vast global capabilities for the collection and analysis of intelligence."[40]

These agencies developed impressive capabilities to intercept masses of information from a range of communications systems such as radio, radar, telephone, email, and other electronic devices.[41] The sensitivities around how technology was used to collect this information produced by necessity a "culture of secrecy," which still pervades national security agencies in all Five-Eyes countries.

The last important factor that helps clarify how intelligence has been used in the national security context is the role collection and analysis plays in this activity. The collection and analysis of intelligence has been the raison d'être of all national security intelligence agencies. This is because the production of focused *intelligence products* (i.e., reports and briefings) has been centered on providing warnings or providing an understanding of threats as well as providing for the operational "disruption" of threats or their prosecution by "covert action."[42]

Intelligence in the Law Enforcement Context

In contrast to national security, it is only possible to generalize about how intelligence has developed in the law enforcement context. This is because the number of policing agencies within the Five-Eyes intelligence alliance countries is so diverse. Take for instance the United States, which has an estimated 18,000 law enforcement agencies – so it would not be possible to discuss how intelligence has been used historically in these law enforcement contexts in that country, let alone across the Five-Eyes nations.

Nevertheless, in general, the historical development of intelligence capabilities in law enforcement agencies shows some cross-pollination of ideas with other intelligence categories such as national security and military intelligence. A good example of this cross-pollination, historically, has been the Metropolitan Police in Britain. For example, one of the first two commissioners of the Metropolitan Police, Sir Charles Rowan, had been a former military officer who brought a lot of his ideas about intelligence from the military.[43] The Metropolitan Police also faced an early threat from Fenians (the Irish Republican movement), which influenced the organization's use of intelligence practices (such as informants and surveillance), that were generally more associated with national security agencies.[44]

While there may have been some borrowing of ideas and influences from the national security context into law enforcement intelligence, it would be safe to say that intelligence during much of the Cold War played only a supportive role in law enforcement agencies. In policing, the main objective was, and remains, to investigate crime and build a case of evidence for prosecution. Intelligence has traditionally been used more narrowly for the purpose of prosecution, but rather than in the broader interest in understanding the threat environment. Up until the late-1960s and early-1970s, law enforcement intelligence was a low technological and localized activity, especially when compared to the high-end technological role of national security intelligence. However, since the 9/11 terrorist attacks, this has changed – what happens locally may be considered a national security issue.

The key message from this discussion is that it is becoming more difficult to define in a succinct way what is uniquely national security or what is law enforcement intelligence practice. This point, as we shall see later, has consequences for the private investigator.

The Intelligence Process

The second way we can define intelligence is by its function, or by describing the processes that are involved. Intelligence advice is referred to as a *product* and provides decision makers (i.e., clients) with insights based on a series of processes. These processes are collectively referred to as the *intelligence cycle*. The intelligence cycle can be depicted in different ways depending on what processes are seen as most important to the production of intelligence.

So, there is not one correct perspective on the intelligence cycle, and more recently, some scholars have begun questioning the utility of thinking about intelligence in this cyclical way.[45] These debates do not concern us here, but a brief understanding of the intelligence cycle is nevertheless helpful for anchoring our later discussions about how various intelligence processes can help private investigators.

It is preferential to keep the number of steps of the cycle as small as possible and Figure 2.1 shows this well. Starting at the *direction* phase, clients ask the private investigator to produce a product that will assist them make a de-

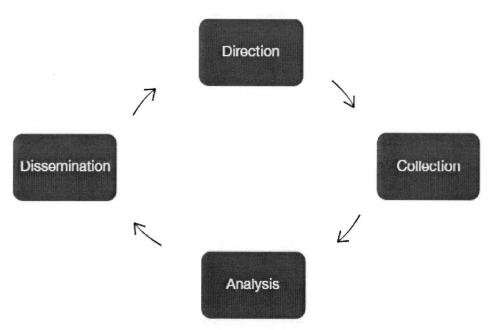

Figure 2.1. The Intelligence Cycle.

cision about the issues that are concerning them. The next phase, *collection,* is where the PI seeks out information from a range of sources that will help answer the question. Collection can be from either open-sources or by covert means.

Open-source information is publicly available and can include research reports, journals, newspapers, statistical data, and many, many other sources. The bulk of information that a PI will use is likely to come from publicly available sources. Information gathering from this source is covered in detail in Chapter 4 of this book.

Covert information is obtained by means that are in some way secret, but in any case, these data are not openly in the public domain. Although covert information can be collected publicly, it is done without the target's knowledge; for instance, through a surveillance operation. If collected by government investigators, its use is usually controlled by legislation, and oversight mechanisms are in place within the agency to monitor any invasion of privacy or the unlawful collection against citizens.[46]

Once sufficient information has been collected, the next step in the cycle is to *analyze* it. This is the "heart" of any intelligence cycle and is what turns information into intelligence. That is, information is useless unless it can be synthesized and its importance assessed. Analysis is also the critical phase of the intelligence cycle because it is here where intelligence can go wrong or fail.

Good analysis should "produce assessments of events, issues and threats that are either correct, or at the very least provide some value for decision-makers."[47] Analytical failure can be the result of a number of things, including insufficient application of appropriate intelligence research methodologies and training.[48]

National security intelligence agencies, and increasingly, law enforcement agencies are developing analytical training programs to help analysts. Some agencies, such as the CIA, started this training in the 1980s with a focus on acquiring a sound understanding of research methods. These research methods are collectively referred to as *structured analytical techniques* and include methods such as *competing hypotheses* and *red cell analysis,* and an increasingly diverse number of other methods, which are designed to get analysts to look at intelligence from alternative perspectives.[49] But there are many other analytical methodologies that can help improve the accuracy of intelligence analysis. In Chapter 5, we look at in detail target profiling.

The final phase of the intelligence cycle is *dissemination*. This involves getting the results of the analysis – the product – to the client. This may seem straightforward, but again relies on having good processes to get products to those that need them in a timely, secure, and legal manner. All national security and law enforcement agencies in the countries of the Five-Eyes intelligence alliance have protocols governing how and what can be disseminated, and to whom. Because of the events of 9/11, progress has been made to improve the intelligence support between agencies in order to enhance their ability to share intelligence, and quickly. The rhetoric has now shifted from a "need-to-know" to a "need-to-share."[50]

Levels of Decision Making

The third way intelligence can be defined is by the kinds of decision-making processes that it supports. Generally, intelligence can support three levels of decision-making – tactical, operational, and strategic.

The role of intelligence at the tactical level is reactive and relates to events as they happen and the intelligence products generated are used to support decisions that need to be made in very short time frames – possibly a day or even a few hours. For example, at the tactical level, an intelligence analyst may collect information reports (which include some crime analysis of "hotspots") and this information would be given to a police commander who needs to decide where to allocate patrols.[51]

At the operational level, intelligence is supporting a broader range of operational level activities, and the time span for providing support to decision makers is typically longer: days or weeks. Operational intelligence support could be applied across more than one local area to have greater impact.

Although we have discussed tactical and operational level intelligence, some scholars combine these under one designation – either operational intelligence or tactical intelligence as the levels of decision making are so similar as to make differentiation hard.[52] Others have opted for a generic term – line intelligence.[53]

At the higher level – the strategic level – the role of intelligence is quite different. It is no longer concerned exclusively with short- to medium-term tactical outputs. At this level, intelligence support focuses on what is driving all the criminal activity. It could be, for example, an increase in cocaine distribution in a major city due to changing social or economic influences regarding the availability of other illicit drugs.

The focus at the strategic level of intelligence is to provide an estimation of a range of political, economic, social, legislative, and other issues will impact on an issue under investigation. Strategic intelligence can then be used to provide warning to decision makers about *indicators* of a trend they may be developing so that something can be done about it before the issue or threat arises. At the strategic level, some of these indicators may still not be fully visible to the analyst, so the challenge for them is to infer the potential possibilities, based on their research and projection from currently available intelligence. Intelligence support provided at the strategic level is normally for senior executives and government officials who are seeking to make relevant policy changes.

INTELLIGENCE AND PRIVATE INVESTIGATION

Using the three intelligence perspectives – context, process, and decision-making levels – provides a useful way for private investigators to reflect on how intelligence could be applied to their operating environments in order to achieve better investigative outcomes. So, we will use each of these perspectives to reflect on how intelligence can be applied to private investigation.

Private Investigation Context

To start our discussion on how intelligence methodologies and processes can be applied to investigative case management is to consider the operating environment. Knowing your business is not only critical to success in general, but it is essential in order to assess how intelligence can support business outcomes. These outcomes can be anything from infidelity to insurance fraud, and from workers compensation to corporate espionage.

The targets that are involved in individual cases as well as the complexity of the cases will dictate the level of intelligence support required. It could be argued that simply putting a target under surveillance, for say, suspected employee theft, is not using intelligence in any meaningful way. And, in a simple investigation, the low-level information gathering required may not resemble anything like the intelligence activities used in more complex cases, or that used by national security agencies.

Intelligence is more than just surveillance and more than information gathering. At its core, intelligence differs from research, information management, and investigative interviewing in that it includes three unique activities in combination. These activities are: (1) interpreting the threat in the context of the issue or problem (sometime referred to as the *security environment*); (2) the use of information gathering methods (e.g., open-source as well as covert); and (3) the operation must be carried out under secrecy.

Of course, what one considers a threat or how secrecy is defined can also be relative, particularly in regards to private investigation. In some private investigations, surveillance, or the use of secret, or privileged information, is not required. The point of this discussion is not to suggest that private investigators do not use intelligence – they do – but even national security and law enforcement do not solely rely on *secret information* to support operational decision making. So, it is important to know whether your investigative context requires intelligence or just good information. Not all pieces of information that are collected during the course of an inquiry will have intelligence value, or need to be/can be "turned into intelligence."

Private Intelligence and Investigation

Reflecting on our earlier discussion of the intelligence cycle, we need to consider how the various phases that make up the cycle improve intelligence support to private investigators? We will start with *direction* setting. The first thing a PI needs to keep in mind is *who* is the client and what is he or she seeking from the investigation. Intelligence support to any investigation must be client-focused and the investigator needs to be clear about what intelligence tasks will best support the client's requirements. From this point, the complexity of the operation will then dictate what kind of intelligence tasks would best support the investigation.

Understanding the client's requirements starts with the consultation process between investigator and client to assess how intelligence can be best deployed (e.g., capabilities and methodologies). It is also possible that there may be more than one client or stakeholder to satisfy so these factors need to be carefully considered during any initial task definition between client and investigator.[54] An investigator employed by an insurance company seeking confirmation of a worker's compensation claim represents a more straightforward deployment of intelligence tasks (i.e., mainly keeping the target under surveillance) than what may be involved with an investigation of an international group involved in the counterfeiting of trademark goods.

The next phase, *collection,* is where the PI seeks information relevant to the issue under investigation using a range of sources and methodologies. Information collection should be planned prior to the start of any investigation, but also requires reviewing throughout the course of the investigation. To begin, the collection process starts with a data collection plan. This is important, particularly in long complex investigations, to ensure information needs are addressed systematically and all potential sources of information are canvassed in a methodical manner. Developing an information collection plan also helps the operative to ask only relevant questions — "what do I need to know and where can I go for this information"?

Information collection can be classified into either open-sources (overt) or covert sources. Open-sources already discussed are very relevant to private investigators. Open-sources can be at a low-level, such as the electoral roll; birth, death, and marriage records; and company registers, but scale upwards to complex data mining searches linking various data-sets.

Apart from the obvious sources, the age of the Internet has resulted in an increasing volume of social media, search engines, and databases available to private investigators. Internet databases such as *CompuServe* and *Google* can help the investigator searching for additional biographical details on a target, including financial and consumer-related patterns. Others such as Lexis Nexus or StratFor provide what is termed *open-source intelligence* on various state and non-state-based risks and threat agents.[55]

Covert sources of information could include surveillance; various electronic devices, including GPS tracking; interview transcripts; and assuming identities in order to obtain information from either the target or their associates (i.e., the use of pretexts). In complex financial investigations, operatives may need to outsource collection efforts to, say, computer forensic specialists, or the like.

Effective intelligence collection also relies on "three criteria being met: the output must be reliable, valid and timely."[56] Although these criteria are collectively important, reliability and validity of data are particularly important. Take, for example, a case where an operative collects information from covert means. Just because information has been collected from a covert source does not make it more correct than data collected from open sources. An important task for the investigator is to test the validity and reliability of all information obtained because if the information is not reliable, it will cause the rest of the investigation to fail, no matter how sound the other aspects of the intelligence process are.

Another critical part of the collection phase is to develop a plan that helps the investigator manage the overall project (i.e., the investigation in its entirety). As with all intelligence collection – national security and law enforcement – there are legislative provisions that govern its collection, and this applies to private intelligence, too. In the government sector, investigators working for compliance and regulatory agencies will generally be governed by specific legislation outlining how potential breeches of their acts can be investigated. Private investigators working in these areas therefore need to be familiar with these provisions and where their powers end and those of a policing agency begin.

The collection of information in the private sector can be as problematic for PIs as for their government counterparts. By way of example, take the case in Britain where the now defunct newspaper *News of the World* erupted into scandal because, it was alleged, that some decision makers within the *News of the World* employed private investigators who used unethical and illegal means to obtain information (i.e., "phone hacking"). This alleged misbehavior has made some corporate clients more wary of using private investigators for corporate intelligence work, with some corporations now asking them to vouch for the "legality of their intelligence operations."[57]

In addition to the legislative constraints, there are also a number of ethical issues, particularly around human rights and privacy that arise when collecting covert or sensitive information. For instance, is it legal, or ethical, for the private investigator to pay people working in banks, passport offices, or the police to access information about the targets of their inquiries? The answer is likely to be "no." Other issues relate to the potential invasion of privacy of other individuals who may be associates of the person under investigation. These legal and ethical issues will be explored more deeply later in Chapter 13 (legal issues) and Chapter 14 (ethical issues).

Once sufficient information has been collected, the next step in the intelligence cycle is to *analyze* it. This is the most important phase of the cycle as it is here where all the raw data *becomes* intelligence. It is at the analytical phase that the private investigator becomes the *analyst*. If the investigation is straightforward, only a small amount of information may need to be collected and analyzed. Under these circumstances, specialized analytical methodologies, such as the use of data mining tools, geographic profiling, or hotspot analysis may not need to be used. In the analytical phase, structured analytical techniques like competing hypotheses (see Chapter 3) and SWOT (see Chapter 5) help the private investigator challenge the tendency to satisfice assumption and perceptions of what is going on; that is conjecture. Using structured analytical methods allows the conclusions drawn from the data to be transparent and hence defensible in court.

During the analytical phase, investigators also need to keep in mind that different types of reasoning will be used – say, inductive reasoning in forming a list of possible motives – whereas in preparing a brief of evidence for the client, deductive reasoning will be used.[58] Intelligence, particularly in more complex investigations, does not necessarily result in a clear, irrefutable picture of what is going on, or who is "guilty of an offense." The private investigator may not be able to rely exclusively on the analytical process to "come up with the smoking gun," rather they may only come up with what is considered the best or most likely interpretation based on the facts. Intelligence provides insight. Intelligence tries to reduce uncertainty. It is not a crystal ball that "tells all."

The final phase of the intelligence cycle is *dissemination*. This phase involves getting the results of the analysis to the client. Hopefully, the client will have provided advice during the *direction* phase, about the form (written or oral) in which they wish to receive the intelligence product. At the tactical/operational intelligence level one of the most commonly used products is the *target profile*. This type of report will be discussed in Chapter 5. The selection of intelligence product type should be in response to the client's preference and what level of decision-making they required.

Levels of Decision Making

The outcome of an investigation is dictated by the client at the beginning of the job (as long as it is legal and ethical . . .). Questions such as "is the client looking for tactical or strategic advice" should be at the fore of the PI's mind when interviewing the client. For a tactical example, a legal firm may hire a private investigator to locate a businessman who has fled the country to avoid a trial for embezzlement. It is tactical because the client's decision is to locate and serve a subpoena on the target. The production of any intelligence in this instance would be short term with an immediate goal.

Alternatively, a client may hire a private investigator to probe a network of employees involved in a complex corporate fraud to see how they are laundering company profits or stealing goods from the production line. This case relies on the collection and analysis of a range of information that will potentially support more than one outcome, and the investigation is likely to be carried out over a longer timeframe – months or even years. Clients may also ask for information from private investigators that allows them to make longer-term strategic decisions about the future of their business or about their competitors, or the threats or risks their business faces.

INVESTIGATIVE INTELLIGENCE WORKSHEET

To conclude, it might be valuable to offer some thoughts on how a private investigator might go about navigating the intelligence cycle for the first time. To this end, Table 2.1 offers a worksheet template that will assist PIs think through the various phases of the cycle and plan their intelligence operation. Although the template is a simplified form of what could be a more involved process, it nonetheless offers operatives a way to start thinking about using intelligence in their investigations. Hopefully, the template will generate ideas about how it could be expanded or tailored to suit the particularities of individual cases.

Table 2.1. An Example of a Tactical Intelligence Worksheet for Locating a "Missing Person" Wanted to Appear in Court

	Investigative Intelligence Worksheet
For the attention of:	Ms. Isobel Trudeau, Chief Investigator, Whitney Global Investigations
Private Investigator:	Mr. Ross Callum
Investigative objective:	Serving of a subpoena to appear in Hampden County District Court
Date:	April 12
Direction:	Ms. Naomi Yardley, General Manager of Wilbraham Enterprises requires subpoena to be serviced on Mr. Freddie Ready to answer a change of theft as an employee. Mr. Ready is alleged to have embezzled $220,000 from the company's account during the time he served as its director of accounting services. It is understood that he has left the United States last month and is rumored to be in the Central American country of Belize.
Collection:	Collect information from target's: • rubbish bins at his last known address; • relatives; • neighbors on either side, behind, and across the road from his last known address; • work colleagues; • members of the bowling club where he was a member; • search of social media websites; and • follow-up on any leads generated through the above methods.
Analysis:	Brainstorm a list of the most likely places the target may have travelled including locations put forward by the client – Belize. Use an analysis of competing hypothesis, assess the information collected in order to determine the most likely place the target could be.
Dissemination:	Client requires a written report as to the likely whereabouts of Mr. Ready in order to assess the likelihood and costs involved in serving him with the legal notice.
Date report required:	May 12

KEY WORDS AND PHRASES

The key words and phrases associated with this chapter are listed below. In one or two sentences, demonstrate your understanding of each by writing a short definition or explanation.

- Covert information;
- Intelligence cycle;
- Intelligence;
- Law enforcement intelligence;
- National security intelligence;
- Strategic intelligence;
- Structured analytical techniques; and
- Tactical intelligence.

STUDY QUESTIONS

1. Describe the difference between the three perspectives for describing the role of intelligence: context, process (i.e., the intelligence cycle), and the levels of decision-making.
2. Explain the difference between information and intelligence.
3. Describe how the security environment has changed since the 9/11 terrorist attacks and provide two implications this may have for private investigators using intelligence collection and analytical methodologies.

LEARNING ACTIVITY

Using the tactical intelligence worksheet in Table 2.1, develop an intelligence plan for locating the missing person in the following scenario: Your client is a successful Massachusetts businessman. He claims his long-term girlfriend went on a vacation to Mexico by herself for a few weeks of relaxation and was supposed to check into an Acapulco hotel, but failed to show-up. Your client reported this to the police, but their brief inquires with the Mexican police indicated that although she entered Mexico, there was no evidence of foul play (despite the Mexican police's failure to locate her). The police in both countries have listed her as one of the thousands of unexplained "missing persons."

Chapter 3

SKILLS REQUIRED FOR INTELLIGENCE-LED PRIVATE INVESTIGATORS

Troy Whitford

INTRODUCTION

Since the terrorist attacks of 9/11, the value of intelligence cannot be understated – that is, the ability to identify, locate, and assess the threats people pose to other individuals, organizations, and the state. Typically, intelligence-led investigations are a blend of sophisticated information gathering processes and intelligence-based analytical methodologies undertaken by government agencies, law enforcement, and defense personnel. Although portrayed in fiction as clandestine operatives equipped with high-tech gadgetry, these bodies are nonetheless well resourced with human capital and these new technologies; they are also supported by legislation that empowers them to effectively target threat-agents, and bring them to justice.

But in the twenty-first century, the value of intelligence has also been recognized by the private and commercial sectors. Intelligence gathering is now an accepted method used by private security and investigative firms to meet demands from a diverse clientele. Subsequently, the challenge for private investigators in the current environment is how best to provide clients with intelligence-based services with limited resources, but all along doing so with only the legal powers that the average citizen[59] of any of the Five-Eyes countries – Australia, Britain, Canada, New Zealand, and the United States.

This chapter will discuss how the private investigator can develop his or her knowledge, skills, and values to provide informed professional intelligence-led investigation services. Developing a sound knowledge base needed for intelligence-led investigations requires a number approaches. In order to identify the various sources of knowledge it is prudent to categorize them into: (a) formal theoretical knowledge; (b) industry-focused knowledge; and, (c) practical knowledge. In the context of this chapter, theoretical knowledge is primarily, but not exclusively, obtained through institutional-based learning at colleges or universities. Industry-focused knowledge is obtained through specialized courses in private investigations and practical knowledge is essentially what is learned "on the job." Naturally, skills are acquired through similar sources as knowledge.

Two particular skills required for intelligence-led investigations are analytical skills and an ability to undertake qualitative research. This chapter will introduce the private investigator to these techniques and encourage further interest and appreciation for analysis and qualitative research methodologies. In addition to developing sound research and analytical methodologies, the private investigator must also develop less tangible skills such as self-reflection and ability to adopt a panoramic view of the investigation being undertaken.

Values are something that can be learned but difficult to teach. Developing a values compass is often acquired over time and through experiences. However, this chapter will challenge the private investigator to move beyond traditional paradigms of "good and evil" or adversarial interpretations of events. Unlike government and law enforcement agencies, private investigators do not always have a clear protagonists and antagonists. In business, politics, and human relationships, roles change as the situation or event presents. In the field of private investigations, there are a multitude of competing interests that need to be acknowledged, understood, and analyzed. The central value that is being canvassed in this chapter is an appreciation that events are often complex and intelligence cannot be discounted because of preconceived views or biases.

Acquiring training to develop new knowledge, skills, and values is essentially eclectic but not unobtainable. A central requirement is the ability to be an independent lifelong learner with an open and critical mind. This chapter will include suggested training options to assist investigative students and established practitioners to develop an independent learning plan and to adopt a lifelong learning philosophy.

DEVELOPING KNOWLEDGE

Knowledge is having facts and information. It is the basis for applying skills and forming values. It is unfruitful to debate what source of knowledge is more appropriate than others. Formal theoretical knowledge, industry-focused knowledge, or practical knowledge are all interdependent and inform each other.

A broad theoretical knowledge based in the social sciences or humanities provides the private investigator with an understanding that allows for greater and more successful interaction with a range of people and organizations. A historical analogy would be religious texts such as the Christian *Bible,* Jewish *Tanakh,* Muslim *Koran,* or Buddhist *Tripitaka.* In early societies, most people were familiar with the verses and central messages of those texts and they were used as the basis of law, science, and philosophy. Today, in a more post-modern age where there are a range of competing ideas, philosophies, and cultural relativity, the central texts that weave the social fabric are more diverse and understanding them requires a greater knowledge base. A well-rounded liberal arts degree that includes some politics, sociology, psychology, economics, and history would provide investigators with an understanding of central ideas and background to understand the society they work within.

Modern intelligence-led investigations are also shaped by the globalization of economic, political, and social systems. It is important to have a broad knowledge of events and how they are often interconnected or at least informed in their genesis to a wider set of political, economic, or social movements. Essentially, ideas, money, and social interaction are more transnational than ever before and having knowledge of how those ideas, transactions, and interactions function is vital to successful intelligence gathering. In addition, the private investigator should develop certain qualities such as objectivity, insights into human nature and cultural differences, and knowing how to ask the right questions.[60] These qualities can be gained through formal study in the social sciences or humanities. Through study at an undergraduate level, students are offered an opportunity to develop knowledge objectively, accept cultural and social differences, and seek answers to questions.

Broadening a theoretical knowledge base can also be achieved through developing an appreciation for wide reading and being aware of changes in financial, political, and social sectors. Subscribing to a range of newspapers and media outlets and developing a regular practice of observing change in society all offer an opportunity to develop a wider knowledge base. It is easy to fall into regular routines using the same news sources and consuming ideas and knowledge that re-enforce our existing thoughts.

However, it is in the interest of the investigator to move outside of his or her intellectual "comfort zone" by viewing and reading material that they would normally discount or dislike. For example, if knowledge is deficient in finance issues, regularly read and view material on finances. Also challenge existing biases by reading publications that are ideologically different or view news material generated from another state or country. The different perspectives will better inform you and give access to more opportunity to understand people from various backgrounds and beliefs.

Industry-focused knowledge provides the technical expertise to undertake investigations. Most states and provinces in Australia, Britain, Canada, New Zealand, and the United States have licensing requirements that investigators undertake a minimum level of formal industry-based education. In Australia, for example, investigators are required to complete a Certificate III in Investigative Services. This course of study includes fifteen core units that are shown in Table 3.1.[61]

Table 3.1.
Core Units of Competency for the Australian Certificate III in Investigative Services

1. Contribute to effective workplace relations	2. Prepare and present evidence in court	3. Develop investigative plan
4. Organize personal work priorities and development	5. Store and protect information	6. Compile investigative report
7. Maintain workplace safety in the security industry	8. Work effectively in the investigative services industry	9. Provide quality investigative services to clients
10. Gather information by factual investigation	11. Locate subjects	12. Conduct surveillance
13. Organize and operate a surveillance vehicle	14. Operate information gathering equipment	15. Conduct interviews and take statements

The knowledge, skills, and values developed through such industry-based courses are self-evident as they contribute to becoming an effective investigator. Perhaps best described (albeit somewhat abstractly) by renowned American private investigator Peter Psarouthakis: "the only difference between a stalker and private investigator carrying out surveillance was that the PI had a license."[62] There is a good deal truth to this comedy. Without sound knowledge through some formally recognized qualification, the investigator is simply a rouge citizen stumbling through a minefield of legalities and ethical dilemmas. Little more needs to be said about the importance of industry-based training; however, it is worth concluding on the necessity of regularly undertaking short courses and workshops to continue refreshing industry knowledge.

Practical knowledge, or informal knowledge, is mostly achieved over time. It is a learning process that takes place outside of educational institutions and basically means "we learn everywhere, from all kinds of experiences and encounters."[63] Practical knowledge can be self-directed and intentional. But, it is important that a plan is established to ensure that the most is being made from the learning experiences encountered through the practical knowledge process. Often people will cite having a substantial amount of practical knowledge because they have been in the same business or industry for decades. However, repetitious experience is not a sufficient basis for gaining practical knowledge. Rather, it is in many respects the opposite. Well-planned practical learning reflects a wide experience across the whole spectrum of the investigative industry.

Traditionally, private investigation is divided into three specialties: factual investigations, surveillance, and locating persons. It is natural that investigators specialize in a particular area. Nonetheless, to increase practical knowledge, the investigator (particularly the new investigator) must be willing to explore unfamiliar areas of investigation and develop a more holistic knowledge and skills base. One method for developing greater practical knowledge is to develop a network of other investigators with a range of specialties. Joining industry forums or *LinkedIn* kind of discussion groups are just a few suggested avenues for developing networks. These networks can provide advice and also the opportunity to take part in investigations that may not normally be considered.

While networking does provide a basis for increasing practical knowledge, it also has a number of other benefits worth mentioning. Intelligence-led investigation is a people-centered process. Knowing people with certain expertise or contacts that can facilitate an intelligence-led investigation are vital resources. Establishing networks takes a considerable amount of effort and time. But with social media, the process is becoming much easier. The private investigator should take time to join relevant online discussion groups and, where possible, attend conferences and seminars. Current technology allows investigations and investigators to cross boarders and create networks with overseas operatives and sources of information.

Globalization has facilitated opportunities to gain an international clientele and conduct international investigations. Since the terrorist attacks of 9/11, ideas, money, and social interaction are transnational. Subsequently, even a domestic investigation may have international leads to follow. Therefore, it is a core requirement to successful intelligence-led investigations that practitioners establish and maintain their own international and national network of expertise and human resources.

DEVELOPING SKILLS

There is a long list of skills that the intelligence-led investigators could gain benefit from having. Yet, there are two key skills which are fundamental to all investigations: qualitative research and analytical skills. Arguably, it is within the gambit of these that there are two skill sets that help intelligence-led investigators break from the traditional investigative practices. One of the fundamental tenants of investigative work is that it only deals with fact. Yet, in intelligence-led investigations, the fact is the basis for *analysis* – the first skill set. Analysis provides insight, and in turn, insight reduces uncertainty. So, "insight and certainty offer mankind the ability to make decisions that enable civilizations to take better control over the unknown."[64]

Intelligence-led investigations are essentially *qualitative research* projects – this is the second skill set. A traditional factual investigation may ask *what, where,* and *when,* but a qualitative intelligence-led investigation will ask *how* and *why* – seeking an in-depth understanding of actions, personalities, or events. The strengths of qualitative research methodology in relation to intelligence-led investigations is its ability to be conducted in natural human settings and it allows for a deeper understanding of subject or event.[65]

There is a range of qualitative research methods used in the social sciences that would have applications for intelligence-led investigations. But perhaps most pertinent is historical research. The analogy between historians and detectives is commonly made in social sciences classes because both will use evidence to piece together an event. Historiography, that is, historical research, is more than gathering historical facts; it also links together those facts to provide an interpretation of the event or subject. Table 3.2 highlights the similarities between conducting historical research and intelligence-led investigations.

Table 3.2.
Similarities Between Historical Inquiry and Intelligence-Led Investigations

Historical Inquiry[66]	*Intelligence-Led Investigation*[67]
Identify an area, topic, or research question	Problem formation
Conduct a background of the literature	Literature review
Determine the data collection process	Intelligence collection plan
Identify and locate primary and secondary sources	Data collection
Confirm the authenticity and accuracy of the source material	Data evaluation and quality control
Analyze the data and develop a narrative exposition of the findings.	Data analysis, inference development and drawing conclusions. Recommendations and report.

Gaining skills in using a qualitative methodology to conduct an investigation can be best achieved through the kinds of social science studies outlined earlier in this chapter. Undertaking research in social science, even at an undergraduate level, provides an opportunity to learn how to frame research problems or projects and develop a systematic approach to undertaking research. The similarities between framing qualitative research and intelligence-led investigations makes the transfer of skills almost seamless.

Within the qualitative research methodology is analysis. There are a number of analytical tools that can be used to interpret information. Depending on the nature of the investigation, an analysis of strengths, weaknesses, threats,[68] and opportunities (SWOT); an analysis political, economic, social, and technological (PEST); force field analysis; network analysis; or an analysis of competing hypotheses can be adopted.[69] The following example is intended to illustrate how using analytical methods can benefit an investigation.

> A client has contracted a private investigator to find out if her husband is having an affair. The investigator conducts some surveillance and finds the husband arrives at an unknown woman's residence at 3:30 pm and leaves at 4:45 pm. The following week, the client's husband returns to the same address at exactly the same time and leaves around the same time. Unable to see into the place of residence, the fact reported to the client was that at 3:30 pm the husband arrived at the women's place of residence and left at 4:45 pm.

In traditional investigations these facts are provided without any analysis and conclusions about the husband having an affair are left to the client. An intelligence-led investigation, however, uses analytical methods to address the client's concern about her husband's fidelity. In this instance, a competing hypothesis analysis could be applied. A competing hypothesis analysis aims to identify all reasonable hypotheses and have them compete against each other for the most likely hypothesis.

For the purpose of highlighting the benefits of intelligence-led investigative skills as opposed to the traditional approach, the following is an outline of the steps involved in applying an analysis of competing hypotheses.[70]

Step 1

The first is identifying all the possible hypotheses to be considered. List possible reasons why the target is regularly attending the residence of the unknown woman. For instance:

- The target is having an affair;
- The target is attending the premises because the women offers services (non-sexual) from a home office such as psychology, astrology, or massage; or
- The target may be offering his services (non-sexual) to a client in their home such as TV repair, computer education tutorial, or simply volunteering to assist around the home.

Step 2

The next step is to list evidence and arguments for and against each hypothesis. The client would be able to assist the investigator to test out the hypotheses by asking relevant questions.

Step 3

This step involves analyzing the evidence to assist in forming a judgment about the likelihood or unlikelihood of the hypotheses. For example:

- While under surveillance, it was noted the target was not in attire that would suggest manual repair work, nor was the target carrying any tools;
- The client had commented that the husband is "anything but a handyman"; or
- During surveillance, it was also noted that other people, male and female, visited the premises often only hours apart.

Step 4

The fourth step is to draw conclusions about the likelihood of the hypotheses trying to disprove them rather than prove them. Just as an example, the hypothesis of the husband undertaking maintenance at the residence could be considered unlikely given the surveillance report and interview with the client. In addition, the number of other visitors to the residence in similar time spans would also go toward disproving the hypotheses that the husband is having an affair.

Step 5

The final step is to report and discuss the likelihood of all the hypotheses and how evidence has contributed or discounted those hypotheses.

Although this is a simplified example, we can see that by using a structured analytical approach to private investigations provides the opportunity to add value to the services traditionally offered by using methods that provide answers to questions. This is in contrast to providing raw facts that are open to interpretation.

With respect to the above example, the client was seeking an answer to her question about her husband's fidelity. The traditional investigator may have simply collected facts and provided them in a report. But the answer to the question would not have been adequately supplied. If the investigator was equipped with the analytical skills to answer the question rather than just supply facts, then there is greater scope to meet the needs of the client. In this case, the husband may have been undertaking private hobby-craft lessons to make a gift for his wife's upcoming birthday and the woman he was seeing was a retired craft teacher who ran classes from her home.

DEVELOPING VALUES

Values are perhaps less tangible than knowledge or skills and are best formulated through experiences and the world we live.[71] Developing values requires self-reflection and a desire to set ethical and personal boundaries. Certainly there are industry-based codes of conduct such as the Australian Institute of Private Detectives national code of practice[72] and in Australia and New Zealand, parts of the United States, and Canada all have licensing requirements which ensure practitioners work within the law. The British are also considering licensing their private investigators.

Nevertheless, values are not laws. Rather, it is a set of ideas, views, and beliefs that formulate what is "right or wrong." Within law enforcement or government intelligence agencies, there are usually clearly established values centered on protagonists and antagonists – those in "the right" and those in the "wrong," or "our side and their side." Private investigations do not always have such distinct adversarial roles. Within the private sector there is the client and his or her case. It is probable during the career of an investigator that he or she will be asked to undertake an investigation that may confront his or her own values.

Some investigators may feel uncomfortable undertaking matrimonial investigative work while others may not feel comfortable working for a foreign company seeking commercial intelligence on a domestic enterprise. Each investigator will have a different set of values and it is not the aim of this chapter to enforce any particular values regarding the kinds of cases investigators should accept. But, there are a few personal reflection methods that investigators can use to develop their professional values when they consider accepting a case. These include consequential thinking strategies and values mapping.

Value Mapping

Value mapping is a self-reflection exercise designed to establish the kind of professional persona required to develop as intelligence-led private investigator. The exercise involves writing down or thinking about a range ideas and beliefs that are important to the investigator's practice. It could be modeling investigative practices on firms or individuals admired in the field.

In addition, reflecting on issues that are important to you such as the kind of politics you are attracted toward, personal religious beliefs, or thoughts about what makes a good community might be considered. These are just examples of the line of questions which can assist in value mapping. At the end of the exercise, themes will emerge that provide a values compass for future reference when accepting cases. The importance of conducting this type of exercise will be highlighted in Chapter 7 where values regarding political intelligence are involved.

Consequential Thinking

Consequential thinking is a process that involves consideration of the pros and cons of an interpersonal act.[73] In the field of intelligence-led investigations, it is a vital tool when deciding courses of an investigation. It can also assist in making a values judgment about accepting a case or dealing with individuals.

Within the investigations profession there is a classic fable that best illustrates how consequential thinking can be applied. The story deviates but the theme is the same. Briefly, it goes as follows:

> An investigator is approached by a male client who says he is searching for a woman who was a previous employee and is owed wages. She had left the company before collecting her pay and he wants to find her address so he can mail the pay check. He explains she was a good employee and a friend and does not like the idea of simply keeping the money himself. The investigator accepts the client's story and proceeds to find the woman. He passes on the address to the client. A week later, the investigator discovers the women he had located was killed in a vicious attack by the client. It becomes apparent that the client was in fact an ex-husband looking for his estranged wife who had left him and went into hiding six months prior. The police learn the investigator was involved in locating the women and is then under police investigation as a possible accomplice to murder. Fortunately, the investigator kept the email communications with the client which proved he was acting on what was thought a simple case of goodwill.

Applying a degree of consequential thinking could provide the investigator some greater options about how to handle the case. The initial step would be to take a "bird's eye" view of the situation. The first step is asking "what is the consequence of accepting the case?" Naturally, there is a business aspect to consider. But under a values framework, further analysis could be applied to better understand the implications of accepting such a case as described above. For example, looking at the case from a broader perspective and applying a hypothesis analysis could provide you with an opportunity to establish if the client had any other motivations, or what impact this case would have on the investigator or target.

As already pointed out, the acquisition of values is a personal on-going learning experience. Working outside of traditional law enforcement or government intelligence agencies means allegiances; ethical practice and choice of client are at the discretion of the investigator. This is both a liberating, yet highly responsible position in which to be placed. Even so, through incorporating a self-developed set of values and applying a degree of consequential thinking, the intelligence-led investigator can develop the tools to work within such an environment.

CONCLUSION

The knowledge, skills, and values for the intelligence-led investigators are diverse. But these elements need to be brought together. Doing so requires a commitment to what is termed *lifelong learning* through formal and informal study methods. To achieve the learning experiences suggested in this chapter, it is essential to develop a personal learning plan. Such a plan will provide structure so that an overview of what knowledge, skills, and opportunities for values development can be acquired. To this end, a template with examples is presented in Table 3.3.

In addition to setting a personal learning plan, it is important to model your professional approach to those existing firms or individuals that have the community's admiration. Examine how successful intelligence-led investigators conduct their business; the knowledge, skills, and values they possess and within your resource capability emulate the positive aspects. The overall skills for the intelligence-led investigator are varied and will essentially require a broad general knowledge, specific research, and investigative skills and values that make investigations ethical in an era with changing alliances and globalization.

Table 3.3. An Example of a Personal Learning Plan

Personal Learning Plan	Improving knowledge, skills, and values			
Current role	Private Investigator			
Key Professional and Career Goals				
Short Term	Develop intelligence-led investigative knowledge, skills, and values			
Long Term	Demonstrate proficiency in intelligence-led investigations			
Reflection	**Action**	**Assistance**	**Achievements**	**Review**
Short Term: What knowledge, skills, or values to I want learn over the next year or two?	What do I need to do to help me reach my goal?	Who might help me? What might help me?	Expected outcomes	Milestones and timescales. Next steps
EG: Develop analytical skills	Knowledge and application of a variety of analytical skills.	Literature on different types of analysis. Discussions with experienced analysis.	Able to use a set of analytical tools in private investigations.	Incorporate analysis into investigations service within 12 months. Look for courses to formalize my understanding of analysis skills.
Long Term: What do I hope to achieve in 5–15 years?	What do I need to do to help me reach my goal?	Who might help me? What might help me?	Expected outcomes	Milestones and timescales. Next steps
EG: Formal tertiary education in humanities or social sciences.	Access to college or university.	Admissions bodies at college or university. Graduates of college or university.	Successfully complete an undergraduate or graduate degree.	Complete within 3–5 years. Assess any other formal education that may be relevant.

KEY TERMS AND PHRASES

The key words and phrases associated with this chapter are listed below. In one or two sentences, demonstrate your understanding of each by writing a short definition or explanation.

- Consequential thinking;
- Knowledge;
- Lifelong learning; and
- Value mapping.

STUDY QUESTIONS

1. Arguably, there are two skill-sets that intelligence-led investigators should have. List these and explain why these skills are important to have. You may provide an example to illustrate.
2. Referring to Table 3.2, compare the elements of historical inquiry and intelligence-led investigation and discuss the similarities.
3. Using the Internet, research the code for practice for private investigators that is promoted by the professional associations in your country. Compare it to a code of practice you have found for one of the other Five-Eyes countries. What is similar and what is different? Overall, are the two the same in intent? Have they attempted to achieve the same outcome?

LEARNING ACTIVITY

Regardless of whether you are new to private investigation or a master practitioner with years of experience, using the personal learning plan template provided in Table 3.3, develop a learning plan for yourself with regard to improving knowledge, skills, and values.

Chapter 4

OPEN-SOURCE INTELLIGENCE

JEFF CORKILL

INTRODUCTION

The image of the private investigator is one often associated with clandestine operations. One can almost imagine an operative posited in a darkened van, cradling a parabolic listening device that is pointed at the target. This is the romantic vision that many fictional stories about private investigators are based.

But, with the rapid increase in published information about people's lives, it is now possible for private investigators to conduct "surveillance" of the target without even physically making sight. This is known as open-source information, or open-source intelligence,[74] and it is used to produce intelligence in the same way covert and clandestine data are used. Private investigators estimate that they can obtain between 70 and 80 percent of the information they need for the average corporate target from open-sources.[75] Open-source information can also be used to complement a PI's covert operations even if it does not account for the majority of data that is obtained.

This chapter introduces the reader to the history of open-source intelligence, the key concepts that underpin it, and how this rich source of information can be incorporated into the private investigative process.

BACKGROUND

Open-source intelligence means many things to many people. Even within the field of intelligence the term invokes different meanings. It would be fair to argue that while the modern concept of open-source intelligence had its genesis in the late-1980s and early 1990s, the reality is open-source was in existence long before that; some would argue it in fact goes back hundreds of years. Since print media has existed, intelligence organizations have collected newspapers, pamphlets, books, and reports all for the purpose of gleaning potentially useful information that might contribute to the production of intelligence products.

The introduction of radio and television saw intelligence agencies shift resources to the monitoring and collation of information broadcast on these media for fusion with that gathered from the print media to be turned into simple intelligence products. Now in the so-called "information age," with the Internet, the breadth and depth of open-source information that is available to the private investigator is almost boundless. It would be fair to say that for some people, the future of the open-source intelligence was crystalized by Steele in his 2001 book in which he foretold of a new world of intelligence collection and production.[76]

So, what is open-source intelligence? Before answering that question one should briefly recap our understanding of what is intelligence. Consider the definition by Gill and Phythian below:

> Intelligence is the umbrella term referring to the range of activities – from planning and information collection to analysis and dissemination – conducted in secret, and aimed at maintaining or enhancing relative security by providing forewarning of threats or potential threats in a manner that allows for the timely implementation of a preventative policy or strategy, where deemed desirable, covert actions.[77]

Richards, in his analysis of what intelligence, identified a number of characteristics that were generally held to be common to a broad cross-section of definitions: "Firstly, intelligence is both a product and a business process. Second, intelligence is the output of the analysis of information."[78]

There are many definitions of what constitutes intelligence; with references to national security, law enforcement, the importance of secrecy, support to policy makers, and clandestine collection of information. All of which might suggest that intelligence has no role to play in investigation and no utility to the private investigator. However, it would be wrong to draw this conclusion; intelligence can be more simply defined as: a product resulting from the collection, validation, integration, and analysis of information and used to support decision making.

If that becomes our working definition of intelligence, then what is open-source intelligence? Simply put, open-source intelligence is information that has been collected from sources available in the public domain – i.e., openly. The key to understanding open-source intelligence is remembering that it is not simply information retrieved from, say, a news service or magazines;

rather it is the result of a process that adds value to these pieces of information. Analysis of this information is the aspect that adds value.

So what is open-source information? And how do we access that information? To understand this we need to understand more broadly the concept of a "universe of information."

UNIVERSE OF INFORMATION

While it is not certain just who it was who coined the phrase "universe of information," the concept is an appropriate one for use in understanding open-source data. The private investigator who understands this concept is more likely to discover useful information than the PI who does not. The universe of information is a metaphoric way of explaining the various domains in which information resides. Therefore, knowing where a piece of information likely resides becomes the key to accessing it quickly and efficiently.

In the first instance, we can consider information residing in one of two domains. The first of these domains is the *internal domain*. This is information we already have; it may reside in files, databases, or even archive boxes. The key is we have it, and all other information then resides in the *external domain*. When we look to the external domain, we can separate this information into two sub-domains. The first sub-domain is what we know as the *public domain*. This sub-domain includes a wide variety of information types stored in all manner of repositories and formats.

Public domain information includes things such as published company reports, news in all its forms, and a wide variety of government publications to identify just a few. What is not in the public domain we can then classify as being in the sub-domain of *restricted,* or *private*. A restricted sub-domain is not necessarily information that could be considered *classified* (in the national security sense) as it may be simply restricted because a fee needs to be paid to access it. For example, many news organizations provide a certain amount of free information on their websites; however, for those prepared to pay a fee, they can gain access to greater detail or more information, or so on.

We can further separate-out this universe of information by considering some of the other domains in which information resides. Take for instance, language – it is an important issue to consider as there is likely a *native language* domain where various pieces of information exist. However, external to a particular native language domain, there will be larger *foreign language* domains. Further, in the present digital world, we have what many look to first to answer questions, the *digital domain,* yet there is still an enormous body of information that exists in some form of *hard copy domain*.

Encompassing all of these domains is the *explicit knowledge* domain which accounts for information that has been codified or recorded in some format. Still, this domain has an allied domain being the *tacit knowledge* domain. It consists of all knowledge internalized in the minds of individuals, and in some cases, cultures and organizations.

Moreover, all of these domains overlap – there is no clear demarcation between them. For example, the internal knowledge domain of an organization will consist of a mix of public domain information available to people inside and outside of the organization; there will also be restricted domain information that is limited to only people inside the organization; and there will also be information restricted to specific individuals or accessible to those by specific approval. Therefore, the key to creating reliable open-source intelligence is understanding where information resides, and then being able to develop an information collection plan to gather it.

Understanding the concept of a universe of information is a good way to conceptualize the complexities associated with all forms of data. The most common approach to satisfying an information requirement has been said to "*Google* it." The trouble is not all information is accessible via an Internet search engine.

Traditional search engines used by the average "researcher" really only addresses information situated in what is sometimes termed the *surface web*. This body of information lies on the surface of the web and is represented by as little as 10 to 20 percent of all accessible data. The other 80 to 90 percent resides in what is known as the *deep web* or the *dark web*. To access this deeper body of information the researcher needs to use specialized search applications or specific databases.

Open-Source versus Covert Collection

It would be a mistake to assume that the primary benefit of accessing open-source information, over covert information, is simply one of cost. Open-source is not synonymous with free information, but while it is true that there is a wealth of information available that is free, there is also a vast amount of information technically in the public domain, but it comes at a cost (e.g., directly in the form of a fee or subscription, or indirectly in the form of time and software to access it). Nonetheless, these costs may be offset by the greater efficiencies achieved by utilizing these assets over covert employment of your own assets.

Nor does access to open-source information by default negate a need for covert collection methods; however, thoughtful utilization of open-source methods and systems may encourage more efficient employment of covert assets. Further, by exploiting open-source means, in the first instance, the private investigator may be able to achieve more when using his or her covert capability following an open-source approach.

ACCESSING THE OPEN-SOURCE DOMAIN

Successful open-source collection requires an understanding of the task at hand and planning. Generally speaking, when an inquiry is undertaken, it is done so with a purpose and it is done for a client. So, rather than use a "shotgun" approach to information collection, the essential elements of information need to be established. This is often called the *information collection plan.* It outlines the pieces of information needed and where these data items reside. But to craft an information collection plan, the private investigator needs to determine why the information is required. Normally, the client is trying to achieve one of the following:

- Who: To identify who is involved in, linked to or doing something.
- What: To identify what is happening or has happened.
- Where: To identify where something is occurring, has occurred, or might occur.
- When: To identify when an event occurred or might occur.
- Why: To determine why something has happened or may happen.
- How: To determine how something is being conducted or occurred (in the past).

In addition, the PI needs to understand the context in which the information will be used:

- Is it for the purpose of informing?
- Is it for the purpose of acting?
- Is it to be evidentiary?

APPROACHES TO OPEN-SOURCE INFORMATION COLLECTION

Successful information collection is a result of planning and methodical application of a search strategy. To formulate an information collection plan of the open-source domains, the following step-wise procedure will help.

Step One. Review the client information requirements and from these extract a set of searchable terms. If the information requirements are deemed to be too complex to be used as search terms in their own right, the PI may need to simplify them, or perhaps break them down into a number of searchable elements.

Step Two. The next step is to consider where to search for the information. This is where an understanding of the universe of information becomes important. Does the PI need to access a specific database, a news service, or can he or she start with a general search using one of the popular search engines, or will the investigator need to peruse social media websites?

Step Three. Finally, determine the time available to carry out your information collection plan. As the client is paying by the hour, the PI needs to be realistic about how much time he or she can spend searching, and the likelihood additional time may reveal information pertinent to the inquiry.

Themes and Key Words

The key to successful open-source information searching is knowing what themes or concepts to use. Breaking-down themes/concepts is known in intelligence work as *thematic analysis.* This then forms the first step of the analytic process − to simplify the search terms and break them down into elements. But this may be more difficult than appears. Practice is important, but here are some hints that might help this learning process.

Examine the information requirement and make a first-pass extract of key themes. These will act as the search's key words. In order to contextualize this, let us consider the following inquiry question: "Is there any evidence that links Perth-based property developers with organized crime?" Such a question might arise when your client is approached to invest a large sum of money in some new property developments. The client may have considerations about the investment being associated with rumors that are circulating about inroads being made into the industry by organized crime.

The initial theme to emerge from this information requirement is that of *property development.* This theme is quite broad; so is the second theme − *organized crime.* However, the limiting theme is the geographic location − *Perth,* which will help to constrain research.

When search themes are broad, as in this case, consider using derivatives that might narrow the focus. For example, *organized crime* may be narrowed to outlaw motorcycle gangs, or ethnic crime gangs, and so on. Each of these themes may then be narrowed further to named groups, such as the Banditos, Hells Angels, or in the case of ethnic crime gangs, Asian crime gangs, or Eastern European crime gangs.

Key Word Searching

Depending on the access the PI has to specific databases, he or she has a choice of using subject-based or key word searches. Subject-based searching has many advantages, but it is probably less useful in the private investigations domain, so we will focus on key word searching. A key word search is based on a premise that the words we search for will occur somewhere in a document, document title, on a web page, or in an index. Key word searching tends to lack precision because a single occurrence of the word in, say, a document will suffice to get a "hit."

While key word searches will work by simply typing in the list of words that have been identified as relevant to the information requirement, it is likely the result will not be that useful. Successful key word searching requires us to craft search statements. To do this requires using *operators* to join search terms, accounting for specific phrases that might be used, and consideration of relevant word variants. This is further complicated by the fact that different search engines, databases, and points of access can all require or use different means of achieving such.

To be successful in accessing open-source information, there is a need to have a basic understanding of how Boolean operators[79] work. These are conditioning statements that allow you to create, refine, and delimit your information searches. The three most commonly used Boolean operators are: AND, OR, and NOT. The use of AND requires that all conjoined words must be present in the document. This is useful when we need to connect concepts. Whereas the operator OR will return all documents where any of the words are present. This is useful when there are a variety of synonyms that might be used to describe the information we are searching for. The Boolean operator NOT allows us to exclude specific words from our results.

The problem with key word searches, notwithstanding the use of Boolean operators, is that for the most part, they will return far too many returns to be useful without refinement. However, specific phrases can go a long way to assisting in that refinement.

In order to generate specific phrases for searches there are a number of options: the PI can enclose the phrase in quotation marks, and/or he or she can use some additional Boolean operators. With the advanced search functions available in some search engines, there are drop-down menus, or dialogue boxes, in which you simply place your phrase. The two Boolean operators that assist with specific phrases are NEAR and ADJ. Use of the operator NEAR will find both words near each other in any order, usually within the bounds of a single sentence. The use of ADJ will find occurrences of the two words adjacent to each other again in any order. But when a specific phrase is placed within a set of quotation marks, only occurrences of the exact phrase will be returned.

The use of the AND and OR operators will produce the widest returns in a search, whereas the use of NEAR or ADJ will restrict your returns, while the use of specific phrases will limit your returns even more so. The key to getting good results is the amount of time and thought expended at the beginning in order to craft a set of precise search terms. So, the private investigator might want to consider searching in stages – first, on the broader concepts, then subsequently focusing in using specific phrases. In some cases, the PI will be able to undertake sequential searches limited to the domain of data already found.

Depending on the search applications used, the private investigator can also refine his or her searches by limiting the results by date. The PI might also limit his or her results to a specific document type, or limit the search to domain or domain type. However, care needs to be exercised when becoming too prescriptive, as the results can miss data that may be of relevance.

Reliability and Validly

Before moving on to consider some of the different applications available to search open-sources, it is worth giving some thought to some simple website evaluation practices. One of the dangers of the Internet is that anyone can represent themselves as an expert and post information. In some ways, the Internet is a great leveller in terms of having a forum to present voice and opinions. But in another way, it is a place where the word of the unenlightened person is equal to the word full of knowledge; so thought needs to go into establishing what is fact, and what is fiction. Or, how does the PI establish what may be considered reliable and valid from that which is likely to be deceitful, deceptive, or a case of disinformation.

Some questions the PI should asks him or herself when evaluating websites include these considerations. Review the URL of the website you are looking at and question whether it is a website or a personal page? What about the domain name? Is it appropriate to the content being displayed? What about the country code – does it clearly identify the entity and owner of the website? Can you identify the author and the currency of the material being displayed?

Sometimes these data items are easy to determine by a quick scan of the material being viewed – look for links to elements such as "about us," or "contact us," or even "background." Importantly, as the PI discovers useful and relevant websites – sites that are trusted – they should be recorded for future reference. The simple use of Internet browser *bookmarks* is a valuable start; the PI could also copy and paste useful URLs into a document. The key is to make sure the private investigator can get his or her way back to them without the need to work through the complete search process over again.

SOME OPEN-SOURCE SEARCH APPLICATIONS

The depth and breadth of open-source search applications that are available to the private investigator grows every year. Therefore, we will restrict our review of these applications to an overview of their use and some ideas as to how they might be employed. The focus will be on cost-free, web-based applications; however, some fee paying options will also be discussed.

One of the open-source intelligence applications that is in ubiquitous use at the time of writing is the search engine *Google*. A search engine is simply an enormous database index of web pages. While the process of indexing is ongoing, the fact is that for the most part when the PI searches using a search engine, he or she is actually seeing a small portion of the world-wide web that was indexed at a specific point in time. Even though this may not be an important issue for popular websites that are updated regularly, it may be an issue with some of the more obscure. Generally, the more websites indexed by a search engine the more up-to-date the index is. This may account in part for *Google's* popularity.

It is important to understand that all search engines are not the same, which is a point easily demonstrated by conducting a simple search on a variety of search engines using the same set of key words. Differences will be seen in terms of the number of pages returned and the order of those pages. Differences will also occur on using the same search engine, but different regional derivatives. Table 4.1 highlights this using the key words *organized crime corruption*.[80]

Table 4.1. Examples of Search Engine Results

Search Engine	Number of Results
http://www.google.com.au	362,000,000
http://www.google.com	7,290,000
http://us.yhs4.search.yahoo.com/web/advanced?ei=UTF-8&fr=altavista&p	41,000,000
http://www.bing.com/	41,500,000
http://www.google.com/blogsearch?hl=en	30,400,000
http://www.youtube.com/	69,300

Each search engine used its own algorithms for determining relevance. As a result, search engines may rank relevancy by currency, or as is often the case, by popularity. In some cases, website owners pay fees to have their information listed in the upper levels of any search results. This highlights the need for thought and planning when it comes to crafting your search terms. It also underscores the need to use several search engines to help locate information. In addition, applications that allow searching of the deep web are as important as searching the surface web.

> **. . . it is widely understood [that search engine] algorithms are based on interdisciplinary concepts borrowed from the likes linguistics, cognitive psychology, mathematics, and informatics (and perhaps others).**[81]

THE FUTURE OF OPEN-SOURCE INFORMATION – SOCIAL MEDIA

Social media has changed the way people connect and communicate because of the influence of websites such as *Facebook, LinkedIn,* and *Twitter.* At the time of writing, their popularity continued to grow at an almost impossible to comprehend rate. Even if these avenues do not continue to succeed, it is likely to be the result of something new that has overtaken them.

Social media is not just a communication medium that appeals to young people, there are plenty of Baby Boomers and Generation X users, too. Social media has been given some credit for facilitating the successful uprisings of the Arab Spring that began in December 2010, later to consume many nations in North Africa, the Middle East, and beyond. This was because information about what was going on in these "closed societies" was made available to the world via social media and allowed people to connect their ideas and plans.[82]

Privacy

One of the most interesting aspects of social media from the perspective of the PI is the fact that in the virtual world of social media, people become far less concerned about their privacy. In fact, many people will say things or post photographs on social media that in the physical world they would never do. Successful exploitation of social media provides an opportunity for the PI to profile a target in a myriad of ways. Notwithstanding the fact that validating information on social media is fraught with problems, the "diamonds," when discovered, are really priceless, and often otherwise unobtainable.[83]

Social media allows private investigators to access two useful information sets. First, media like *Twitter* enables the PI to access opinion and commentary on things that may be of interest to an inquiry. Media such as *Facebook* and *LinkedIn,* give the private investigator access to more useful personal information and allows him or her to see connections between people, to access photographs of these people, and to some degree obtain insight into how people might be perceived by, or perceive others.

LinkedIn profiles provide a potential wealth of information about an individual. Most of these profiles are accompanied by a personal photograph which could provide, say, a point of comparison if a private investigator needs to confirm an identity. Most profiles then provide the professional role and title of the individual as well as details of the professional employment history, education, and particular skills they possess (or claim to possess . . .). Some will also have testimonials or recommendations by others in their network. A *LinkedIn* profile can provide a rich vein of information for further lines of inquiry.

In comparison, a *Facebook* profile provides an insight into the private side of an individual; here the PI will likely find images not just of the person of interest, but possibly of his or her associates, friends, and relatives. The person of interest's personal thoughts could also appear on a *Facebook* website that discuss issues and people whom they like, and dislike, and why.

While social media offers the private investigator a potentially enormous opportunity to investigate all manner of individuals, the reality is somewhat more complex. Accessibility of data on platforms such as *Facebook* will depend on the level of privacy controls used by each individual. Where individuals limit access to their personal data by making it "private" or limiting access to specific circles of friends, it therefore becomes difficult to access by a third party (i.e., including the private investigator). Fortunately for the PI, not all members of a circle of friends will be so privacy conscious and often information becomes available to us through the posts of others. That is, the PI can "observe" their target indirectly via another person in the circle.

There are a variety of software applications available specifically to assist the private investigator find information on people, notwithstanding the websites specific to commerce and industry which allow the PI to check details of company directors, or websites that allow one to check on an individual's criminal history. Software and search facilities have a history of evolving very rapidly; however, there are various websites where individuals and organizations collate useful lists of online resources. A typical example is the British website *www.uk-osint.net,* which has lists of searchable websites and search engines, both fee paying and free to access.

Let us now look at how the private investigator might track down an individual via the Internet. We will look at two of the many options that are available, one being a free option and the other being a subscription service. Of course, in the first instance, the PI might look for people using the inbuilt search functions available on websites like *Facebook* or *LinkedIn;* however, generally speaking, in both cases, the PI will need to create an "identity" on those websites themselves.

Two websites that provide a large selection of useful search facilities to perform such functions as tracing a person of interest are *Pipl* and *Spokeo*. Much like the search engines *Google, Yahoo,* and others, conducting searches in these may produce different sets of results (due to the search algorithms used). Both of these search facilities have limitations, though. Still, both do have quite reasonable coverage of the United States. On both search engines, the PI will see that they have a variety of options to search for their target.

A search at *Pipl* begins with a name and there is an option to include a location if known (to help narrow the results). Once the private investigator has obtained the search results, he or she can then refine the search, if need be, by selecting the advanced search options. Narrowing the search results could be done by selecting such data items as an email address, a nickname, or via keywords; all of which will help if the target has a common name like "John Smith" (which, by the way, surprisingly only returned 180 matches at the time of this writing[84]). As well as getting links to the websites at which John Smith is mentioned, the PI also gets access to any images that might be posted to the website.

On *Spokeo,* conducting the same search of John Smith generated in excess of 50,000 hits; all of whom were situated in the United States. *Spokeo* enables the private investigator to take a number of different options when commencing a person of interest search. Searches can be conducted on a name, an email address, a telephone number, a "user name," an address, or even the name of friend or associate or the target. The benefit of *Spokeo,* given it is a paid subscription service, is in the enhanced interface that is provided. That is, results are associated with a map, which in turn allows the PI to locate a specific address, and if the relevant information exists, it will provide a synopsis of the area in which the target lives, family composition, and more.

Tracing an individual via his or her digital footprint on social media is not necessarily simple. *Facebook* and *LinkedIn* together provide access to profiles of in excess of a billion people. Each is searchable but requires the PI to have his or her own "online identity" to exploit them. *Pipl* and *Spokeo* provide an alternative means of accessing person of interest data; however, they are limited in their coverage. The key to searching for people is maximizing the number of identifying elements that can be exploited. This is no different in the physical world where several pieces of personal identification are required to ensure positive identification. So, in cyber space, a name is good, but a name and an email address is better.

KEY TERMS AND PHRASES

The key words and phrases associated with this chapter are listed below. In one or two sentences, demonstrate your understanding of each by writing a short definition or explanation.

- Deep web;
- Digital domain;
- External domain;
- Hard copy domain;
- Internal domain;
- Key words;
- Open-source information;
- Operator;
- Reliability and validly;
- Search engine; and
- Surface web.

STUDY QUESTIONS

1. Examine the search page for *Google* with the advanced search page for *Yahoo*. Explain how the *Yahoo* search page enables you to create your search terms without the need to use Boolean operators.
2. Why is it important to understand your client's intent prior to beginning your information search strategy?
3. If you have a *Facebook* or *LinkedIn* profile, examine it critically. Ask yourself "what does it tell people reading it about me." Find a profile of someone you know and examine it too critically. What are you able to learn about him or her? Now would you change anything you have posted in your profile?

LEARNING ACTIVITY

Assume you have a client who is a U.S.-based investor and she has become aware of the potential investment opportunities in Perth, Western Australia due to the mineral resources boom in that state. She is interested in opportunities for property development in and around the Perth metropolitan. However, she has also heard that there may be some issues linking organized crime to the property industry. Your client wants to know what, if any, risk she might be exposed to if she partners with property developers in Western Australia. In completing this activity, first consider what might be inferred by your client's concerns? Is she intending to avoid unnecessary risk, and in particular avoid partnering with anyone who might be linked to organized crime? What then are your information requirements – compile an information collection plan. Hint: one information requirement that you might come up with might be: "Is there any evidence of links between Perth based property developers and organized crime?"

Chapter 5

TARGET PROFILES

Tony Buffett

INTRODUCTION

Background

A private investigator driving around a sun-drenched city in the latest model European sports sedan is a fiction of television. The post-911 private investigator needs thinking skills not conspicuous glamor. In order to meet this need, this chapter discusses a structure for such thinking. It is a simple framework for what PIs do (or should do. . .) – perhaps unconsciously – and uses fact and reason to draw conclusions. This technique is known as the *target profile.*

In the simplest of terms, private intelligence is the result of two actions: the first is the collection of information regarding a target, and the second, the conversion of those raw data items into a focused *intelligence product* – a report or briefing. Although the term is used widely, it is worth clarifying – intelligence products are reports, briefings, messages, dispatches, summaries, articles, and the like.

By-and-large, the majority of information used in private intelligence comes from public sources. Public sources are termed *open-source intelligence* which was discussed in the preceding chapter. But suffice to say that open-source intelligence accounts for ". . . 90 percent of all information that you and your [client] need to make key decisions and to understand your [target] . . . is already public or can be systematically developed from public data."[85]

As the Chinese military strategist Sun Tzu is reported to have written: "Know the enemy, know yourself; your victory will never be endangered."[86] In order to do this, the private investigator should not only be aware of what

a target profile is; he or she should be able to produce a profile in order analyzing any given situation. So, as nice as a luxury European car would be, it
is not as useful as a structured way of thinking.

Profiles and Assessments Support Investigations

Any investigation that is deemed to be problematic or complex would benefit from some type of intelligence support. It has taken decades for policing
organizations to recognize the value intelligence plays in investigations, but
now that they have, it is doubtful whether any law enforcement agency would
conduct an investigation that has some level of complexity associated with it
without intelligence support.

It could be argued that the private investigator has been thrust into this situation by a combination of events – changes in the law, the nature of law
breaking, and the complexities of communications, and financial transactions,
to mention a few. But, if intelligence is not driven by the collection of evidence or to deliver a prosecution, why then did intelligence inculcate the investigative environ? Although the products provided by the intelligence function ultimately assist in the outcome of an investigation, it is designed to help
decision-makers understand the issue being probed and to select options as to
the directions the investigation needs to take.

Even though intelligence is the result of the process known as the *intelligence
cycle* (see Chapter 2), it is an iterative process where the outcome does not end
at the conclusion of the investigation. The collection of information and the
meshing of the various parts of information enabled the production of a larger understanding of the target or the issue under investigation. For instance, it
could be said that the benefits of the analytical process include: helping decision makers deal more effectively with uncertainty; provide timely warning of
threats; and support a range of operational activities relative to the target or
problem under consideration.[87] This is where the target profile comes into the
picture.

The Language of Assessments
Although intelligence analysts use phrases in their reports
such as: *it is estimated,* or *it is considered* along with terms
that convey probability, such as *likely,* it is important to understand that these phrases are not referring to facts, but
judgments. Although judgments can be based on facts, the
two are different.

TARGET PROFILES

What is a target profile? A target profile is a report that contains at its heart an analysis of an individual, a group, or a network (which could include companies, or issue motivated groups – see Chapter 7 for more details on issue motivated groups). We will call this a *target-of-interest*.[88] The expressed purpose of the target profile is to establish a basis for some form of intervention with regard to the target. As such, the target profile will usually contain recommendations about future informational requirements that might be necessary to implement a tactical response.

But the target profiles' central function is to assist decision makers understand the key issues and think through what future actions, if any, might be required to deal with the target-of-interest. So, the target profile should ideally enable a clear understanding of the target-of-interest. In doing so, it also makes clear what the profile *does not* provide; that is, the gaps in the intelligence profile. Identifying what is not known about the target is equally critical.

Context

The key to any operative's credibility is his or her ability to provide an intelligence product that is both ethical and accurate. Part of the private investigator's business acumen is to provide his or her client with outcomes that are based on fact and reason.

The target profile should be developed through the application of analytical methods. The profile will remain a "live document" throughout the investigative process. This means that any new data that is the product of the analytical process against the target should be included in the target profile and this information assessed as to its effect on the operational context of the investigation. Not all targets will require a profile.

Critical to the development of the profile is the risk the target presents to the investigation. As a result of conducting a SWOT analysis in conjunction with link analysis, the target may be assessed as a minimal risk to the investigation and as such not be considered (at that time) requiring further development. However, the individual may figure as part of the associate group of the key target.

The target profile is developed to assist the investigator in not only the decision-making process, but also in the development of courses of action for the investigative outcomes. To that end, as previously discussed, the need to ensure the communicative process between the analyst and the investigator is critical. Within this context, the development of the profile will be defined and the profile will be developed in a timely and efficient manner.

Initial Considerations

Although we will discuss what are seen as the key parts for a profile, it should be said that there is no definitive outline for the target profile. Nevertheless, the profile needs to highlight a number of important items. These pieces of information will be discussed shortly; however, when developing the target profile, the PI needs to be mindful of these central tenants:

- The target profile needs to be easily understood by the decision maker. In other words, the report should be clearly written and to the point;
- It should only contain maps, photographs, or other material if it will help support the decision-making process, not confuse it (and certainly not to "pad-it-out"); and
- The report should be able to answer the "so what" or "what if" questions relating to the target-of-interest.

The target profile's constituent parts are arranged in a funnel shape, taking the decision maker from the background of the issue under investigation through to the specific recommendations. In the process, the target profile should provide the facts and the analysis (i.e., the reasoning) on which the options are based.

Parts of a Target Profile

In order for the target profile to take the decision maker through the facts surrounding the target-of-interest, and arrive at a logical conclusion about some course of action, the report needs to be structured. In structuring the report, the PI will need to include different pieces of information, each with a specific purpose. That is, in order to draw a conclusion at the end of the report, and therefore make a judgement as to what to do about it, there needs to be facts, and these facts need to be analyzed. Analysis in this sense is arranging facts to produce meaning. Facts alone are just that – a pile of information. It is not intelligence. Although there may be other report forms for doing this, the structure suggested below is a suitable *pro forma* for achieving this result.

Introduction. This section simply lists the operative who developed the target profile and for whom it was developed. This information helps with filing and retrieval.

Background. As this section sets the scene, it needs to contain broad-based information. This information might include the following: the objective and scope of the report; explanation about why the target is being investigated; and the reasons as to why the target has been chosen for investigation. This latter issue is important in ensuring the process and the product are both ethical and lawful.

Personal Details. From the general scene setting of the background section, the report moves into a number of specific information items, starting with the personal details of the target. If the target-of-interest is a group or gang (i.e., a *group-of-interest*), then this section might include details about the group. The personal details section might then follow this group or gang details section. Data items could include a description of the person's physical attributes, aliases, occupation, driving licence details, as well as home and business addresses.

It is likely that a target-of-interest may have some association with a business. It is difficult to think of any situation where a person acting criminally has no connection with some business enterprise – either directly, indirectly, or consequentially. So, if the target-of-interest has such an association, then those details could be listed in a separate section of the report entitled "business details," or if they are only incidental, they could be incorporated in this section.

A clearly articulated social insight into the target should be included. This should highlight places the target frequents, known associates, connections within businesses and community. This information should present a picture of the target and the environment that he or she feels comfortable in.

Criminal History. If these data are available, this section should highlight the criminal history of the target. The inclusion of any convictions recorded, court appearances, or key issues that will help in the analysis stage with regard to considering the impact of these events on operational safety are appropriate.

Issues that may impact include whether the target has a propensity for violence; whether he or she (or the group or gang) own or have access to firearms, and what connections the target has within the criminal environment.

Because private intelligence relies heavily on open-source information, it is unlikely that an operative practicing within one of the Five-Eyes countries will have legal access to restricted government information of this sort. So, to be able to obtain information about a target's criminal past, the private investigator will need to rely on public databases.

Local, state/province, and national newspapers report on a range of crime and criminal stories. So, in the process, people's names, offenses, court convictions, and probation and parole details are usually reported as part of the public record. But not all are. Nevertheless, it is a source of information that cannot be overlooked. There may be other databases – like sex offenders' registers, and perhaps additional sources depending on the jurisdiction, and these should be explored, too.

Surveillance. If any surveillance has been conducted against the target, then this information should be included in this section. This information is important as it might provide insight into, say, the target's social patterns or the physical environment which he or she traverses. Not only should this section of the report provide observations made by surveillance, but information about the target's practice of countersurveillance or other counterintelligence actions. For instance, does the target, check for surveillance when driving in a vehicle; does the target only use telephones in public areas; or use public Internet for emails; and so on.

Target Analysis. This is the part of the report that turns the facts listed in the previous sections in to intelligence. Analysis allows the private investigator to draw conclusions so he or she can answer the "so what" and "what if" questions.

A popular analytic technique to use for a target profile is an analysis of strengths, weaknesses, opportunities, and threats.[89] It is abbreviated as SWOT and requires a minimal amount of training. A SWOT analysis can also show missing data – termed *intelligence gaps* – as well as acting as the foundation for formulating recommendations and identifying additional information for collection.

SWOT analyses can be used with unstructured data (i.e., qualative data) and structured data (i.e., quantitative), so it is very flexible. Only three steps are involved in conducting this type of analysis:

1. Articulate the aim or objective of the investigation (in military terms, this is known as the *end-state*);
2. Consider the facts that are listed in the various sections of the report (i.e., personal details, business details, criminal history, surveillance, and possible others), and take these facts and place them under the appropriate quadrant of the SWOT (see Table 5.1[90]). Note that strengths and weaknesses relate to issues internal to the investigation, whereas opportunities and threats are external. Depending on the meaning assigned to the fact, some facts may be applicable to more than one quadrant; and
3. Consider each quadrant for strategies that might present as ways of achieving the aim or objective. For instance, consider how:
   • the strengths can be used to achieve the aim or objective;
   • the weaknesses can be overcome;
   • any opportunities can be utilized; and
   • threats can be mitigated.

Table 5.1. SWOT Analytical Matrix

	Analysis of Strengths, Weaknesses, Opportunities, and Threats	
	Supportive	Detrimental
Internal	*Strengths* are the attributes associated with the [issue/problem/agency/etc. under investigation] that are conducive to achieving the end-state.	*Weaknesses* are the attributes associated [issue/problem/agency/etc. under investigation] that are detrimental or may prevent achieving the end-state.
External	*Opportunities* are the conditions [legal/criminogenic/social/economic/political/psychological/etc.] that would assist achieving the end-state.	*Threats* are the conditions [legal/criminogenic/social/economic/political/psychological/etc.] that might be detrimental to the way the agency carries out its operations.

Recommendations for Action. Once the analysis is performed, then some course of action needs to take place. This is the planning section of the report. This is where the private investigator reviews the conclusions he or she drew from the SWOT and translates them into options for action.

But as with many things in life, there is never just one option; there is a range of options – from doing nothing, all the way up to a resource-demanding option. Each option presented should be couched in terms of how it might achieve the aim or objective (i.e., the end-sate). Recommendation of additional information can be presented here if intelligence gaps were perceived.

The target profile should provide realistic courses of action that afford a number of options. Ultimately, the target profile is designed to assist in developing an understanding of an individual or group. So, care should be taken not to "guide" the profile in a particular direction through preconceived ideas or bias. The data should speak for itself.

Attachments. If there is material that may be overwhelming or easier to show in diagrammatic form, then consider placing this material in an appendix to the report. If this is done, the appended material should be referred to the material in the body of the report under the appropriate section heading. Material that falls into this category includes maps, photographs, and charts.

EXAMPLE OF A TARGET PROFILE

Introduction

This profile was developed on April 1, 2013 by licensed private investigator Mr. Dolan Earlwood. The profile was developed for Whitney Global Investigations, Brimfield, Massachusetts, for its client Prudent Car Insurers, Brookfield, Massachusetts.

Background

This profile is raised against the target Freddie READY.

Mr. READY is suspected of being involved in a car theft ring based in the Boston area but appears that that illegal enterprise may be expanding to the Sturbridge, Massachusetts area.

It is understood that READY has developed associations with a group of males in the Sturbridge area who own a large industrial-type garage on the outskirts of the township. The client, Prudent Car Insurers suspects that READY may be expanding his car theft activities to include central Massachusetts where Prudent Car Insurers has a substantial client base.

The objective of the target profile is to determine what actions, if any, may benefit the client as a major motor vehicle insurer.

Target's Personal Details

Personal Details

Personal details of READY were obtained through public records searches and genealogical databases as well as from surveillance.

Name: Freddie READY
Date of birth: April 1, 1966
Place of Birth: Cambridge, Massachusetts
Height: approximately 5'10"
Weight: about 200 lbs
Last known address: 123 Fake Street,
Cambridge, Massachusetts
Married/Family: Not known but currently lives alone.
Marks: Scar on left cheek (confirmed by surveillance operative)

Criminal History

As search of the online newspaper database showed that READY was:

- convicted in June 2010 for motor vehicle theft and was sentenced to six months imprisonment;
- arraigned for receiving stolen goods (car parts) in January 2011 but charges drop for insufficient evidence; and
- was again convicted of motor vehicle theft in November 2012 and sentenced to 8 months imprisonment.

Surveillance

Whitney Global Investigations conducted physical surveillance on READY during the week beginning March 4, 2013 and observed:

- On Tuesday March 5, 2013 READY drove to Sturbridge along US Route 20. During the trip, the target did not use his rear view mirrors or alternate his speed or any other evasive tactics. Once at Sturbridge, READY drove directly to Big Al's Diner on Main Street where he met two males standing outside, appearing to be waiting for him.

- The three went in and sat at a booth at the rear of the diner. During the meeting, the three men only drank coffee. All three took turns placing telephone calls on their cell phones. While this happened, the other two men sat and listened – no conversation took place. After each man had used his phone in turn, the three would conduct a discussion.
- After the meeting that lasted 54 minutes, READY got in his car and drove east along US Route 20 towards Cambridge-Boston.
- The operative followed the two men in their car to a large industrial garage located further along Main Street to the west, but on the outskirts of the town. The men drove slowly and at one stage, pulled over to the side of the road and waited for 3 minutes before proceeding along Main Street in the same direction. There was no signage over the build or any other means of identification. As this part of the town is semi-rural, there were no street numbers and the operative had to estimate that the property number was an even number (i.e., north side of the street) and in the low 700s. The two men who met READY went inside and while the operative remained in a stakeout position (for 45 minute), no one entered or exited the building. Both men stood at the door to the building for about 2 minutes and looked up and down the street several times. About 5 minutes later, one of the men opened the door enough to stick his head out and looked around the parking lot at the front, then closed the door.
- On Thursday, March 7, 2013, READY received a visit at his Cambridge home from one of the two men met on the Tuesday. This male is likely to be Shandon ROSQUE as the sign on the side of the F100 pickup truck he was driving stated "Shannon ROSQUE, Collision Automotive Body Shop, 720 Main Street, Sturbridge, MA."

Target Analysis – SWOT

Strengths

- READY does not appear to know that he is under surveillance.
- The two men who met READY have both recognized that there is active surveillance on them.
- The location of the garage suspected to be involved in this alleged car theft has been located.
- The enterprise carried on at the garage is likely to be automotive collision repair.
- The name of one of the two Sturbridge garage men has tentatively been identified (Shannon ROSQUE).
- Vehicles known to READY and ROSQUE's vehicles have been identified.
- Much of READY's personal details have been compiled.

Weaknesses

- Nothing is known about the relationship between the Sturbridge men and READY.
- Ownership of the garage is not known.

- Confirmed identity of the one Sturbridge men is known and the other only tentative.

Opportunities

- More can be learned about the intentions of the three if the two Sturbridge men can be identified.
- More could be understood about the intentions of the group if the function of the garage can be learned (e.g., is it a car *repair* shop or a car *dismantling* shop).

Threats

- The two Sturbridge men present as being suspicious of surveillance and have practiced countersurveillance maneuvers.
- Unsure whether ROSQUE and his associate in Sturbridge have a history of violence or of criminal activity.

Conclusions

These data do not indicate that READY is involved in any illegal activity that involves stealing cars. However, his meeting with the two males in Sturbridge on March 5 and 7, 2013 and his subsequent meeting with ROSQUE may indicate that the three are in the early planning stages of, perhaps, a car re-birthing enterprise in central Massachusetts.

The present data indicates that READY does not have a history of violence.

As READY has twice been convicted of car theft, it could be concluded that he has good understanding of the illegal market for motor vehicles. Because he was arrested for receiving stolen goods (i.e., car parts), he is likely to have contacts in this type of enterprise.

Nevertheless, there is no evidence that READY, ROSQUE, and the other man are planning any illegal activity, though there is sufficient cause to reasonably suspect that they are planning such activity.

Recommendations for Action

If the objective of the target profile is to determine what actions, if any, may benefit the client as a major motor vehicle insurer, then there are a number of actions that can be taken:

1. Do nothing – *Not recommended* as this would not achieve the goal of the investigation.
2. Conduct a physical surveillance of the garage with the express aim of obtaining information about the two men that READY met with and the function of the garage – *Recommended.*
3. Conduct public records research on the two men's identities and backgrounds once these facts are known (as per recommendation 2 above) so that a target profile can be developed on each person – *Recommended.*

KEY WORDS AND PHRASES

The key words and phrases associated with this chapter are listed below. In one or two sentences, demonstrate your understanding of each by writing a short definition or explanation.

- Analysis;
- Intelligence product;
- Open-source intelligence;
- Target-of-interest; and
- Target profile.

STUDY QUESTIONS

1. List the four quadrants of a SWOT analysis.
2. Describe what each of the four descriptors of SWOT means.
3. Describe how each of the four SWOT descriptors is used to contribute to the overall analysis.

LEARNING ACTIVITY

Although the example discussed in this chapter involved the notional case of organized motor vehicle theft, consider the purposes of this exercise a matter involving the sale of counterfeit trademark goods, say, T-shirts. Suppose you are the private investigator assigned to make some initial inquiries into the allegation by the trademark's owner. List the public sources of data you could exploit to provide information for each of the report's headings (i.e., the sections on personal details, criminal history, and surveillance).

Chapter 6

FRAUD INTELLIGENCE

REBECCA VOGEL

INTRODUCTION

Traditionally, the role of the private investigator was largely one of performing a reactive activity. That is, the private investigator was usually hired to solve a case involving any number of crimes, particularly fraud; such as workers' compensation fraud, welfare fraud, tax evasion, and insurance fraud. However, since the attacks of September 11, 2001, private investigation has undergone a transformation due to advances in technology and has moved toward more proactive, intelligence-led role. In today's technology-driven society, the role of the private investigator has, by necessity, changed to combat the complexities of today's iterations of fraud, including more intricate types of what could be called traditional fraud.

The advent of smart phones and related technologies have afforded the private investigator almost instantaneous access to information. This includes the complexities of worldwide communication, global money transfers, international travel, and the ability to use technology to create or alter identities. By way of example, take the case of Frank W. Abagnale who was the subject of the 2003 motion picture entitled *Catch Me if You Can.*[91] Mr. Abagnale altered his identity numerous times in order to swindle people out of millions of dollars via his many identities – a pilot for Pan Am, medical practitioner, and lawyer.

Recent high-profile, large-scale scandals involving fraud have highlighted the growing incidence of corporate deceptions. Such cases include Tyco International, Enron, Adelphia, and Worldcom. Moreover, the Global Financial Crisis (GFC) of 2007–2012 spawned an entire multi-faceted industry engaged in mortgage and foreclosure fraud. However, in the world of the private investigator, there are as important, but somewhat smaller in scale, instances of fraud that deal with individual cases of mortgage and foreclosure fraud, identity fraud, theft of services (e.g., utilities, telephone, and computer processing time), tax evasion, credit card fraud, wire fraud, and insurance fraud.

FOCUS

Our exploration of how intelligence can form part of the PI's investigative methods will be grounded in the framework of the intelligence cycle. The intelligence cycle was discussed in Chapter 2 (Investigative Intelligence) and comprises direction, collection, analysis, and dissemination. To begin our discussion of how intelligence methods can be used in each phase of the cycle, we will view this cycle through what could be considered is a prism of its function, thus allowing the reader to contextualize private intelligence and investigation.

There are clear parallels to be drawn between the methods used in intelligence work and those that could be used by the private investigator to solve fraud cases. For instance, intelligence-led policing has changed the nature of policing practices from what was largely a reactive process to one that is pre-emptive. Intelligence-led policing uses targeted, intelligence-based operations to detect and deter crime. Similarly, the use of intelligence methods by the private investigator can form part of a paradigm shift from reactive to active inquires. This shift in approach can only be beneficial to the PI's clients by helping avoid fraud in their businesses. Strategies involving fraud prevention and disruption at the "front-end" can be marketed to the PI's clients.

Although fraud takes on many different forms, we will focus our discussion on two types. First, we will examine identity fraud and then we will discuss economic espionage. The reason these two aspects of fraud investigation will be the center of our deliberations is that identify fraud is the chief enabler for all other forms of fraud. The reason economic espionage is the second focus, is that although this type of crime has been around for decades, arguably, it has accelerated in the post-9/11 world. These topics will be couched in the framework of the intelligence cycle. Doing so allows us to examine intelligence methods that can be linked to each phase of a private investigator's fraud inquiry.

IDENTITY FRAUD

Identity theft is a term currently in vogue, but in fact, it is not possible to "steal" a person's identify. It is simply an act of *impersonation*. That is, person

A assumes another person's identify (e.g., person B) in order to fraudulently obtain goods, services, or other benefits that are entitled to person B. In years gone by, this was done by way of a fake ID and was also known as *paper tripping.*[92] Arguably, the most common example of this is obtaining credit cards to make purchases, or to obtain a bank loan.

Identity theft is the primary enabler of fraud because it provides the necessary anonymity for criminals to carry out their monetary theft. Hence, many of the Five-Eyes countries have moved to insisting on a system of improved identity checking. This usually includes providing birth certificates, citizen certificate or passport as "primary documents," along with a number of "secondary documents" in support – such as, a driver's license, employee ID card, marriage certificate, bank account cards, and so on. The rationale behind the use of these cross-verified documents is that it makes it far more difficult to impersonate another person (or, a completely fictitious person).

There is a wealth of information available for criminals to "harvest" and we are often our own worst enemies when it comes to providing opportunities for others to impersonate us. Prior to computer databases and the Internet, this was mainly done by visiting cemeteries and searching graves for a person of the same sex and about the same age. Once located, a copy of the birth certificate could be obtained. This "primary document" could then be used to obtain any number of "secondary documents."

However, identity theft is now perpetuated through the popularity of social media websites or from customers' personal information stored online in commercial databases. There are frequent media reports about breaches of computer security that have resulted in hackers gaining access to enormous numbers of customers' names, addresses, email addresses, as well as credit card details, and in some cases, even Social Security numbers.[93]

The profits to be made through identity fraud have inspired criminals to perpetuate increasingly more complex methods of stealing personal information. Often, the victim remains unaware that his or her details have been used fraudulently until substantial amounts of money have been stolen from them.

"Identify theft can go on for months or even years before you become aware that you are a victim. When an identify thief is running up debt in your name, you may not be aware of it until you apply for some type of credit yourself."[94]

In recent years, the marked increase in the number of individuals not covered by health insurance has spawned a "medical identity fraud" trade. This is characterized by individuals who deceitfully receive medical treatment, or obtain pathology tests, or have prescriptions filled by using the identity of an individual who has insurance coverage. The unfortunate result of this type of fraud is that the victim of the fraud then has the medical details of the fraudster on his or her medical records, which may detrimentally affect future medical insurance applications or premiums.

As lucrative as obtaining cash, consumer credit, and bank loans can be, a more lucrative area is stealing intellectual property. This includes the illegal use of others' ideas that are protected by patents, trademarks, and copyright. It is usually perpetrated by acts of espionage by people who have legitimated access – insiders.

INSIDER ESPIONAGE

Theft of trade secrets and other forms of intellectual property (IP) is generally termed *economic espionage*. It is a crime often perpetrated by individuals who are termed *trusted insiders*. These insiders may be permanent or temporary staff, or even contractors, or suppliers who have access to a business' information. They do this by using their inside knowledge of the business's processes, procedures, and policies to access electronic databases to obtain information that can be sold to competitors.

The information that falls into the category of being commercially valuable includes production plans, product launch dates, pricing schedules, advertising campaigns, customer lists, research and development findings, supply sources, personnel details, or anything that could benefit a competitor.[95] Insider theft also includes the theft of personal information, such as customer credit card details or other customer identifiers, which could subsequently be used fraudulently. Theft of company assets or materials has also been a common occurrence that is prevalent today as it has been for decades.[96]

Various situation factors can influence the prevalence of insider theft, such as technology, social factors, and the state of the economy. An insider's personal financial stress can serve as the impetus to commit intellectual property theft from his or her employer. Table 6.1 shows the motivations and opportunities that contribute to insider espionage.[97] Fraud researchers have determined that "perceived pressure" is common to all fraud, whether it is based in financial problems, frustration with the job or the boss/co-workers, or a challenge in "beating the system." Nonetheless, the operative word is *perceived*, and the pressure these people experience need not be "real pressure."[98]

Table 6.1. Motivations and Opportunities for Insider Espionage

Motivations		Opportunities
Increasing prevalence of financial crisis		Advances in information technology
Increasing prevalence of gambling disorders		Expanding market for . . . information
Diminishing organizational loyalty	Increasing vulnerability to insider espionage	Globalization of scientific research and commerce
Ethnic diversification of . . . workforce		More frequent international travel
Increasing popularity of global values		Global Internet expansion

Kramer and Heuer's study regarding the contributing factors to insider espionage found that there are increasing opportunities and motivation for insider fraud.[99] According to their research, employees living in the United States have a:

> . . . greater opportunity to establish contact with foreign entities and to transfer information to them through traveling internationally more often and by participating in international research and business ventures more frequently. [The] Internet can now be used to transmit massive amounts of digitized information simultaneously. [In addition,] American employees are more often encountering situations that can provide motivation for this crime. More insiders are experiencing financial problems and gambling addiction, both of which can provide impetus for workplace theft. Loyalty to organizations is diminishing and a greater proportion of American workers are at risk for becoming disgruntled.[100]

The risk of this particular type of fraud is high. In a speech in July, 2012, the Director of the National Security Agency and head of the U.S. Cyber Command, General Keith Alexander, estimated that the theft of intellectual property by cyber means cost the U.S. economy US$250 billion a year.[101] As such, corporate fraud remains one of the FBI's "highest priorities"[102] and will likely to continue this upward trend.

The U.S. Federal Bureau of Investigation (FBI) outlines six countermeasures that it recommends businesses take if they have concerns of economic espionage and these comprise the following:

1. Recognize there is an insider and outsider threat to your company;
2. Identify and evaluate trade secrets;
3. Implement a proactive plan for safeguarding trade secrets;
4. Secure physical and electronic versions of your trade secrets;
5. Confine intellectual knowledge on a "need-to-know" basis; and

6. Provide training to employees about your company's intellectual property plan and security.[103]

INTELLIGENCE METHODS

Direction

A client will approach the private investigator with a problem – a gap in his or her knowledge that he or she hopes the PI will be able to provide an answer to. In the case of the matters being discussed here – whether economic espionage or not – they are likely to be related to helping the client detect, deter, or disrupt some sort of fraudulent activity.

The direction phase is important in setting the expectations of the client, determining what information the client requires to make a decision, what will be needed to communicate effectively during the course of the inquiry, and determining the format that the information will take when reported at the end of the investigation.

In the past, a sizable proportion of the private investigator's work came directly from attorneys or insurance companies; the instructions they gave were usually clear and concise, so therefore the evidence was often specified. As the lawyers in, say, a civil prosecution will have already identified the actions/behaviors that are at the center of the wrong, it will almost always lead to the gathering of specific evidence – for instance, photographs/video footage of the alleged fraudster being of able-body, in the case of a worker's compensation claim.

However, with cases of economic espionage, a company may not know that its intellectual property has been illegally acquired and sold/traded to a competitor. Like identity theft, it could be years before one realizes that something is amiss.

In cases where the client approaches the private investigator, the PI needs to ask questions and record instructions so that he or she is sure of what is being asked of them, and what the client's expectations are. This should be in writing, even if the inquiry has some degree of urgency attached. For instance, the PI could use his or her handwritten notes that outline the nature, extent of the inquiry, scope, duration, and any issues of confidentially that can be made at the time of interview, and sign and date them. The PI could then ask the client to sign them also. More formal typed instructions could then be sent to the client in the PI's house-style report and letterhead, confirming their handwritten instructions.

Common to all investigations are the following elements – PIs can selectively determine which ones apply to the investigation they are about to undertake:

- Client's details and address;
- Contact person during the investigation;
- Client who has authority to initiate the investigating (if a business or body corporate);
- Aim of the investigation (i.e., a specific allegation);
- Scope (that is what will be investigated and what will not);
- Start and finish dates;
- Budget payment schedule for the investigation (usually on a retainer paid in advance);
- Who not to approach (issues of confidentially);
- Cover story to be used/pretext, etc.;
- Name of any suspects and evidence to support these assertions; and
- Timing of progress reports (and whether oral or in writing).

To make this direction setting phase of the intelligence cycle easy, a form could be designed and a number of copies printed. Then, as needed, the private investigator could complete the sections of the form, and strike out those that are not required depending on the assignment.

Collection

In cases other than those where an attorney has specified the types of evidence he or she needs for their prosecution, the private investigator is likely to have to determine the information needed. Therefore, the information gathering methods and procedures will, in large part, be determined by the allegation(s) made.

It is understandable that collection is seen as one of the most important phases of the intelligence cycle. It is often one of the more exciting aspects of PI work – the one glamorized in fiction. This is because the pieces of information gathered in the course of an investigation form the basis on which all *intelligence products* are produced. Here, we are referring to a "product" as a report, document, or oral briefing that provided insight, or helps answer the inquiry's central question/allegation.

A data collection plan will be necessary to start the process of prioritizing collection targets. Although the first collection method that comes to most peoples' minds is surveillance – that is, an operative with a camera and telephoto lens – but this may not even feature in an inquiry (Figure 6.1). Open-source data collection should always be a PI's first "port-of-call." This is because a very large percentage of information used in the production of intelligence comes from open-sources.[104] The exploitation of Internet-based information, particularly social media, should form part of an information collection plan. These data can be used to compile background information on the possible identities of perpetrators. Recall the discussion in Chapter 4 about open-source information and the example of how such information was used to help develop a target profile in Chapter 5. These same lessons apply here in relation to fraud intelligence.

Figure 6.1. Physical surveillance was previously the PI's main collection method (photograph courtesy of Hank Prunckun).

However, one of the most difficult pieces of information to obtain is that of a person's or group's *intent*. People behaving fraudulently will naturally try to hide their identity and activities, and will most likely be alert to any attempts to discover what they are doing. The private investigator may need to deal with denial, deception, misinformation, countersurveillance, as well as other counterintelligence measures employed by the perpetrator. Fraudsters employ numerous operational security measures to avoid detection. Regardless, it is possible to show intent using the weight of evidence that can be collected – in a court of law, the preponderance of such information is hoped to lead the "reasonable person" to conclude that intent has been established.

But if not, then covert information collection methods offer another avenue to establish intent. The methods by which information can be collected are numerous – pretext calls, cover stories, and discreet physical and optical surveillance all form part of the PIs repertoire of techniques. Take, for instance, these examples of some approaches to covert information gathering – the private investigator could interview trusted employees off-site about their knowledge of any activity regarding insider theft, missing inventory, employees showing signs of financial stress, the transportation of inventory from the premises, or the actual sale of goods manufactured by the company, and so on. This type of collection can take place without the knowledge of the perpetrators.

The PI can also look for evidence of disgruntled employees who may decide to target their employer's confidential information or intellectual property. The collected information gleaned from open-sources, surveillance, or discreet interviews with employees can now be analyzed in the next phase of the intelligence cycle.

Analysis

Analysis is at the center of intelligence work. It is at this stage that the raw information is turned into intelligence. But, in order to do this, the private investigator needs to take all the information he or she has collected and "distill" it into an assessment or report. It is this intelligence product that is then provided to the client.

There are many methods to analyze information. Essentially, these are divided into two groups – methods used to analyze structured data and methods used to analyze unstructured data. In the research, of which intelligence work is a specific sub-set, this is known as quantitative methods and qualitative methods, respectively.

The method used to analyze the information collected will therefore depend on the type of information the operative has – structured or unstructured. An example of the former might be a list of telephone numbers a suspect phoned from the company's officers over a number of weeks or months. An example of the latter could be a set of notes about various people who work in the office taken during a series of discreet off-site interviews.

Rather than attempt to go into detail about the various methods for analyzing data, suffice to say that there are a number of texts that can guide private investigators who are just embarking on intelligence work.[105] What we will discuss, however, are some of the key issues that often cause analytic products to veer off course.

Analytic Traps

Analytic traps are states of mind where reasoning appears to be logical, but there are limitations or flaws in the thinking process. Some of these traps include mirror imaging. This is where the PI assumes that the person or group that is at the center of an inquiry shares the same traits, values, and thought processes as the operative.

Layering is another trap. This is where conclusions derived by others are used as a basis for the PI's own judgment and analysis.

Group think is where the private investigator lapses too quickly into agreement with colleagues without critically questioning the information, the processes, or the conclusions.

Bias is another common trap. These not only include personal and professional biases that may color the PI's reasoning, but also cognitive biases, such as confirmation bias. This is where the operative discounts evidence that goes against the investigative hypothesis (i.e., the allegation) and only considers those pieces of information that support the hypothesis.

As analytic methods are essentially ways of thinking, then it is important to use approaches of taking the raw information gathered in the course of the investigation and using ways to make sense, or derive meaning from this. This takes critical thinking skills and problem-solving skills that allow the PI to draw inferences from these data in order to help the client understand the issue under investigation.

It is also about being able to detect anomalies or inconsistencies in the data, as well as detecting emerging trends or patterns of behavior that might indicate fraudulent behavior (e.g., when details do not match up). By way of example, let's look at this illustration. Should company telephone call records be used to canvas calls made by employees (assuming this is legal in your jurisdiction); inconsistencies or anomalies may produce leads for further follow-up.

Even though these aberrations in the records could flag issues, there is also the possibility that they may turn out to be nothing more than false positives. Anomalies that are detected need to be interpreted in reference to the validity and reliability of the data. Associated with the issue of anomalous data is the challenge of dealing with, sometimes, large data-sets – that is, the "needle in a haystack" syndrome.

Dissemination

The final phase of the intelligence process is dissemination; providing the client with a report or briefing on the outcome (or progress) of the inquiry. The information provided needs to be what is often called "actionable." In other words, it is important that the information presented is done so in a timely manner so that the client can act on it.

Clearly, as soon as a fraudulent situation has been identified, conveying this information to the client is critical, since the sooner corrective action can be put in place, the less damage that can be caused. This underscores the importance of the first phase of the intelligence cycle – direction setting. By establishing direction and developing a relationship with the client at the beginning helps facilitate smooth communication at the end of the inquiry.

Key to the communication process is the ability for the intelligence product to provide context; that is, explain what all the information means and the implications of the conclusions drawn. This will include outlining the validity and reliability of the information, and what level of certainty/uncertainty can be placed on the inquiry's findings. These are not trivial matters, as the client will need to make decisions based on the private investigator's report.

The client's decision, in turn, may carry hefty legal and economic consequences – so the PI's report needs to be accurate. Nevertheless, being able to providing a client with an intelligence report that indicates reasons to deny a particular individual access to the company database is very powerful advice (e.g., due to a questionable background check that indicates a history of being untrustworthy).

FUTURE CHALLENGES FOR FRAUD INVESTIGATION

Advances in computer technology have overwhelmingly contributed to the improved ways business is conducted. New efficiencies have created opportunities for broadening and growing particular markets, and these are very positive developments. However, these same advances in the information processing environment have acted as a force multiplier by affording enormous opportunities for fraudulent exploitation. The modern cyber-environment has simultaneously generated new hazards and risks, and these have accentuated traditional security weaknesses. The nature of risks associated with the new technology is correspondingly fluid.

Cyber-enabled fraud represents a considerable confounding effect for private investigations because of its sophistication. Cybercrime has emerged as a serious risk to organizations and it ranks as one of the top four economic crimes.[106] Combatting cyber-enabled fraud presents numerous challenges for commercial enterprises – international jurisdictional issues, links with organized crime, terrorists, gangs, and other illicit organizations. Perpetrators persist because of the potential profits to be made.

It therefore makes sense that identity fraud will continue to be a key challenge for all forms of fraudulent behavior. The power of social media is likely to be exploited by criminals to ascertain personal identifier information, as well as general background information. The relative ease with which this information can be harnessed will makes it a first-stop for criminals.

There are likely to be new types of fraud that will emerge, and most of these will be cyber-enabled. More developments in technologies that are only in their infancy at the time of this writing will create additional opportunities for criminals to commit fraud. These yet to declare challenges to the cyber security environment will necessitate the private investigator to be skilled in computer technology. Of course, the PI will need to use his or her traditional skills, but by employing intelligence-led practices, the operative positions him or herself to better detect the fraudulent practices that will emerge tomorrow.

Organized crime, particularly transnational organized crime, is likely to increase. PIs will be called upon to combat the continuing increases in the cost of fraud to society, as well as the broader implications of fraud, such as the nexus between organized crime and terrorist financing. This blurring of what used to be quite separate functions of law enforcement and national security intelligence with the function of private investigation is likely to continue.

Without doubt, the human component required in fraud intelligence and investigation will endure. Although new technologies that can assist the PI – such as visualization software and algorithm-based programs, and analytic software for interrogating large data-sets – will enable PIs to identify potential fraudulent behavior quicker, it is consider that fraud detection will still need a private investigator with expert knowledge, in addition to intuition, to determine patterns and anomalies of fraud. And for sure, technological advances in software will continue to enable the private investigators to develop leads that were unheard of by the Sam Spades of yesteryear.

IMPLICATIONS FOR PRIVATE
INVESTIGATION – "BEST PRACTICE"

The potential for private investigation as a discipline to be actively involved, rather than traditionally reactively involved, in addressing the problem of fraud is enormous. Just as perpetrators of child pornography websites and banking scams are often at the technological leading edge in using new techniques to hide or mask their activities (techniques which are then mimicked and then seen months later more broadly in other organized frauds), the private investigator could position him or herself to exploit the new technological era.

This could be done by, say, becoming an integral part of their clients' security plans by providing surety that they will be *less surprises* (with the hope that it might be *no surprises*). But to do this, the private investigator will need to use intelligence methods to identifying emerging trends in fraud and to help his or her client mitigate these risks. As with the many countries with advanced economies that are moving at what seems to be lightning-speed to exploit technological advances, the private investigator will need not only to understand these developments, but to anticipate them.

The increasing cost of cyber espionage to countries with advanced economies mandates that businesses actively engage employees in a security culture that forms part of the company's core values in order to protect proprietary information. In this regard, the private investigator could be engaged to perform risk assessments by looking at the general security hazards, but in particular, the potential damage to the client in the case of fraud.

The private operative should be able to convey this information to staff through the company's security training program. Training programs are important features for creating a culture where employees understand the risks and potential for fraud.

In addition, education focused on the private investigation is growing. Similar to the expansion of tertiary education for criminal justice and criminology, where policing and forensics classes have become required aspects of such degrees, private investigation degrees may emerge where subjects in critical thinking, analysis, research skills, and data mining are the norm.[107]

Employment of private investigators is expected to grow 21 percent over the decade leading to 2020 – a much faster growth rate than the average for all occupations.[108] Increased professionalism via college or university education is a logical corollary to this increase.

Although investigation of fraud has progressed to sophisticated heights since the days of the simple paper-based fraudulent check-passers, it still requires the private investigator with detailed, expert knowledge of the fraud environment to detect, and deter threats. Using an intelligence approached based on that used in other environments – national security, military, law enforcement, and corporate – private intelligence provides PIs with the potential to operate as an integral part of the larger crime solution that includes fraud.

KEY WORDS AND PHRASES

The key words and phrases associated with this chapter are listed below. In one or two sentences, demonstrate your understanding of each by writing a short definition or explanation.

- Confirmation bias;
- Cyber-enabled fraud;
- Economic espionage;
- Identity fraud;
- Intelligence product;
- Intellectual property (IP); and
- Mirror imaging.

STUDY QUESTIONS

1. Explain what is considered to be the primary enabler for those who are intent on committing fraud?
2. Explain what a trusted insider is and what types of crimes they usually perpetrate?
3. Discuss three of the common analytical traps analysts can fall into when looking at raw information.
4. Describe some of the future challenges for curbing fraud.

LEARNING ACTIVITY

Consider the issue of identity theft. Using what is presented here in this chapter as a "springboard," conduct further research into the ways perpetrators acquire false identity. Explain how fraudulent acquisition is done and discuss the current safeguards in place to mitigate such fraudulent schemes. Do you think the current measures are adequate? If not, can you suggest realistic ways to prevent this from happing, yet still allow people with legitimate need to access relevant documents?

Chapter 7

POLITICAL INTELLIGENCE

Troy Whitford

INTRODUCTION

Gathering political intelligence has been an important part of the repertoire of government-based intelligence agencies and law enforcement personnel for decades. Broadly, political intelligence is the process of gathering information about a political organization's capabilities, threats, or policy platforms. This information can come from either closed or open-sources, or both. Political organizations include recognized legitimate governments and political parties, oppositional movements, minor political parties, as well as activist, or issue-motivated group (IMG).

This chapter explores the applications of political intelligence as sought by the private sector and highlights the range of sources available in gathering political intelligence. It also examines some methods for gathering intelligence such as covert surveillance, interviews, networking, and background checks. The chapter concludes by examining some of the ethical considerations regarding political intelligence gathering but hopefully instills the idea that the private investigator, as a political intelligence operative, is free to traverse domestic political boarders.

BACKGROUND

In the twenty-first century, there has been an increase of interest from the private sector wanting to access political intelligence. The motivations for the private sector to seek political intelligence are diverse but are often based on reducing risk or ensuring security of assets and information.

Essentially, the business sector is seeking to minimize risks when considering new investments. Companies want to be assured about the stability of government where they will invest their capital or want to know what government or opposition parties will do in terms of policy, legislation, and regulative activities. From a security perspective, the business sector wants to protect assets from competitors or IMGs. Political intelligence on IMGs provides information for security risk assessments and options for lawfully countering any threats.

Other political groups will use political intelligence gathering to undertake candidate or incumbent analysis of either their own political representatives or opposition candidates. They will also seek out information that will discredit politicians or political party policy. Most political organizations tend to undertake political intelligence gathering operations in-house through the establishment of special units within the government or political organization.

Political intelligence firms rely primarily on open-source material (see Chapter 4 on open-source intelligence). This includes keeping subject files on political groups and individuals based on media reports, website content, or anything in the public domain. However, they also collect information from political insiders, including politicians, their staff, and employees of the public/civil service.[109] Sometimes information is given to a political intelligence operative knowingly, while other times it is obtained covertly. This is not unlike information gathering for other types of inquiries.

POLITICAL INTELLIGENCE OPERATIVES

Political intelligence operatives have traditionally been independent policy research providers or lobbyists, and law firms. However, the intelligence-led private investigator with an understanding of politics is also well suited to provide political intelligence to a range of clients. The investigator in the political intelligence field is able to operate freelance, and unlike policy research groups or law firms, has the benefit of not being associated with the lobbying industry. The PI who is working as a political intelligence agent is also free to move between different organizations without bringing attention to him or herself. Another advantage for the private investigator undertaking political intelligence activists is the wide range of methods at their disposal.

In most of the Five-Eyes countries, it is only the government licensed private investigator who can undertake covert surveillance, background checks, or conduct counterintelligence assessments for fee or reward. Therefore, the private investigator who works as a third-party contractor would be conducting their activities within legal boundaries that political organizations or companies could not. Representatives of corporations, or other political organizations, that embark on political intelligence using covert surveillance activities will essentially be viewed as stalkers, or risk being identified, and put through legal and media scrutiny. Nevertheless, the benefits of political and corporate groups recruiting the private investigator as political intelligence operative far outweigh the risks of using someone who is not formally trained.

BRIEF HISTORY

Gathering political intelligence has for the most part been the domain of nations and states. Predominately, it's because the aim of political intelligence is to provide knowledge for protecting existing political entities or countering emerging political forces. In most liberal democracies, the gathering of domestic political intelligence has been seen as the more deviant aspects of policing. The notion that the state should gather information or conduct surveillance on domestic political groups is in contradiction to perceptions of freedom of political association, and expression of ideas, and free speech. Further, state-sponsored activities to disrupt those groups through infiltration or spreading disinformation is often akin to what would be expected of a totalitarian regime rather than the democracies of, specifically, Australia, Britain, Canada, New Zealand, and the United States, but also other nations with advanced political systems.

A central criticism to domestic political intelligence gathering is that it often is unable to distinguish between lawful dissent of a radical nature and political violence.[110] Despite the general unease regarding political intelligence gathering in liberal democracies, the practice had flourished throughout the twentieth century. For instance, the British *Special Branch* had assigned a mandate to make inquiries into what was described as subversive groups in Britain from around 1910, and later during the First World War, for "all domestic non-military espionage activities."[111]

The Australian Security Intelligence Organisation (ASIO) was established in 1949 and since that time has been active in gathering information on individuals, including writers, actors, and political organizers.[112] The U.S. Federal Investigation Bureau's Counter Intelligence Program – COINTELPRO[113] – is perhaps one of the better known domestic political intelligence gathering and covert action programs which aimed at disrupting the Ku Klux Klan during the late-1960s.[114]

The importance of political intelligence has certainly gained renewed emphasis in the years since the 9/11 terrorist attacks. State intelligence agencies have been active in gathering information on individuals and political groups who may pose a threat to national security. But there has also been a rise in the number of private intelligence companies offering political intelligence services. These private entities are staffed former government intelligence personnel, academics, journalists, former diplomatic and military personnel, as well as private investigators. It is predominately the business sector that is making the most of private political intelligence services, but there is also a trend in government intelligence agencies to outsource their political intelligence gathering activities, and organizations wanting to keep government honest.

APPLIED POLITICAL INTELLIGENCE

There are a number of applications for political intelligence. The most infamous application for political intelligence is for financial gain. In 2012, the role of political intelligence gathering in the United States came under Congressional scrutiny with allegations that political intelligence operatives were providing "insider" legislative information to Hedge Fund supervisors and investment banks.[115]

Such a practice had become commonplace, but there were concerns that these practices were being undertaken covertly and in many instances, legislators or their staff did not know they were talking to political intelligence operatives. Such scrutiny of political intelligence and the trading of political information had led to calls to establish a political intelligence operatives' register similar to lobbyist registers that are features in Australia, Canada, New Zealand, and the United States. Nonetheless, less contentious and more broadly used political intelligence operatives will often undertake such inquiries as:

- in-depth incumbent and candidate analysis;
- provide reports on the policy agenda of political organizations or governments; and
- conducting security threat analysis which assesses the capabilities and intent of issue-motivated groups towards specific companies, or industry groups (see Chapter 8 regarding anti-terrorist and anti-gang intelligence in this regard).

Candidate or Incumbent Research

Undertaking candidate or incumbent analysis is often the job of political organizations seeking to endorse one of their own candidates or attempting to discredit the incumbent legislator. Usually, these kinds of analysis are undertaken by members of the organizational wing of a political group or party. Often they rely upon open-source material such as media reports, speeches, and analyses of voting records of various legislative houses or chambers. However, with the advent of personality politics or what is also known as presidential-style campaigning (in countries that have a Westminster system of government) – where the focus is in on the individual rather than the political party – the need to understand the values and attitudes of candidates and incumbents are vital to political organizations seeking to win government. Essential to campaigning is a candidate's or incumbent's credibility and image. When a voter chooses a candidate he or she is assessing which is more creditable.[116]

Increasingly, notions of credibility are centered not only around political and policy decisions made by the candidate, but also business and personal dealings they have made prior to seeking or gaining public office. Yet, despite such a shift toward personalized or presidential-style campaigning, political organizations have not attempted to professionalize the "backgrounding" of potential candidates or current legislators. Instead, it is often political staffers who are charged with such activities.

Take for instance in 2012, the Australian Prime Minister was tarnished with reports that her ministerial staffers had been instructed to "gather sensitive information on shadow ministers."[117] Earlier in 2011, the premier of the Australian state of Queensland, Mr. Campbell Newman, expressed his concerns and dismay when learning that his Liberal National Party had paid a former Labor party staffer to "compile a dirt file on Labor members of parliament."[118] This staffer was alleged to have been paid A$3,000 to provide this type of information.[119]

In the United States, the story is not dissimilar. In 2012, news reports highlighted how the Democrat Party was active in gathering information on possible running mates for Mitt Romney. Such information includes previous policy statements, voting records, and personal preferences that "might paint the candidate in a poor light."[120]

Then there was the infamous Watergate Affair. During a political espionage operation associated with the 1972 Republican Party's Campaign to Re-Elect the President (CREEP) operatives broke into the Washington D.C. headquarters of the Democrat Party and placed illegal listening devices. The operation ended in failure – the arrest of the operatives – and the conviction and/or jailing of dozens of people who were either involved with the operation or its cover-up. It culminated with the resignation of President Richard Nixon.[121]

The public tends to view the operation of "dirt units" or candidate and incumbent analysis as the more seedy side of political campaigning, and in many cases, conducting such research can have a detrimental impact on those who have compiled it. Further complicating the issue of conducting in-house candidate and incumbent analysis is that most political staffers are publicly funded. Using public funds for such activities could be seen as a misappropriation of funds and resources.

In addition, while often enthusiastic about such projects, political staff are ill-equipped and untrained in gathering and handling domestic political intelligence.[122] Often they are responsible for media leaks regarding political intelligence activities and in some cases are simply disgruntled former employees of politicians. Take for instance the case of Donald H. Sergretti who, during the 1972 U.S. presidential election campaign, and clouded by the zeal of political ideology, offered to conduct "opposition research" to help Richard Nixon's re-election. "His goal [however] was to create as much bitterness and disunity within the Democratic Party as he could."[123] Sergretti was "Recruited by [H.R.] Halderman's appointments secretary, Dwight Chapin, for the political game of 'dirty tricks.'"[124]

***Dirty tricks* is a euphemism for *political sabotage*. It is not only unethical to practice this type of operation, it is likely to be illegal. Government licensed private investigators should never engage in such activities. They should remain objective and abide by the ethical standards discussed in Chapter 14.**

Given the sensitivity and importance of gathering political intelligence, arguably it is the private investigator who is best equipped to undertake such work. The intelligence-led private investigator has the training to gather and analyze information from a range of sources. He or she is also able to conduct surveillance and undertake discreet interviews. The investigator should also be apolitical in his or her profession and bound by a code of conduct that respects confidentiality. These traits would be uncommon amongst political staff and therefore open to greater criticism. A further benefit is that through outsourcing this kind of intelligence gathering activity, the political organization responsible for commissioning the research can remain distant from the process.

For the intelligence-led private investigator to work in the field of candidate and incumbent analysis, the operative must have a strong understanding of politics. The PI's understanding of political interaction needs to be at a level where it is possible to undertake detailed social network analysis – that is, the ability to understand the relationships between politicians and other politicians, and/or individuals though charting who knows or associates with whom.[125] Arguably, post-9/11 political reporting in the media has become more biased and superficial. To gain a true understanding of the machinations taking place within politics, the private investigator must have established contacts in political circles. Open-sources, like the media reports and public records, will only provide part of the overall picture. Reliable contacts need to be identified and cultivated.

But developing such contacts can also be fraught with problems and requires a good deal of tact and discretion. A world leader in political and business intelligence, Hakluyt & Company Limited[126] was exposed in 2008 after sending an email to journalists in the Australian Parliamentary press gallery. Hakluyt & Company Limited was seeking information for a client concerned about new health care reforms canvassed by the Australian Government at the time. They were seeking to enlist the support of a journalist to gather information on the proposed health reforms. However, efforts failed to recruit the journalist and instead Hakluyt & Company Limited's approach was made public.[127] Such miscalculations of judgment are not only damaging to the reputations of such firms, but also create a hyper-awareness of political intelligence gathering and subsequently the activity becomes more difficult to carry out.

Sources of Political Intelligence

Open-source methods for gaining political intelligence for candidate and incumbent analysis is straightforward as it often begins with compiling a history of the subject. Today, most political parties require their candidates to fill out extensive forms outlining past criminal convictions, business dealings, employment history, and political affiliations. These documents provide a basis for further inquiries and background research. Nonetheless, it is likely that an ambitious candidate may omit certain offenses or dealings. Whatever the reason – pride, embarrassment, or just forgetfulness – even minor criminal offenses, such as driving while under the influence of alcohol, or previous political party affiliations, can provide a rich source of additional information.

That is why whatever is recorded on the background document requires checking. Simply, the role of the private investigator undertaking candidate analysis is conducting a background check. It is a common activity for PIs, but made easier because candidates and incumbents will have a public profile. Often they will be known in their local communities, perhaps a member of the chamber of commerce or a sporting group. They may have also spent time on local or county governments honing their political skills. Past college or university political affiliations also provide some insight. During those years, subjects are often more radical in their outlook and tend to publish in student-based journals, articles, blogs, and letters to the editor. Also pertinent are committees, associates, political newsletters subscribed to, and so on. These activities are often on the public record and easily located by a trained government licensed private investigator.

Undertaking analysis of an incumbent is often easier than candidates. They will often have a website and are searchable through media databases and parliamentary or congressional records. The aim of incumbent analysis is not necessarily about finding sensitive information, but, perhaps, how often they attend parliament/congress/senate sessions and what legislation they have voted in favor or against. Essentially, the analysis can be an assessment of what they have done or have not done during their term in office, and a comparison made against what they promised (i.e., an analysis of the data).

The skills of the private investigator are easily transferred to candidate and incumbent analysis. But, it is often difficult to convince political organizations that this is a service that requires a professional approach undertaken by an expert in the field. Unfortunately, too many political organizations consider that this kind of research can be undertaken by anyone and therefore do not actively outsource these inquiries. Nevertheless, given the rise in profile of "dirt units" and other political gathering operations, it may be worth political organizations' rethinking the practice, or at best, understanding that such operations require a specialization and high degree of confidentiality that can only be found through employing the skills of the private investigator.

Political Intelligence and the Business Community

Any business operation wanting to invest either domestically or overseas requires a substantial amount of knowledge about those they are proposing to deal with. As the Hakluyt & Company and the earlier Wall Street examples illustrate, there are businesses that want to know the political climate associated with the venture before making any investment. Placing aside the ethical issues canvassed in the introduction and examined later in this chapter, there is a clear market for the private investigator that can provide political intelligence to the business sector. In comparison to the political sector, businesses are more comfortable in outsourcing intelligence gathering activities. The business sector can see a clear cost/benefit value of spending, say, $20,000 to gain information that will assist an investment gain $100,000 profit, for argument's sake.

The practice of intelligence gathering, private investigation, and commercial espionage by businesses has a long history. The private investigator had often been at the center of countering insider treason, industrial theft, and elicitation. PIs have also conducted business intelligence-gathering operations that have involved examining public records, annual corporate reports, market reports, speeches, and sales data.[128] So, not surprisingly, is the business sector's reawakening interest in political intelligence. This interest has focussed predominately on policy decisions and has tended to coincide with the emergence of globalization. Political intelligence for the business sector is focused on regulation or deregulation. Knowing if a government is going to nationalize an industry or deregulate an industry can have particular consequences for investment decisions.

Investigative Neutrality

One of the acknowledged leaders in the field of political intelligence gathering (i.e., global geopolitical intelligence) for the business sector is the Stratfor Global intelligence group. The Stratfor group was established in 1996 by George Friedman, a political scientist.[129] On a subscription basis, the group provides geopolitical analysis and political intelligence using open-source monitoring as well as its network of people in key positions around the world.

After Wikileaks[130] had exposed the contents of a number of emails between the Stratfor group and its client's,[131] questions arose regarding the independence of this private intelligence firm. The emails showed that the company lacked true global independence and was described as "advancing US corporate and government interests at home and abroad," as well as "enhancing government secrecy."[132]

Stratfor's alleged lack of independence as a political intelligence-gathering operator proved problematic for journalists and other researchers who relied upon Stratfor's intelligence as it was subsequently seen as less creditable and unbiased. The criticism that has emerged regarding Stratfor Global is that it was simply an extension of the United States intelligence community. This criticism tarnished the prospect of Stratfor gaining non-American clients because its information and analytical products it marketed were not truly candid and neutral. Without a sense of neutrality and assurances that the information was without bias, it was not reliable enough to provide businesses with the confidence needed to make critical investment decisions.

Issue-Motivated Groups

Another use for political intelligence, which has emerged during the twenty-first century, is the undertaking of threat assessments by companies of issue-motivated groups.[133] In many cases, issue-motivated groups seek to disrupt production, interfere with online communications, and generally aim to create a lack of confidence in the business enterprise. IMGs are often identified through their militant approach to protest and activism. At the time of writing, it was the mining and energy sectors that were often targeted by groups that adhered to an environmentalist agenda. However, groups like the online activist *Anonymous*[134] or the *Occupy Movements*[135] are loose confederations of a variety of groups that are more difficult to understand and require ongoing monitoring.

Open-Source Intelligence

Gathering information on IMGs requires planning and ongoing assessments. Understanding the leadership, organizational structure, and political goals are just the basics and found through Internet research. This kind of political intelligence is gathered by accessing online open-source material, such as social media, and other sources discussed in Chapter 4 on open-source intelligence.

Increasingly, sites like *Facebook* and *Twitter* are providing the platform for IMGs to organize and plan demonstrations and therefore open to intelligence gathering. Regardless, detailed monitoring requires greater effort. To provide relevant and timely intelligence on IMGs, it is necessary to understand the structure of social networks, the dynamics of the personalities leading the target group, and its membership. Subsequently, infiltration or surveillance of these groups can be required. Some private intelligence companies are already undertaking such measures. By way of example, the London-based firm Executive Analysis Ltd[136] is a specialist intelligence company that reportedly uses surveillance and civil unrest analysis to provide information to its clients regarding IMGs.[137]

PIs as Political Intelligence Subcontractors

Given the difficulties in gathering detailed political intelligence and the awareness these groups have of being under scrutiny by government law enforcement and intelligence agencies, it is not surprising that gathering political intelligence on IMGs is contracted out to the private sector. Government intelligence agencies tend to monitor these groups by outsourcing the work to private intelligence companies, for instance, the Australian-based private intelligence agency National Open Source Intelligence Centre (NOSIC).[138] NOSIC ". . . provides state and federal agencies with a dedicated open source Issue Monitoring, research and analytical support capability. . . . NOSIC aims to provide Open Source Intelligence (OSINT) on the identity, capability and intentions of organizations or individuals that engage in radical activism, criminal (terrorist) activity or unlawful behavior motivated by politics, ethnicity, religion, radical dissension, hate or financial gain."[139]

However, accepting government work may often lead to criticism that the investigation is simply an extension of the government's view, and subsequently, an extension of the political party that is in power. In such cases, it would be prudent for private intelligence firms to consider the pros-and-cons of accepting a government contract.

Selected Examples of IMG Targets

Although the potential list of targets for political intelligence is long, here are a few broad categories that could generate others for consideration:

- Animal rights groups;
- Anti-abortion militants;
- Anti-drag net fishing campaigners;
- Anti-mining activists;
- Anti-nuclear promoters;
- Anti-whaling protesters; and
- Pro-environmental/ecology collectives.

Analytic Products – Target Profiles

As discussed in Chapter 5, the *target profile* is a useful format for compiling a report regarding political intelligence. Although considered in terms of a target-of-interest, IMGs, as well as other political targets, are also suitable subjects for this type of report.

ETHICS AND VALUES OF POLITICAL INTELLIGENCE GATHERING

There is a stigma around gathering domestic political intelligence in liberal democracies. Political expression is seen as a fundamental human right. In many cases, it is easy to reconcile this ethical dilemma when a political organization is conducting activities that are also contradictory to human rights, such as racially-based hate groups, or groups that commit violence. However, gaining political intelligence on politicians, parties, or groups that are acting within acceptable behavioral norms, or that are acting within their legal rights, is more problematic.

The private investigator who gathers political intelligence for third parties is not bound by the loyalties in the same way law enforcement or intelligence personnel are expected to be loyal to the executive branch of government.

Each PI has to make a judgement regarding not only the ethics of accepting a case involving political intelligence, but also personal safety. In some respects, making this type of decision requires an almost mercenary approach. While politics is driven by ideology, the private investigator should essentially remain ideologically neutral and focused on delivering the service to his or her client. Before embarking on political intelligence work, it would prove useful to undertake a value mapping exercise to establish the operative's suitability for such work. This value mapping process is discussed in Chapter 3.

CONCLUSION

In sum, this chapter highlighted some of the features of political intelligence and its applications for political organizations, as well as the business sector. It can also apply to individuals and groups who monitor the integrity and veracity of political leaders and their parties, as well as related applications.

The key to working in the field of political intelligence is having a strong understanding of the political process, the political actors, and the networks that operate across a variety of political communities. This requires establishing and cultivating contacts, and developing target profiles by being an avid observer of politics.

An underlining theme of this chapter has been to encourage neutrality when gathering political intelligence while maintaining a high degree of professional ethical standards. While government contracts and affiliations can be a lucrative market for the private investigator, these will, in the long term, impact on the operative's ability to gather critical information and present it with credibility. Professional judgment needs to be exercised at all stage of an investigation – from contract acceptance to the delivery of the final report.

KEY TERMS AND PHRASES

The key words and phrases associated with this chapter are listed below. In one or two sentences, demonstrate your understanding of each by writing a short definition or explanation.

- Political intelligence;
- Incumbent and candidate research; and
- Issue-motivated groups.

STUDY QUESTION

1. Research what private firms conduct political intelligence. List three and discuss the types of services/products they offer clients.
2. How might candidate analysis establish credibility for a candidate?
3. Why is neutrality in political intelligence gathering important? List some strengths of maintaining neutrality.
4. What are some of the ethical issues to consider when conducting political intelligence gathering?

LEARNING ACTIVITY

You have been asked by a corporate client to provide information on the interest-motivated group "National Anarchist." Using web-based open-sources, provide a target profile (see Chapter 5 for the detail on compiling this type of report) on the group including its ideology, history, leadership, and the activities of the group, as well as other key issues that need to be considered.

Chapter 8

ANTI-TERRORIST AND
ANTI-GANG INTELLIGENCE

HANK PRUNCKUN

INTRODUCTION

O ne of the prominent features of the post-9/11 world is the expansion of
investigation services from the traditional – missing persons, workers
compensation claims, and character inquiries – into what has been termed
anti-terrorist investigations. Some private investigation agencies now offer this
service to individuals, groups, and organizations. This type of investigation is
sophisticated and takes the form of an intelligence inquiry.

But it is not only terrorists to whom these investigations can apply – they
are equally applicable to gangs and threats posed by organized criminal
groups because the underlining factors that make them a threat to a client are
common to all (i.e., a *threat-agent*). In this sense, the concept of a gang is more
than the hip hop group that hangs around a street corner, but non-state actors
that have at their core the aim to project community insecurity so as to control a geographical location or market (legal or illegal).[140] For instance, the
United Nations Office on Drugs and Crime reported that gang-related violence has a long history associated with the marketing of drugs, especially
"crack."[141] Other studies have established links between crime gangs and terrorists, and gangs and the underground financial economy. This relationship,
state such studies, is part of the underpinning of their illicitly acquired
wealth.[142]

> "With many criminal gangs taking on the characteristics of transjurisdictional criminal enterprises, the need for information sharing and analysis of threats is essential."[143]

"Criminal gangs commit as much as 80 percent of the crime in many communities, according to law enforcement officials throughout the nation."[144] It is no surprise then that criminologists have pointed out that: "Concerns over urban decay, societal collapse, and the subsequent need for combat and high-intensity policing operations to stabilize cities falling into such darkness and despair have been uttered for almost two decades now."[145] So, although this chapter will discuss intelligence inquires in relation to these threat-agents, the methods discussed can be applied to allied issues of concern, such as investigating the possibility of riots or other forms of civil unrest – protests, occupations, marches, demonstrations, sit-ins, pickets, and so on – anything that has a threat and vulnerability associated with it.[146]

In order to meet this challenge, today's private investigator needs to be able to understand the threat environment and be able to conduct this type of investigation. Being able to conduct an anti-terrorist or anti-gang investigation, as well as being able to prepare a report, requires an understanding of two analytic methods – threat analysis and vulnerability analysis.[147]

> The term *anti-terrorism* means defensive measures whereas the term *counterterrorism* involves offensive measures taken to "prevent, deter, pre-empt, and respond to terrorism."[148] However, counterterrorism has gained a foothold over anti-terrorism in today's security lexicon. Nevertheless, anti-terrorism is used in this text as it is the more accurate term for the private investigator to use.

THE TWO-PHASE INVESTIGATION

Investigating a suspected terrorist cell is not like investigating a civil dispute between two businesses. Terrorists by definition have a political agenda and are motivated by political ends.[149, 150]

Unlike two disputing parities in a civil action, terrorists operate underground, making their actions known only when it is too late to respond, or respond effectively. Nevertheless, their political agenda may impact on your client – for instance, businesses that trade overseas may be a target, or a company that has officers or associates who travel overseas, or businesses that produce goods or provide services that are at odds with a person or group's ideology, and the list could go on. If a terrorist decides to strike, his or her actions could impact on a client's interests, facilities, products, services, personnel, and families. How does the private investigator provide a report on whether his or her client faces a threat from terrorism or is vulnerable to an attack, kidnapping, or other danger?

Although not politically motivated, gangs pose a similar problem. Gangs could present dangers for individuals and businesses from random attacks (e.g., car jackings) to systematic crimes (e.g., kidnapping and extortion). Not a week passes that the news media does not report a story of, say, a shootout with cartel members, gangs attacking public transport facilities, or retaliatory killings, public feuds involving violence, and the list goes on. How does the private investigator assess his or her client's potential threat from gangs or how a client may be vulnerable?

A gang is a group of people who seek to control a geographic area or a market. A gang has a hieratical structure with leaders at different levels. Other members perform various support functions. Collectively, the gang engages in violent activities as a way of pursuing undertakings such as drugs and arms trafficking, human trafficking, theft and "fencing," extortion, gambling, loan rackets, illegal alcohol and tobacco, prostitution, kidnapping, and more.

There are two phases to these types of investigations. Both phases are integral to developing a report on the dangers faced. The first phase is to carry-out a threat analysis, and the second is a vulnerability analysis. These intelligence techniques can be linked to form a set of methods for investigating the threat of terrorism or gang violence.

In summary form, these steps are:

1. identify and assess the threat(s); and
2. assess the vulnerabilities to these threat(s).

Consider the following abbreviated example of how these steps could be applied by the private investigator in response to a client's request for an investigation into a suspected threat posed by a criminal gang with alleged ties to domestic terrorists:

1. Threat – attack on personnel employed at one of the business's regional offices; and
2. Vulnerability – employees as they enter and exit the building.

Although these steps are presented sequentially to form an integrated approach to anti-terrorism/anti-gang activity, either one of these assessments can be carried out on its own as a stand-alone investigation. Or, either one can be applied to hazards other than terrorism or gang violence. For instance, a threat assessment could be conducted on its own in relation to a person or group who is presenting as if they may act in a criminal manner.

> *Terrorism* is a term that can refer to a number of forms of violent extremism – for instance, Islamic or other religious ideological extremism; right-wing, left-wing, or political extremism.

THREAT ANALYSIS

Although the term *threat* is used in different ways and in different contexts, it needs to be made clear that a threat is a person's resolve to inflict harm on another. So, a threat needs to be made by a person or an entity controlled by a person or people (or in the case of political intelligence as discussed in Chapter 7, to adversely affect another person, group, or the community). A threat cannot be made by a force of nature or otherwise – these are *hazards, risks,* or *dangers.* This distinction becomes clear when viewed this way – a force of nature or other hazard cannot be a threat as it cannot form intent, and intent is one of the essential factors that characterize a threat.

Having said that, threats can be made against most entities – people, organizations, and nations. That is why this type of investigation can apply to terrorist activity, as well as gang-related activity (it could apply to other criminal activity such as organized crime). The making of threats is attributed to *threat-agents*. Threat-agents do not have to openly declare their resolve to cause harm in order to constitute a threat, though explicit words or actions make it easier for the investigator to identify and assess the threat-agent.

An investigation into threats involves the analysis of two key factors – the need for a threat-agent (which could be a person, group, or a body corporate/organization) and an object of the threat (i.e., the target – which does not have to be a material target such as a shopping mall or an individual – can be intangible such as the threat to national security or the security of a particular venue or event). Stated another way, a threat-agent who has intent and capability must be able to harm something. By way of example, a threat-agent could be an ideologically driven individual who is intent and capable of inflicting harm upon, say, a group of people, or a gang of criminals who have an intent and capability to disrupt civil society, and so on. The potential harm can be in many forms and can be suffered either physically or emotionally/mentally.

"Fighting terrorism is like being a goalkeeper. You can make a hundred brilliant saves but the only shot that people remember is the one that gets past you."[151]

When the private investigator assesses a threat-agent, he or she is gauging whether the threat-agent has the *capability* and *intent* to produce harm to a target. In this context, the target is likely to be the PI's client or the client's physical or intellectual property. To weigh-up whether the threat-agent has capability and intent, the private investigator needs to establish two elements for each of these factors: *knowledge* and *resources* for capability, and *desire* and *expectation* (or *ability*) for intent. These considerations are shown diagrammatically in Figure 8.1. As an equation, threat is expressed as:

$$capability + intent = threat$$
or more specifically
$$(knowledge + resources) + (desire + expectation) = threat$$

Desire can be described as the threat-agents' enthusiasm to cause harm in pursuit of their goal. Expectation is the confidence the threat-agents have in that they will achieve their goal if their plan is carried out. Knowledge is having information that will allow the threat agent to use or construct devices or carry out processes that are necessary for achieving their goal. Resources include skills (or experience) and materials needed to act on their plan.

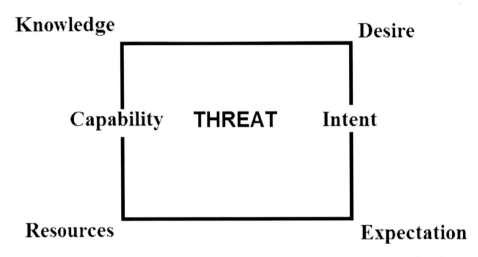

Figure 8.1. The threat quadrangle – a logical model of how threat is analyzed.

IDENTIFYING THREATS

One way of identifying potential threats is to contextualize threats into what is termed *threat communities,* that is, to brainstorm categories of potential threats to the target – from the obvious to the obscure. In this way, the anti-terrorist investigation will be sure to canvass all possible sources of harm (but note we are discussing *threats* here, not *hazards*). Some examples of external threat communities relating to, say, a client's business might include:

- Animal rights militants;
- Anti-Semitics;
- Colombian, Hispanic, Middle Eastern, Russian, and other ethnic gangs;
- Domestic anarchists;
- Eco-terrorists;
- Environmental militants;
- Insurgents and guerrillas of various descriptions;
- International or transnational terrorists;
- Motorcycle gangs;
- Neo-Nazis;
- Prison-based gangs;
- Racists groups;

- Religious extremists (of various beliefs);
- Street gangs;
- White supremacists; and
- Xenophobes.

When brainstorming the list of potential threats, do not overlook threats from within. This applies to targets that are businesses, groups, or organizations rather than targets that are individuals for obvious reasons.

These threat communities can be subdivided into more distinct groups if there is a need – for instance, rights campaigners can be classified into political activists, religious activists, single-issue activists (anti-whaling, animal rights, anti-abortion, environmental, etc.). But bear in mind that membership of one threat community (or sub-community) does not exclude that person or group from being a member of another, or several other threat communities.

"Some 33,000 violent street gangs, motorcycle gangs, and prison gangs with about 1.4 million members are criminally active in the U.S. today."[152]

To better understand the "who" that comprise a threat community, the private investigator needs to compile a *threat profile*. The profile needs to be adequate (perfection is rarely, if ever, obtainable) in order to understand the threat environment. The threat profile aids the next phase in anti-terrorism investigation – that is, the vulnerability analysis. In the meantime, consider the threat profile shown in Table 8.1 as an example that demonstrates the important aspects of a fictitious threat-agent (the order can be rearranged to suit the target of the PI's investigation, and other factors can be added if these are deemed inadequate to communicate the message).

ASSESSING THE THREAT

A model for calculating threats might look something like the model depicted in Table 8.2 (i.e., a threat summary). Though models such as this do not eliminate subjectivity, using a model forces the private investigator to be transparent about how he or she has calculated threat and, in doing so, is able to defend his or her conclusions.

Table 8.1. Threat Profile for the Notional Terrorist Group

Summary	Observations
Desire	
Targets	Objects that represent Western businesses that represent liberal values.
Target characteristics	Symbolic and iconic objects that afford high visibility and hence extensive coverage in the world's media.
Tactics	Targets property owned or operated by Western interests, especially mining, exploration, critical infrastructure, and communications networks.
Affiliation	Semi-autonomous.
Recruitment	Semi-illiterate local ethic populations.
Expectation	
Motivation	Radical religious ideology.
Intent	Extensive destruction.
Tolerance to risk	High.
Self-sacrifice	Very accepting.
Willingness to inflict collateral harm	Extreme.
Knowledge	
Planning	Based on target acquisition intelligence through fixed and mobile surveillance, informants and open-source data.
International connections	Training and ideological support through affiliates.
Resources	
Weapons	Improvised explosives and small arms.
Financing	"Donations" from wealthy ethic sympathizers.
Skills	Attack vector dependent: • Computer-based – extremely low; • Electronic/communications – low to moderate; • Small arms – high; and • Explosive – very high.

It is important to note that there is no weighting attached to what constitutes, say, an acute or high level of intent. That is because one cannot say, for instance, how many media announcements it would take from a terrorist group to represent such a desire (which contributes to intent). The same can be said of capability in this model. Ideally, some form of conditioning statement would be attached to each of these scale categories so that the client knows what is meant by acute desire, high desire, medium desire, and so forth; and the same for capability. An example of how such a conditioning statement scale that could be constructed is shown later in this chapter, in Table 8.5 (note: constructing such a conditioning statement scale for this table forms the learning activity at the end of this chapter).

In addition, models do not eliminate miscalculations because of inadvertent skewing. Note in table 8.2 that intent is calculated by adding desire with

Table 8.2. An Example of a Threat Summary

Threat Community Summary for a Regionally-Based Neo-Fascist Group		
Scale	*Scores*	*Tally*
Desire		
Negligible	1	
Minimum	2	2
Medium	3	
High	4	
Acute	5	
Expectation		
Negligible	1	1
Minimum	2	
Medium	3	
High	4	
Acute	5	
Total Intent		*3*
Knowledge		
Negligible	1	
Minimum	2	
Medium	3	
High	4	4
Acute	5	
Resources		
Negligible	1	
Minimum	2	
Medium	3	
High	4	4
Acute	5	
Total Capability		*8*
Threat Coefficient		*11*

expectation, and in turn, this sum is added to the sum of knowledge and re-sources (and will range from a low of 4 to the maximum of 20). The process of adding limits the spread of values, whereas the process of multiplying any of these scores would increase the values. For instance, if all scores were mul-tiplied – that is, substituting multiplication for addition – as per the equation, the range would be spread from 1 to 625.

The precision of this wide range of values diminishes the analyst's ability to accurately determine either intent or capability. Therefore, it is suggested that adding all values, rather than multiplying them, will reduce the spread and, therefore, maintain the threat coefficient as an indicator rather than pro-mote it as a reflection of its absolute condition. (Even if the private investigator multiplied desire and expectation, and knowledge and resources but added the resulting sums, it would still yield a very wide spread – from 2 to 50 – as would the opposite, that is, multiplying the sums that comprise intent and capability, from 4 to 100.)

Having said that, two additional issues need to be noted: (1) there is still a need to provide conditioning statements so that the client understands what is meant by a medium threat intent and capability (e.g., along the lines of Table 8.5), and (2) "unknowns" are not accommodated in this model. It is very important to understand this last point as it is not possible to use models to assess any phenomenon in categorically or absolute terms. This is because not all the influences can be known (termed *variables* in intelligence research), what has been termed *Black Swans;* that is, random events with devastating consequences.[153]

The threat coefficient obtained from this analysis is then compared against a reference table to gauge where it sits on the continuum of danger of attack. The scale suggested in Table 8.3 can be varied with additional qualifiers, or it can be collapsed if the number is deemed too many. Likewise, how the incremental breakdown of coefficients is determined will depend on whether the agency is willing to accept the risk that a threat-agent may slip under its gaze by raising the categories of negligible and minimum. In the end, the number and their descriptors need to make sense in the context of the asset being protected. That is, each of the descriptors needs to have a conditioning statement attached to it to define.

Table 8.3. An Example of a Threat Coefficient Scale

Threat Level	Coefficient
Negligible	4–6
Minimum	7–10
Medium	11–15
High	16–18
Acute	19–20

VULNERABILITY ANALYSIS

The traditional definition for the term *vulnerability* is that a person, place, or thing is susceptible to either physical or emotional harm. In short, vulnerability is a weakness in an *asset* that can be exploited by a threat-agent (the term *asset* is being used in this context to denote a resource that requires protection). Viewed another way, vulnerability is an asset's capability to withstand harm inflicted by a threat. Harm can be anything from experiencing a minor nuisance event to a situation that is catastrophic.

Vulnerability is a function of several factors – attractiveness of the target, feasibility of carrying out an attack, and potential impact. This model is shown diagrammatically in Figure 8.2. Usually, these factors entail such considerations as status of the target, potential for the attack to succeed, potential for the threat-agent to get away with the attack, and potential to inflict loss. These factors can be weighed against measures to mitigate loss and to deter or prevent attack on an entity.

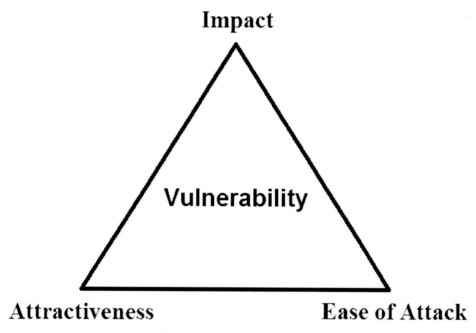

Figure 8.2. Vulnerability triangle – a logical model of how vulnerability is analyzed.

Formulae-based analyses are popular among law enforcement and security agencies engaged in investigating terrorism, and although these vary from agency to agency – or as we are discussing here, from private investigator to private investigator – they follow a basic stepwise formula:

1. Define what constitutes an asset (critical infrastructure, transport network, food chain, distribution hubs, any of the essential services – e.g., electric power, gas, potable water, sewerage – or a person or group of people, etc.);
2. Sort these assets into categories;
3. Assign a grade or level of importance to each asset; and
4. Identify potential impact on the asset if it suffers harm.

As there is no one single criterion for calculating vulnerability because each class of asset may require special considerations to be taken into account (and there may be agency protocols that take precedence also), one general approach is to use a model such as:

target attractiveness + ease of attack + impact = vulnerability

To operationalize *attractiveness,* the private investigator could ask questions along the following lines and tabulate the results to insert into the model:

- Is the target readily recognizable? Rather than answer this question in a dichotomous way (i.e., using nominal data – yes/no), the private investigator could use ordinal data to give greater precision to the overall vulnerability indicator,[154] for example: is the target recognizable internationally in the same way the Sydney Opera House is, or is it recognizable only nationally, state-wide, or just locally? (See Figure 8.3.)
- Is the target the subject of media attention/coverage? Again, the private investigator could construct a scale of attention from rarely to frequently/weekly. Coverage could be in the local press or through to global newscasters, including on-line news reporting.
- Does the target have a symbolic status in terms of historical, cultural, religious, economic, or other importance? The private investigator could assess this factor as having no symbolic status to possessing more than one prominent aspect.

Figure 8.3. Sydney Opera House – an internationally recognized venue (photograph courtesy of Hank Prunckun).

Attractiveness needs to be placed in context with the threat-agent. Say, for instance, some Islamic extremist groups may see assets that represent Western culture or symbolize Western values as attractive.[155] To operationalize the concept *ease of attack,* the private investigator could ask these types of questions:

- How difficult would it be for the threat-agent to predict the peak attendance times at the target? Establish a scale from certain (as in the case of published opening hours) to very difficult (in the case of a training center located in a remote area and opened only for *ad hoc* lectures).
- Are there security measures in place (e.g., calculated on a scale of low to high deterrence or low to high prevention)?

Questions that probe the existence and extent of controls (or lack thereof) can also be asked to gauge ease of attack. On the one hand, if there is a high degree of control effectiveness, this will usually reduce ease. On the other hand, if there is a low level of control effectiveness, it will increase ease. The private investigator should be mindful that, with some targets, even a small reduction in control effectiveness can result in a disproportional increase in ease of attack. Impact could be operationalized by questions like:

- What are the numbers of people frequenting the target, if in the case of a place or thing, or have access to the target in the case of a person or group? Establish a scale ranging from a few daily/weekly/monthly to hundreds or thousands daily/weekly/monthly. Are these same people attracted from the local community, or are they international tourists?
- In dollar terms, what would the financial impact of an attack be if the asset was disrupted, incapacitated/injured, or destroyed/killed? Or it could be put in terms of hours without operation, units of production, and so on. Impact is predicated on an assumption that terrorists want their attacks to result in large numbers of deaths (or a single death that will have a high symbolic or strategic impact). This may be true in the al-Qaeda-focused climate that existed at the time of this writing, but such an assumption may not always be valid; for instance, there may exist a nationalist-focused group that seeks to destroy infrastructure rather than kill people. In such a case, these terrorists may view heavy public traffic as an inhibitor to ease of attack. The two paradigms could be described as *effect-based attacks* versus *event-based attacks.*[156]

A template for calculating vulnerability might look something like that shown in Table 8.4. The vulnerability coefficient derived from this analysis is then compared against a reference table to gauge where it sits on the continuum of susceptibility to attack. The scale can be increased with additional qualifiers, or it could be collapsed if the number is deemed too many. In the end, the number and the descriptors need to make sense in the context of the asset being protected (the left-hand and center column of Table 8.5). Qualitative descriptors (i.e., conditioning statements) can be added for each category as shown in the right-hand column of Table 8.5. Note that *consequence* is not a factor that is considered in a threat assessment. It is, however, considered in a risk assessment.

Table 8.4.
A Vulnerability Analysis of Client's Regional Office Personnel to Gang Violence

Scale	Scores	Tally
	Attractiveness	
Negligible	1	
Minimum	2	
Medium	3	
High	4	4
Acute	5	
	Ease of Attack	
Negligible	1	
Minimum	2	
Medium	3	
High	4	4
Acute	5	
	Impact	
Negligible	1	
Minimum	2	
Medium	3	
High	4	
Acute	5	5
Vulnerability Coefficient		13

KEY WORDS AND PHRASES

The key words and phrases associated with this chapter are listed below. In one or two sentences, demonstrate your understanding of each by writing a short definition or explanation.

- Attractiveness;
- Capability;
- Coefficient;
- Desire;
- Ease of attack;
- Expectation;
- Impact;

**Table 8.5. An Examples of a Set of Vulnerability Coefficients
with Qualifiers (i.e., Conditioning Statements)**

Vulnerability	Coefficient	Qualifier (i.e., conditioning statements)
Negligible	1–3	• Can only be attacked successfully if the threat-agent has an acute threat coefficient; or • Has little or no importance; or • The range security measures make attack very difficult; or • If attacked, the target will suffer little disruption or harm (i.e., has significant redundancy and/or has sufficient capacity to continue functioning).
Minimum	4–6	• Can only be attacked successfully if the threat-agent has a high coefficient (or greater); or • Has limited importance; or • The range security measures make attack difficult; or • If attacked, the target has a large measure of redundancy and/or has a large capacity to continue functioning.
Medium	7–9	• Can only be successfully attacked if the threat-agent has a medium coefficient (or greater); or • Has reasonable amount of importance associated with it; or • The range security measures make attack moderately difficult; or • If attacked, the target has a moderate measure of redundancy and/or has a large capacity to continue functioning.
High	10–12	• Can only be successfully attacked if threat-agent has a minimum threat coefficient (or greater); or • Has a sizeable amount of importance associated with it; or • The range security measures make attack undemanding; or • If attacked, the target has little redundancy and/or has little capacity to continue functioning.
Acute	13–15	• Can only be successful attacked if threat-agent has a low threat coefficient (or greater); or • Has a very high level of importance associated with it or is an internationally recognized symbol; or • The range security measures are non-existing; or • If attacked, the target has no redundancy and/or no capacity to continue functioning.

- Intent;
- Knowledge;
- Resources;
- Threat-agent;
- Threat community;
- Threat profile;
- Threat; and
- Vulnerability.

STUDY QUESTIONS

1. An investigation into possible threats to a client comprises an assessments of two factors – intent and capability. These two elements comprise two further factors each. Discuss these four factors and explain how their interaction results in a threat.
2. An investigation into a client's vulnerability comprises an assessment of three factors – attractiveness, ease of attack, and impact. Discuss these factors and explain how their interaction results in identifying vulnerabilities for attack.
3. Review the list of external threat communities cited in this chapter. Brainstorm possible additions to this list – say, three to six additional threat communities.

LEARNING ACTIVITY

Using Table 8.5 as an example, construct a set of condition statements that could accompany each of the categories in Table 8.2 so that the client knows what is meant by high intent, low intent, and so forth. Do the same for capability.

Chapter 9

ILLICIT ORGANIZATIONS AND
FINANCIAL INTELLIGENCE

LEVI J. WEST

BACKGROUND

Crime and Terror – Funding Mechanisms

The decades since the end of the Cold War have brought substantial changes to the structures of international trade, economics, and business. The globalization process has lifted countless numbers of people worldwide out of poverty and provided opportunities for economic growth and innovation to remote corners of the globe. It has also resulted in greater levels of interconnectivity, increased access to modern communications technology, and the emergence of multinational corporations with annual turnovers larger than many sovereign states.

The process has also involved the deregulation of international financial markets, and what Naim referred to as the "dissolve[ing] of the sealants that governments traditionally relied on to secure their national borders."[157] Ultimately, the globalization process has served to empower individuals across the world to increase their wealth, and improve their standards of living. Indeed, there are few places that have not been touched by the globalization project.

There has, however, been a concomitant development, and increased prevalence of, international *illicit* trade, economics, and business. This specific area of crime – distinct in many ways from its predecessors – has succeeded in permeating almost every facet of legitimate business through adaptive organizational structures, increasingly sophisticated techniques for the transfer and laundering of illicit finance, and the leveraging of the aforementioned breakdown in national borders.[158] In what Gillman et al. refer to as "deviant globalization," a multitude of actors and practices have emerged. Gillman et al. define this phenomenon as:

> The unpleasant underside of transnational integration. . .the cross-border networks that produce, move, and consume things as various as narcotics and rare wildlife, looted antiques and counterfeit goods, dirty money and toxic waste, as well as human beings in search of undocumented work and unorthodox sexual activities.[159]

Most importantly, this process has also produced opportunities for increased cooperation between, and in some instances, the merging of criminal enterprises with terrorist operations. In such cases, both are seeking to leverage the industry that results from the trafficking of a multitude of illicit and licit products.

Aims

What does this new situation mean to private investigators that have traditionally carried-out after-the-event investigations? It means that they need to understand that there is now a distinction between what they have hitherto considered a demarcation between organized crime and terrorism, and that this came about in the post-Cold War period, particularly in the post-9/11 world. Unlike the private detective depicted in Dashiell Hammett's *The Assistant Murder,*[160] the post-9/11 private investigator is now exposed to a new and far more complex world of crime and criminally.

This chapter will focus on, first, explaining these complexities so that private investigators are aware of the environment into which they now work. Second, it will introduce the reader to the intelligence-based approaches used to investigate economic crimes. Although, this chapter will not make the private investigator proficient in economic crime investigation, it will nonetheless expose the reader to the essential elements of this approach so that they can operate with more confidence.

TRADITIONAL ORGANIZED CRIME

Shelley, of George Mason University, described traditional organized crime groups, or what she has termed *older* organized crime groups as:

> . . . often (existing) in long-established states, have developed along with their states and are dependent on existing institutional and financial structures to move their products and invest their profits . . . rarely do the large established

crime organizations link with terrorist groups, because their long-term financial interests require the preservation of state structures. Through corruption and movement into the lawful economy, these groups minimize the risk of prosecution and therefore do not fear the power of state institutions.[161]

Further to this description of traditional organized crime, Wagley, writing for the Congressional Research Service, identified the following:

> Traditional groups have a hierarchical structure that operates continuously or for an extended period . . . They may have repeatedly laundered their assets through legitimate businesses.[162]

These conceptions of organized crime describe traditional organized crime groups, motivated primarily by profit, requiring a stable and corruptible state through which to launder their finances, and with little or no interest in a political or ideological agenda. It is this distinction that has informed much of the separation between law enforcement and national security investigations and intelligence gathering, and in turn, the distinction between the investigation of money laundering and of terrorist financing. As will be identified below, these distinctions are becoming increasingly blurred, if not obsolete.

PRE-GLOBALIZATION TERRORISM

Terrorism, as distinct from organized crime, has a history that dates back at least as far as Romans occupied Jerusalem and its evolution has continued to reflect the changes that have occurred in the social, economic, and political context in which it occurs. While much has changed in relation to the ideologies and methodologies of terrorists and terrorist organization, the dramatic changes that occurred as a result of the end of the Cold War have had important implications for efforts to deal with terrorist activities. This change was primarily in relation to what Gupta calls the "lifeblood of terrorist groups,"[163] that is – money.

The Cold War had offered an extended period of substantial state-sponsorship for terrorist organizations, with many states utilizing terrorist organizations and armed groups more generally, to wage proxy warfare in numerous third-world locations.[164] With the collapse of the Soviet Union and the subsequent end of the Cold War, terrorist finance was "privatized" in the sense that terrorist organizations needed to provide their own funding mechanisms to support both their operations and their organizations. This shift resulted in terrorist organizations developing, or rediscovering, a number of avenues through which to raise funds, increasingly leveraging the globalization process to improve their capacity to raise and transfer these funds.[165]

It is important to note that traditional conceptualizations of terrorist organizations held that they avoided criminal activities (in the sense of for-profit criminal behavior) due to the risk of detection or exposure. As long as alternative methods of financing such as state-sponsorship or easily obtained donations from diaspora communities continued, terrorist organizations were able to avoid criminal activity for the purposes of raising funds, maintain ideological purity, and to focus primarily on operational concerns. The end of state sponsorship, in conjunction with the overwhelming opportunities presented by globalization, converged to bring about a new model of terrorist organization, and more specifically, terrorist financing. This occurred in parallel with substantial changes in the nature of organized crime.

THE EMERGENCE OF TRANSNATIONAL ORGANIZED CRIME

In contrast to the nature of traditional organized crime, and as a function of the impact of globalization on the world of illicit business, organized crime has experienced a significant shift in its structure, capability, and increasingly, in its purpose. Shelley, in her important work on the changing nature of organized crime, identified the contrast between the traditional structures of organized crime referred to above, and the new organized crime groups. She states that:

> In contrast, the newer transnational crime groups, often originating in post-conflict situations, thrive in a state of chaos and ongoing conflict . . . where the shadow economy is dominant, the crime groups are dominant actors in the shadow economy. The newer crime groups in ungovernable regions are now forging alliances with terrorist organizations . . . neither the criminals nor the terrorists need fear ineffective and corrupt law enforcement regimes in conflict regions.[166]

These new organizations, referred to as Transnational Organized Crime groups (TOCs) have emerged as a genuine international security issue, with increased focus and resources being deployed by international agencies, national governments, and private corporations. While trafficking in illicit (and licit) goods is not new, the scale, ability, and ease with which these new, often networked and flexible organizations are able to engage in their business is arguably unprecedented, as is their ongoing cooperation with and increasing fusion with terrorist organizations. Most important is the shift in the relationship these organizations have with the state. Whereas traditional organized crime sought a relatively stable, albeit corruptible state, TOCs seek instability or conflict as this environment provides them with appropriate operating space in which to conduct their illicit business.[167]

TERRORIST FINANCING

Freeman identifies four primary mechanisms for the funding of terrorist activities: (1) state sponsorship; (2) illegal activities; (3) legal activities; and (4) popular support.[168] Although state sponsorship has diminished substantially since the end of the Cold War, some terrorist groups retain relationships with states. Established relationships exist between Iran, Syria, and Pakistan and a variety of prescribed terrorist organizations, as well as with private funding by some wealthy members of certain Middle Eastern states.[169]

> **The World Bank defined terrorist financing as: "The financial support, in any form, of terrorism or of those who encourage, plan or engage in terrorism."[170]**

State sponsorship, along with popular support, and the use of legal activities, have all been dramatically affected by the post-9/11 response to terrorist financing.[171] The concerted effort on behalf of the international community to make the use of alternative remittance systems and other mechanisms for the channelling of funding to terrorist groups more difficult has made illicit activity all the more attractive. Illicit activity remains the most accessible avenue for generating funds, and in conjunction with a number of other appealing elements, forms the centerpiece of the terrorist financial portfolio. Shelley identifies five reasons why illicit activity proves so appealing to terrorist organizations and these are:

1. rapid and repeatable income stream;
2. allows groups to diversify source of income;
3. diversification of risk;
4. funds remain in illicit economy, limiting exposure and security risk, and
5. enhanced operational capabilities.[172]

ILLEGAL ACTIVITIES

Research shows that terrorist organizations have been engaged in a variety of illicit activities as a means of generating finance for their operations. Having been required to engage in illicit activity for revenue generating purposes, a terrorist organization is then faced with the decision as to which particular illicit activity it will engage in. Part of this decision-making process will consider the skills required by the participants, the financial investment needed to establish or continue the activity, and the existence of competition in the marketplace. Research in the latter part of the 2000s is represented in Table 9.1. This table is based on the findings of Picarelli and Shelley[173] and highlights the diversity of criminal activities that terrorist organizations are able to consider when making investment decisions, the appeal of some illicit activities over others, as well as identifying some of the vulnerabilities that are manifested as a function of terrorist engagement in illicit activity.

Table 9.1. Picarelli and Shelley's Comparison of Possible Terrorist-Related Criminal Enterprises

Crimes	Capabilities	Entry Costs	Opportunities
Narcotics Smuggling	Expertise required for production, but little to no expertise required for transport or distribution	Moderate financial outlays. Likely barriers due to high competition	Limited for production of agriculturally based drugs. Open for transportation and distribution assuming demand is present
Commodity Smuggling	Little expertise required	Moderate to acquire commodities. Barriers include access to commodities or linkages to those with access	Limited markets and opportunities to access resources
Goods Smuggling	Little expertise required	Low, though some types of goods might require some financial outlays or present competition barriers	Nearly unlimited
Migrant Smuggling	Some knowledge of border controls required	Low, though some borders might require access to fraudulent documents or payments to border guards	Somewhat limited due to the nature of global migratory flows
Trafficking in Persons	Expertise required in the recruitment and exploitation phases	Moderate costs and barriers depending on the form of exploitation. Low for recruitment and movement phase	Nearly unlimited

Table 9.1. Picarelli and Shelley's Comparison of Possible Terrorist-Related Criminal Enterprises *(continued)*

Crimes	Capabilities	Entry Costs	Opportunities
Extortion	Little expertise required	Low costs and barriers, save for competing sources of private protection	Nearly unlimited in areas where the authority of the central government is poor
Kidnapping	Little expertise required	Low cost and few barriers	Nearly unlimited
Intellectual Property theft	Moderate technical expertise required	Moderate costs for access to technical equipment for production. Few barriers for distribution save costs of acquisition	Nearly unlimited
Counterfeiting	Moderate technical expertise required. Expertise dependent on level of awareness of counterfeit instruments	Moderate to high costs for access to technology and defeating anti-counterfeiting measures	Limitations directly related to the quality of the counterfeit instrument
Fraud	Little expertise required	Low costs and few barriers	Limited only by the prevalence of targets for the fraud
Credit card theft	Little expertise required	Low costs and few barriers	Nearly unlimited
Armed Robbery	Little expertise required	Costs related to measures required to defeat security measures	Somewhat limited to the range of potential victims present in the area of operation

THE 1980s AND NARCO-TERRORISM

The 1980s witnessed a dramatic expansion in demand for cocaine products in the United States, and as a result, production and exportation of these products from their source countries increased.[174] One of the most important developments that occurred as a result of the massive growth in the cocaine industry in Latin America was the cooperation that emerged between the Colombian drug barons and the Revolutionary Armed Forces of Colombia (FARC).

Napoleoni details the 1984 raid by Colombian police on a remote drug storage facility in the Colombian jungle that produced the evidence of structured cooperation between these two organizations. The Colombian state's elite forces that landed in that raid fought a 100-man FARC commando unit who were defending the 13.8 tons of cocaine (approximately US$1.2 billion street value) that was seized. In addition, the raid unveiled documentary evidence of agreements between the barons and the FARC for the provision of armed security.[175] The scale and value of this single incident demonstrates the utility of the narcotics industry to terrorist groups. This cooperation was the beginning of a broader trend of terrorist engagement in the narcotics industry specifically, and a more structured and sophisticated engagement in illicit activity more broadly.

Islamic Movement of Uzbekistan (IMU)
"The insurgent group with the deepest reach in the drug trade is unquestionably the Islamic Movement of Uzbekistan (IMU). With a network of fighters extending from South Waziristan up through the former Soviet republics, the IMU was cultivated by [Osama] bin Laden in the 1990s to develop roots in Central Asia. He may have recognized the group's earning potential: Interpol and the DEA report that the IMU controls as much as 70 percent of the multibillion dollar heroin and opium trade through Central Asia."[176]

In the post-9/11 security environment, there has been a convergence of factors that have made the narcotics industry even more attractive to terrorist groups. The launching of more sophisticated countermeasures by national governments and international organizations has limited the capacities of terrorist groups to move and launder funds through legitimate businesses and entities. In addition, greater attention has been paid to the charity organizations and other entities that served as conduits for donations from diaspora communities.

In conjunction with the continued limitations of state sponsorship, data indicates that trafficking of narcotics has become increasingly valuable to terrorist organizations. In addition to the scale and value of the international narcotics industry, the reasoning that terrorist groups undertake when determining how to generate an income to sustain their organizations will be examined in the next section.

CRIMINAL ACTIVITY AS AN INCOME GENERATOR FOR TERRORISTS

Terrorist organizations use of illicit activity to generate income occurs for a number of rational reasons. In addition to the simple "return on investment" considerations, terrorist groups will also make assessments in relation to a number of other considerations. These considerations also mean that different terrorist organizations, operating in different environments, will make different decisions about which particular form of illicit activity will best suit their operational needs.

Freeman provides a matrix which serves to identify the key considerations that a terrorist group will engage in when determining the particular mix of investments in illicit activity. Like legitimate investments, each containing different levels of risk and return. Freeman identifies the following six criteria:[177]

- Quantity – what amount of money that be generated by the particular activity?
- Legitimacy – does the activity compromise the ideological position of the group?
- Security – what are the security and exposure risks of particular activities?
- Reliability – how consistent is the activity in generating income?
- Control – what is the impact of the activity on the command and control of the group?
- Simplicity – what are the outlays, costs, establishment requirements of the activity?

It is likely that it will be a combination of these different considerations that informs the decision making of terrorist organizations in generating their illicit income. In conjunction with Shelley's five-point list regarding engagement in criminal activity, a picture of terrorist group business decision making begins to emerge.

The examples demonstrate the preparedness of terrorist organizations to either cooperate with, or become players in, the international narcotics industry and in criminal behavior more extensively. As a Stratfor briefing by Stewart detailed:

> Terrorists also are funded through illegal activity, including large-scale narcotics sales, which are frequently used by the Revolutionary Armed Forces of Colombia and the Taliban. Hezbollah generates revenue through cigarette tax fraud and through selling counterfeit goods and fake prescription drugs. Kidnapping is also an age-old method of funding terrorism.[178]

SOME THINKING ABOUT TERRORIST USE OF CRIME

Freeman divides terrorism financing into operational and organizational categories. In doing so he refers to the relatively low costs of operations, even those he refers to as "strategic level attacks."[179] As Table 9.2 shows, the return on investment for terrorist organizations is substantial, especially when considered in conjunction with the calculations undertaken by Mueller and Stewart.

Table 9.2. Estimated Cost of Major Terrorist Attacks[180]

	Attack					
	New York 1993	Dar es Salaam/ Nairobi 1998	US 9/11 Attacks	Bali 2002	Madrid 2004	London 2005
Cost	$18,000	$50,000	$400,000	$20,000	$60,000	$15,000

The attacks of 9/11 cost an estimated US$400,000, yet according to Mueller and Stewart, "leaving out the costs of the terrorism-related (or terrorism-determined) wars in Iraq and Afghanistan, and quite a few other items that might be included – the increase in expenditures on domestic homeland security over the decade exceeds [US] $1 trillion . . . This has not moved the country into bankruptcy, Osama bin Laden's stated goal after 9/11, but it clearly adds up to real money, even by Washington standards. Other countries like Britain, Canada, and Australia have also dramatically increased their expenditures."[181]

The exceptional profits generated by terrorist engagement in illicit activities can be viewed as providing an exceptionally effective business model. The capacity to generate high incomes from illicit activity, and maintain low costs and high returns in regard to terrorist activity, provides terrorist groups with a disproportionate advantage when considered alongside the state. These figures become especially pertinent when governments are operating in a fiscally constrained environment and are under both budgetary and political pressure to minimize spending. Thinking about terrorist finance in business terms can be helpful in gaining a clearer picture of the decision-making processes and the selection of particular activities in regard to revenue generation.

CONTINUUMS AND NEXUSES

Research during the 2000s has identified a growing trend toward cooperation and the possibility of convergence of terrorist groups and transnational organized crime groups.[182] This approach has its roots in the work of scholars such as Mainwaring and his research into what he labelled as "gray area phenomena."[183] This work has contributed the development of a greater appreciation of the complexity of contemporary security threats, and the role of violent non-state actors. In establishing a theoretical framework for understanding this process, scholars have developed what is referred to as the crime–terror nexus. Makarenko, one of the foundational thinkers in this area, defines the nexus as:

> . . . a security continuum with traditional organized crime on one end of the spectrum and terrorism at the other. In the middle of the spectrum is a 'grayarea' – where organized crime and terrorism are indistinguishable from one another.[184]

This relationship is shown in Table 9.3, which is based on the model developed by Makarenko.[185]

Table 9.3. Makarenko's Logical Model of the Crime-Terror Nexus

Organized Crime			*Convergence*			*Terrorism*
1	2	3	4	3	2	1
Alliance with terrorist group	Use of terror tactics for operational purposes	Political crime	"Black Hole" syndrome	Commercial terrorism	Criminal activities for operational purposes	Alliance with criminal organizations

The nature of analyzing groups on the continuum is that they rarely remain static. This is increasingly so for networked organizations which, unlike hierarchical organizations with complex bureaucratic structures, are able to more easily adapt and evolve to suit their operational environment. Makarenko developed four general categories for the analysis of the relationships between different groups operating in this fluid space, namely:

> **Alliances**: . . . criminal groups forming alliances with terrorist organizations, and terrorist groups seeking alliances with criminal organizations. The nature of alliances between groups varies, and can include one-off, short-term and long-term relationships. Furthermore, alliances include ties established for a variety of reasons such as seeking expert knowledge (i.e., money-laundering, counterfeiting, or bomb-making) or operational support (i.e., access to smuggling routes).
>
> **Operational Motivations**: . . . criminal groups have increasingly engaged in political activity in an effort to manipulate operational conditions present in the rising numbers of weak states; whereas terrorist groups have increasingly focused on criminal activities to replace lost financial support from state sponsors.
>
> **Convergence**: . . . refers explicitly to the idea that criminal and terrorist organizations could converge into a single entity that initially displays characteristics of both groups simultaneously; but has the potential to transform itself into an entity situated at the opposite end of the continuum from which it began.
>
> **Black Hole syndrome**: . . . situations in which weak or failed states foster the convergence between transnational organized crime and terrorism, and ultimately create a safe haven for the continued operations of convergent groups. The 'black hole' syndrome encompasses two situations: first, where the primary motivations of groups engaged in a civil war evolves from a focus on political aims to a focus on criminal aims; second, it refers to the emergence of a 'black hole' state – a state successfully taken over by a . . . group.[186]

The convergence and "black hole" points on the continuum represent those points at which transnational organized crime groups and terrorist groups may reach their greatest levels of lethality, and the point at which they pose the greatest threat to national and international security. A terrorist group that successfully incorporates involvement in illicit activity will have the capability to generate substantial illicit funds, compensating for the diminution of state support, and the difficulties and risks of remaining engaged with the obtaining of support from a sympathetic diaspora community. In addition, a terrorist group with limited external considerations in regard to legitimacy, or the impact of excessive brutality due to their financial independence is able to mount more deadly attacks with less consideration of the broader consequences to their support base.

Transnational organized crime groups which reach this point on the continuum will begin to see it as being in their interest to foster instability within their geographic area of influence, providing them with operating space in which to engage in whichever particular illicit activity, or group of illicit activities, they have chosen to specialize in. The example below, of the Indian organized crime group known as D-Company has evolved from its beginnings as a small scale organized crime group focused primarily in India before elements within the group were radicalized by political and religious events in India.

Over time, D-Company increasingly became involved with politically and religiously motivated terrorist groups, thus shifting them towards the convergence point on the continuum. Of particular interest is the developing relationship between D-Company and the Pakistani intelligence service, the Inter-Service-Intelligence[187] is an example of a group that has come to display elements of the "black hole" scenario. This is a concerning development in the nature of organized crime and of terrorism, as it fuses with the interests of state infrastructures in fragile, weak, or collapsed states. In 2012, Naím wrote on this phenomenon and coined the term *Mafia State,*[188] which he defined as scenarios in which:

> . . . government officials enrich themselves and their families and friends while exploiting the money, muscle, political influence, and global connections of criminal syndicates to cement and expand their power. Indeed, top positions in some of the world's most profitable illicit enterprises are no longer filled only by professional criminals; they now include senior government officials, legislators, spy chiefs, heads of police departments, military officers, and, in some extreme cases, even heads of state or their family members.[189]

In his article, Naím identified a number of states as qualifying as examples of Mafia States: Bulgaria, Guinea-Bissau, Montenegro, Myanmar, Ukraine, and Venezuela. In these examples, he states that: "the national interest and the interests of organized crime are now inextricably linked."[190] In Makarenko's 2004, article he provided a similar list of states which he determined to be examples of the black hole point on the crime–terror continuum, namely: "Afghanistan, Angola, Myanmar, North Korea, Sierra Leone, and Tajikistan. Furthermore, [it includes] areas in Pakistan (the Northwest Frontier Province), Indonesia, and Thailand – where government control is extremely weak."[191] The recent findings of Naím endorse the earlier diagnosis by Makarenko and demonstrate not only increased cooperation between transnational organized crime and terrorists, but also with nation-states.

Dawood Ibrahim and D-Company

- 5,000-member criminal syndicate operating mostly in Pakistan, India, and the United Arab Emirates
- capable of smuggling terrorists across national borders, trafficking in weapons and drugs, controlling extortion

---

Continued on next page

and protection rackets, and laundering ill-gotten pro-
ceeds, including through the abuse of traditional value
transfer methods, like hawala. By providing those organizations with funding, contacts, and logistical support,
it amplifies their capabilities and durability
- reportedly involved in several criminal activities, including extortion, smuggling, narcotics trafficking, and contract killing . . . reportedly infiltrated the Indian film¬mak-
ing industry, extorting producers, assassinating directors, distributing movies, and pirating films
- considered to have . . . strategic alliance with the ISI as
well as developed links to Lashkar-e-Tayyiba (LeT)
- finance LeT's activities, use its companies to lure re-
cruits to LeT training camps, and give LeT operatives
use of its smuggling routes and contacts . . . network
might have provided a boat to the 10 terrorists who
killed 173 people in Mumbai in November 2008
- D-Company's own terrorist endeavors, its deep pock-
ets, and its reported cooperation with LeT and al-Qaeda, present a credible threat to U.S. interests in South
Asia.[192]

BEST PRACTICE: INTELLIGENCE

Williams provides some salient observations in regarding the nature of the
relationships between terrorists and transnational organized crime groups. He
stated that:

> If the politicization and radicalization of organized crime groups becomes
> more frequent, then the capacity of terrorists to carry out large scale attacks
> will be significantly augmented. There is an upside to this however. If ter-
> rorist networks integrate transformed criminal enterprises or even individual
> radicalized criminals, then the opportunities for infiltration by law enforce-
> ment – with all the benefits of good human intelligence – might be increased.
> The more immediate danger however, is that the terrorist use of organized
> crime activities will render the attack on terrorist finances by governments in-
> effective and ensure that the funding for further attacks. . . remains readily
> available.[193]

While these observations provide some optimism in regards to the capacity to interdict and mitigate the activities of terrorist organizations and transnational organized crime groups, the emergence of the mafia state or black hole phenomena is a particularly unsettling development which presents a substantial threat to international peace and security, as well as having weighty implications for personal security. There are, at least, some avenues through which information can be gathered that can help in the intelligence process to build a picture of these activities, and of the future activities of these groups, including the individuals behind them.

It is important to remain cognizant of the gravity of the challenge that is presented by this element of illicit finance. Extensive efforts have been made, especially in the decade since 9/11, to achieve greater international and private sector cooperation in relation to traditional terrorist financing, such as state-sponsorship, the use of charities, and non-traditional remittance systems.

Williams identifies a number of dimensions to financial transactions that can provide useful insights into the behavior of terrorists and transnational organized criminals. He identifies a number of aspects of behavior that can assist in building a more complete assessment of behavior. Within this list, he suggests the following considerations:

- "Changes in financial flows within terrorist networks . . . might suggest that new targets have been identified or that the terrorist network and its leadership have shifted their priorities;"[194]
- "Channelling of funds in an otherwise unexpected direction can be a clue to an impending operation;"[195] and
- Criminal activities leave a trail that allows investigators and intelligence analysts follow in order to obtain a more accurate picture of at least one segment of the overall terrorist network.[196]

For the post-9/11 private investigator, this means that their normal pre-investigation planning needs to be more robust. Although their data collection plan that forms part of their overall investigation plan will remain essentially the same, it does mean that their understanding of the business activities that are at the center of the allegation/suspicions need to be developed. They need to know about processes and procedures that will allow them to understand, and hence, trace the flow of money.

As with any investigation plan, PIs need to know where to go to obtain information to help answer the investigative question, but these aspects are more critical with financial investigations, and compounded with cases involving illicit organizations that operate clandestinely. The sources of such information would not be those normally encountered in traditional investigations; these may include banks, credit bureaus, accountants, state regulators agencies, and numerous commercial and industrial enterprises.

With regard to the outcome of the investigation, the private investigator needs to bear in mind that his and her investigation may end in a prosecution, so they must be clear from the start what the charges may be so that the elements of the alleged offense(s) can be proved, and that this proof complies with the law of evidence – e.g., showing knowledge, willingness, and intent. This also means knowing the defenses to the allegations and gathering evidence that will negate this type of legal maneuvering in court.

At the center of the investigation is the intelligence process that will assist in sorting what could be voluminous amount of raw data, and once collated, provide analytic methods for making sense of it. This insight can provide not only information about the crimes, but generate future leads for additional information gathering.

Gone are the days where a private investigator can sit ". . . tilted back in his chair, feet on desk"[197] and solve a crime. The post-9/11 PI needs to understand not only intelligence techniques, but needs to be abreast of the wider crime landscape in which he or she must operate. That landscape now inescapably includes illicit organizations and complex financial transactions.

KEY WORDS AND PHRASES

The key words and phrases associated with this chapter are listed below. In one or two sentences, demonstrate your understanding of each by writing a short definition or explanation.

- Black hole syndrome;
- Convergence;
- Crime–terror nexus;
- Globalization;
- Hierarchical organization;
- Mafia state;
- Narco-terrorism;
- Networked organization;
- State-sponsorship;
- Terrorist finance; and
- Transnational organized crime.

STUDY QUESTIONS

1. Explain how organized crime has been impacted by the globalization process?

2. Explain how has the financing of terrorism been impacted by the globalization process?
3. Describe some of the benefits of networked structures for terrorist and transnational organized crime groups?
4. Explain why illicit activity is appealing to terrorists as a mechanism for raising finance?
5. Describe the types of relationships can form between terrorist groups and transnational organized crime groups?

LEARNING ACTIVITIES

1. Identify an existing terrorist organization and select a particular illicit activity from the list in Table 9.1. Apply Freeman's framework, as identified in this chapter, to this activity to determine whether this particular terrorist organization would decide to engage in the particular activity you have selected.
2. Undertake some research into the drug cartels in Mexico. After reading up on their activities, utilize the ideas contained in this chapter to try to identify a mechanism for framing and understanding the behavior and decision making of the Mexican drug cartels.
3. Select five terrorist organizations from the U.S. State Department's list of proscribed terrorist organizations. After reading group profiles on these organizations, determine where, or if, you think they should sit on the crime–terror continuum (Table 9.3).

Chapter 10

COUNTERINTELLIGENCE

Petrus C. Duvenage

INTRODUCTION

Counterintelligence is arguably the most complex and least understood of all intelligence disciplines.[198] It defies easy description because of its multi-faceted nature. The following observation by Miler, at the height of the Cold War, is of even more importance in the post-9/11 context:

> It is not easy, nor can one feel confident, to re-enter this world where, it has been said, the tortuous logic of counterintelligence prevails. . . . Unfortunately, there seems to be no easy way to explain counterintelligence . . . because effective counterintelligence is a combination of so many aspects. . . .[199]

In the private investigation industry, counterintelligence is often sensationalized and misrepresented in the popular media – it is certainly distorted in fiction. Counterintelligence is portrayed as spies outgunning spies. This is, of course, not the reality. For others in the corporate world, counterintelligence could have the much more mundane connotations of being principally about computer passwords, restrictions on the use of computing equipment, security guards, access control, guard dogs, and the like. This is also a skewed view.

Whereas other chapters focused on the gathering and analyzing positive intelligence for a client, this chapter centers on the private investigator's role in protecting the client's information from the intelligence collection efforts of others, as well as protecting the PI's own operations through the application of countermeasures.

COUNTERINTELLIGENCE AND THE PRIVATE INVESTIGATOR

The relevance of counterintelligence to the private investigator can hardly be overemphasized, especially in the post-9/11 world. In the years since these terrorist attacks, the world has seen an escalation of profound security measures by governments, companies, and individuals. In conjunction with this trend, we note that the information glut, together with the Global Economic Crisis (GFC) has raised the premium on quality intelligence – be it from governments, or companies. Espionage operations to obtain such intelligence are usually facilitated by technological advantages as well as the propensity towards insider spying, and the latter is similarly on the increase. Consequently, the private investigator is confronted with unprecedented challenges, but presented with lucrative opportunities, too. That is, if the private investigator understands counterintelligence.

Although difficult to substantiate with exact figures, many private security practitioners will agree that the market demand for investigation services with a counterintelligence bearing is in increased demand. Examples are requests for investigations into leakages of sensitive information, suspicions of industrial espionage by competitors (and foreign nations), and some types of due diligence investigations. The private investigator's ability to capitalize on this market demand (and to effectively conduct such investigations) depends on having an understanding of counterintelligence theory and practice.

Other chapters in this book have emphasized the importance of confidentiality in private investigation work. Even the chapter on open-source information gathering showed how easy it is for an investigator to obtain information about a PI's client with little risk of exposure. So, investigators can maintain a level of confidentiality through the application of counterintelligence principles and countermeasures. But what is counterintelligence?

UNDERSTANDING COUNTERINTELLIGENCE

If counterintelligence were, as it is held in popular media and fiction, only about spy versus spy, it would already have been a complex phenomenon to explain. Counterintelligence is, however, much more much intricate. Even amongst scholars, counterintelligence is a contested concept. Nevertheless, there is a relative degree of consensus that counterintelligence's primary mission is to safeguard an entity's (e.g., person, organization, company, or a nation state's) information against hostile intelligence activities such as espionage. There is also agreement that counterintelligence is much more than protecting information through passive, defensive security measures (i.e., *de-*

fensive counterintelligence). However, opinions diverge on the role of security within counterintelligence.

There is a school of thought within business intelligence that categorically excludes security from counterintelligence. In his aptly entitled contribution, "Confusing Security with Counterintelligence Could Wreck Your Afternoon," Nolan provides the following differentiation: "Security seeks to *protect* a firm's assets, counterintelligence seeks to actively engage and *neutralize* a competitor's collection effort."[200] Security, explains another exponent of this thinking, is of a passive nature and strives to reduce corporate vulnerabilities as well as to protect a firm's tangible and intangible assets (such as sensitive information) through a combination of policies, procedures, and practices – on a lighter note referred to as "gates, guards, guns, and dogs."[201] Corporate counterintelligence is of an offensive nature and aims to neutralize a competitor's collection efforts through "a variety of imaginative, flexible, and active measures."[202] One of the "most proactive, aggressive, and effective" of these is "deception."[203]

The contention that counterintelligence excludes security is prevalent within intelligence studies discipline and with many of the intelligence services of the world's advanced economies. For instance, in the United States context, Godson distinguishes between, on the one hand, "security procedures" and "countermeasures," and on the other hand, "counterintelligence."[204] In contrast to these security procedures and measures, Godson asserts, counterintelligence "involves active efforts to identify, neutralize, and possibly exploit foreign intelligence services."[205]

An opposing view posits security procedures and measures as an integral part of counterintelligence. This view does not dispute counterintelligence's offensive role. It just argues that counterintelligence comprises a whole range of actions that ranges from the passive defensive to the active offensive. This position can be explained by means of the well-known analogy – counterintelligence consists of both relatively non-aggressive measures (the "shield") and aggressive measures (the "sword"). In combat, the sword and the shield function in synergy. The shield is primarily designed for defense but in the hand of a master can be used offensively, too. The shield has security as one of its composites. The sword is an offensive weapon (stab-and-cut) which can also defend (block) from an attack. Authoritative contributions underpinned by the above are those of Taylor[206] and Wettering.[207]

Counterintelligence's offensive and defensive *foci* are at the core of Prunckun's theory of intelligence.[208] This is probably the first coherent theory of counterintelligence as his theory captures counterintelligence's essence in a manner that transcends tactical discourses on what methods and procedures should or should not be defined as part of counterintelligence. He argued that to separate defensive counterintelligence (including security) from offensive counterintelligence is an error. This is because many defensive counterintelligence tactics and strategies can act as triggers to alert the offensive side of the practice. That is, if an attempt by an adversary to penetrate a client's information defenses can feed the offensive counterintelligence side by ". . . revealing an opponent's information voids as well as highlighting their capabilities and possible intentions."[209] Although Nolan called the ability to engage and neutralize a threat-agent's collection effort "counterintelligence," Pranckun stated that it is better termed *counterespionage,* or simply, *offensive counterintelligence.*[210]

Given these views on defining counterintelligence, one way to clarify the issue for the private investigation context is to define it in simple terms. So, for purposes of this chapter, counterintelligence will be described as any actions, processes, and methods that will provide protection for information assets by defensive means as well as offensive methods. Now that this has been established, what are the essential elements of counterintelligence?

COUNTERINTELLIGENCE FUNDAMENTALS

To be of value to the private investigator, the fundamentals of counterintelligence require some "unpacking." This is because we are still dealing with a generalized concept. While this unpacking may appear somewhat theoretical, doing so allows us to explore the precepts that underpin the practical counterintelligence work that the private investigator will do. So, what then are these fundamentals?

- Counterintelligence protects *valuable information – selectively.* Counterintelligence can seldom protect all information. One of the most challenging parts of counterintelligence work is identifying the information that warrants protecting, and subsequently, deciding with what measures (offensive, defensive, or a combination of these two) this is going to be done. In simple terms, valuable information consists of those assets which are critical to a company's functioning, competitive advantage, and even its existence.
- *Counterintelligence protects the C-I-A of information.* In a long-gone world with information stored in paper files, microfilms, and in cabinets, the role of counterintelligence was to safeguard the information's from physical harm and unauthorized disclosure; that is, the *confidentially, integrity,* and *availability* of information, or C-I-A. In the digital age, the confidentiality of information is interwoven with its integrity. Information should thus be trustworthy in that it is free from malicious tampering. Information's utility is moreover depended on its availability to au-

thorized users who access this information through systems. Since these three aspects cannot be separated, the C-I-A of information is a counterintelligence issue.[211]

- For counterintelligence to protect information, it needs to ensure the safeguarding of the custodians, systems, and processes in which the information resides as well as the physical premises within which these are located. Information, to state the obvious, does not exist amorphously and loose standing. It is located in systems (including physical records and information technology [IT] systems), processes (such as communication), and humans. Institutions and individuals are custodians of information. Counterintelligence therefore has a hand in safeguarding the relevant institutions, strives to ensure the integrity of humans/personnel, and should oversee the security of systems and processes.

- Implicit to the above is the notion that counterintelligence protects against *internal vulnerabilities* and *external threats*. The compromising of information through human negligence or insecure systems is an example of an internal risk. External threats are posed by a wide array of hostile actors employing diverse methods. These are termed *threat-agents,* as discussed in Chapter 8 ("Anti-Terrorist and Anti-Gang Intelligence"). Because threat-agents are, arguably, at the center of all attempts to penetrate an entry's information defenses, we will discuss them now.

THREAT-AGENTS

Threat-agents can engaged in several types of adversarial intelligence activities. Such activities include espionage, influencing, disinformation, and attacks on systems and processes. In the course of his or her work, the private investigator may encounter one or more of the following threat-agents:

- **State-sponsored intelligence**. From an American perspective, incidents abound of state-sponsored intelligence – People's Republic of China espionage targeting firms and technology.[212] Espionage, we all are aware, knows no few boundaries and is rife between foes and so-called by allies. France was, for example, recently accused of aggressively targeting America for espionage and infiltrating companies such as IBM, Texas Instruments, and Corning.[213]

- **Private enterprises**. These are widely used by statutory intelligence services in the gathering of economic, technological, and other categories of intelligence. The Federal Bureau of Investigation (FBI), for example, estimates that the People's Republic of China utilized more than

3,000 businesses in the U.S. as "front companies" for espionage.[214] Businesses themselves, without a clear affiliation to a state, however, remain responsible for the majority of cases of industrial espionage. This is clear from the following statistics the U.S. Office of the National Intelligence Executive provided in relation to attempts to illegally acquire sensitive technology from and within this country:

[F]oreign state actors accounted for about one-fifth of suspicious incidents and government-related organizations accounted for another 15 percent . . . Commercial organizations and private individuals with no known affiliation to foreign governments together account for nearly half – 36 percent and 12 percent respectively – of all suspicious incidents. In another 16 percent, the contractors were unable to determine the affiliation of the foreign parties involved in the elicitation.[215]

The extent of espionage that competitors engaged in against rivals therefore exceeds that of the other actors discussed here. Such espionage can be conducted by the business entity itself, contracted to individual private investigators or outsourced to specialized firms.

- **Crime syndicates and gangs**. These are known to possess intelligence capacities with an international reach that includes the Chinese triads, the Russian and Italians mafias, the Japanese yakuza, Columbian cartels, and Nigerian criminal organizations. As far back as 2004, the FBI forecasted that "criminal groups will expand their intelligence capacities to thwart law enforcement investigations."[216] The FBI also reported that, in addition to crime syndicates, organized groupings posing similar threats are – street gangs, prison gangs, outlaw motorcycle gangs, and neighborhood/local gangs.[217] The expanded capacities of these threat-agents are now, as in the past, directed against targets with financial and other resources worth exploiting – individuals, non-government organizations, as well as private and corporate enterprises.
- **Terrorists**. Such groups' possession of intelligence capacities is well-known and requires little further elaboration – take for instance the now publicly available, so-called *al-Qaeda Training Manual*[218] that outlines a range of intelligence and espionage methods. So, suffice to say that these capabilities can also be deployed against companies as well as any individual, or organization.
- **Journalists**. Several source types and methods employed by the investigative journalism industry mirror those of intelligence services.[219] The resultant media reporting, in which sensitive information is compromised, has far-reaching implications for governments and private business. The U.S. government, for one, voiced concern over the "hundreds of serious press leaks . . . that have collectively cost the American people hundreds of millions of dollars, and have done grave harm to na-

tional security."[220] The relationship between "journalism" and organizations that are set up for the express purpose of publishing leaked information are also well documented – for example, Wikileaks.[221]

- *Political activists.* In a similar vein, mounting mobilization by activists and non-governmental organizations around issues such as the environment bring them in conflict with businesses. Take for instance Greenpeace's on-going campaign against Japanese's whaling. Be it with the help of insiders, through cyber-surveillance, or via open-sources, this conflict may result in an individual or company's confidential information being compromised. By way of example, Kush, in his book *The One-Hour Activist,* explains how to conduct "opposition research" using open-source information gathering.[222]

The complexity of the counterintelligence task confronting the private investigator is compounded by the expanding arsenal of technical methods and means at the disposal of threat-agents. These are highly sophisticated and usable by anyone with even a small level of technical expertise, and at declining cost.

In 2007, Joel F. Brenner, the then U.S. National Counter-Intelligence Executive, remarked: "Governments no longer have a monopoly over world-class collection vehicles, like satellites, and word-class communications equipment."[223] Within the cyber environment, the level of expertise required by, and the financial cost to, threat-agents intent on exploiting an individual, organization, or company's information barriers has decreased sharply.

According to those who have studied the issue,[224] from around 1990, when cyber was in the general public's view still in its infancy, the level of knowledge needed to breach simple defenses, such as password protection, was high. However, as the years progressed, the sophistication of attack tools has turned this relationship around – that is, far less knowledge is needed to attack complex security systems.

The simultaneous growth in open-source information gathering during the first decade of the twenty-first century does not translate as a diminishing priority to collection by human agents (abbreviated, HUMINT). On the contrary, all indications are that human intelligence collection efforts intensified during this time also, with respect to both state-based and non-state-based threat-agents.[225] Open-source information gathering and human intelligence gathering are not a zero sum equation. There is no indication that internationally espionage is on the decrease. So, a client will likely expect you, the private investigator, to be familiar with this trend's implications so you can advise on the key methods for counterintelligence.

KEY METHODS FOR COUNTERINTELLIGENCE

It is imperative that the post-9/11 private investigator be familiar with the clusters of key methods for counterintelligence. Counterintelligence, to recapitulate, protects information from threat-agents – internal and external. This is done defensively, offensively, and through a combination of these two approaches. As with many trade and professional practices, counterintelligence can be categorized into various methods. Here we will examine the six key clusters.

Method 1 – Physical Security

Defensive counterintelligence measures (that is, passive) starts with the physical security of facilities where valuable information "is produced and stored."[226] This cluster of methods includes access and movement control, perimeter security, alarm systems, safes and vaults, fire prevention measures, key control, regulating the areas where the computer servers are housed, and so on. The nature of assets protected by physical security is multiplying. The post-9/11 challenge to physical security is encapsulated in the following quotation from the Commission on the Intelligence Capabilities of the United States Regarding Weapons of Mass Destruction report:

> [Physical] security, as a discipline, has historically been dominated by "police" type management, processes, and enforcement approaches. Although the police function is still required, today's security vulnerabilities are increasingly technical in nature and related to information technology systems, software, and hardware.[227]

Method 2 – Information and Systems Security

The quotation by the Commission on the Intelligence Capabilities of the United States Regarding Weapons of Mass Destruction rightly posits physical security as interlinked with information and systems security. A *system,* as used in this context, is deemed as referring to a variety of, by lack of a better word, techno-electronic systems. Examples are technical surveillance countermeasures (abbreviated, TSCM), communication security (COMSEC), and cybersecurity (CYBSEC). Note should be taken that technological advances have in some respects blurred the distinction between the security of information (in whatever format) and the security of systems. Communication and information systems are, by-and-large, an aggregate.

Method 3 – Personnel Security

However well-protected information might be by internal and external measures, the fidelity of personnel with access to information remains a critical factor in counterintelligence. Within the cyber field, the human factor is frequently viewed as the weakest point. Instead of technical methods to breach a cyber-network, the use of pretexts are used to gain information used to obtain access to systems.[228]

Within the statutory milieu, several of the most damaging espionage breaches followed insiders volunteering their services to foreign intelligence services, while numerous others involved foreign intelligence services' recruitment of insiders. It can safely be assumed that this also applies to the corporate environment. The importance of pre-employment and in-service personnel security is consequently self-evident. Methods utilized as part of determining the security competence and suitability of personnel include: biographical verification, criminal record checks, lifestyle and financial analysis, interviews, and polygraph tests.[229] Furthermore, personnel security has background investigations as a specialized function.[230]

On June 10, 2008, a British senior civil servant working in the Cabinet Office's intelligence and security unit transported and left classified documents on a train. While the act was unintentional, it followed the official's breach of several information-security regulations on this, and other, occasions. This documentation contained intelligence on "al-Qaeda's vulnerabilities and the competence of Iraqi security forces" and was classified "UK Top Secret Strap2 Can/Aus/UK/US Eyes Only" [i.e., Canadian, Australian, UK and US Eyes Only].[231]

Method 4 – Investigation

The uncovering during an investigation of an employee involved in unauthorized collaboration with a competitor should not have disciplinary action and criminal prosecution as default actions. Instead, this uncovering opens up exciting opportunities to initiate offensive counterintelligence activities against the competitor.

Therefore, investigation has its pillars in both of counterintelligence's offensive and defensive modes. Furthermore, it attests to the inseparability and blurred distinction between relatively non-aggressive and more aggressive counterintelligence collection methods. Through investigation as part of personnel screening, and probes into the breeches of security regulations, indications of possible adversarial espionage activities could for example emerge. Such indicators provide grounds for more aggressive investigations. The latter could take as premise the analysis of existing information as generated by, *inter alia,* information systems security and personnel security. Movement and key control registers, closed circuit television (CCTV) footage, and records of access to digital databases serve as examples of information generated by the security function. As a basis for more aggressive investigation, counterintelligence draws on all the collection instruments used within the positive intelligence realm.

Method 5 – Collection, Surveillance, and Sources

Depending on the specific case, a combination of human intelligence and open-sources information collection sources and methods is usually employed in investigations. Surveillance as a collection method demonstrates the interaction between open-source human dimensions. Marx,[232] as well as Gill and Phythian,[233] rightly point out surveillance as a value-laden concept with diverse denotations within the academic milieu. In the concrete sense of observing the activities of an espionage adversary, surveillance is one of the most common counterintelligence collection methods.[234] Although they overlap, three subcategories of surveillance can be distinguished, namely: (a) static surveillance; (b) mobile surveillance; and (c) electronic surveillance.[235]

More varied than surveillance is the range of human sources (HUMINT) that could be employed as part of counterintelligence collection. Within the statuary environment, human sources include, but are not limited to, peripheral agents, agents-in-place, access agents, moles, defectors, double agents, multi-turned agents (for instance triple-agents), agents *provocateur,* "walk-ins," agents of influence, unwitting agents, penetration agents, infiltration agents, false flag agents, witting agents, and "sleepers."[236] Although they could be labelled otherwise, these types of human sources are used in the corporate counterintelligence environment.

Method 6 – Neutralization, Deception, and Exploitation

The collection of information has as one of its aims to detect and determine hostile intelligence activity. Frequently, this detection's means and its ends are simultaneously defensive and offensive. On a more passive level, the information could prompt the enhancement of physical security measures. Offensively, the information is at the core of assailing the informational integrity of an adversary through manipulation, disruption, and neutralization (through, for example, criminal prosecution).

Earlier in the chapter we discussed the concept of deception as one of the "most proactive, aggressive, and effective" of counterintelligence measures.[237] Whatever measures employed, the private investigator will be well-advised to be familiar with the legal prescripts in this regard.[238] Corporate clients could outsource services to the private investigator precisely because the actions required are in the gray area. This can be done in a manner that allows the corporate client to deny soliciting illegal services.

Summary

This discussion of the key counterintelligence methods, albeit in a cursory way, shows that the practice of counterintelligence is multi-faceted. It also highlights the issues that defensive and offensive counterintelligence measures operate in a convergent way that defies strict compartmentalization. As such, separating these two dimensions could result in a fragmented counterintelligence practice – leaving an individual, organization, or business vulnerable to any number of threat-agents. For this reason, the various counterintelligence methods should be viewed as part of the counterintelligence process.

THE COUNTERINTELLIGENCE PROCESS

Business intelligence practitioners view counterintelligence as following a series of actions performed in a sequential order, forming a cycle that intersects with, but differs (in the nature of activities performed) from, the *intelligence cycle* of positive intelligence discussed in Chapter 2 of this book.[239] As a base for discussing the process in this book, we will use the "protective competitive intelligence" model, widely employed by corporate intelligence practitioners, as a guide. This process is highly pertinent to private investigators' work and consists of the following steps:[240]

1. Identify critical information requiring protection in order to develop a protection plan (i.e., step 4);
2. Appraise the threat posed by the various threat-agents;
3. Assess the vulnerabilities[241] that increase the risk[242] of information being compromised;

4. Using the six key methods for counterintelligence, develop a set of countermeasures to protect critical information;
5. Implement the recommended countermeasures; and
6. Continually assess and adapt the implemented countermeasures to accommodate the changing environment.

You would have to agree that this is a simple and uncomplicated process, but it masks a range of complex issues at each stage. Take for instance, step one – identifying those pieces of information that require protection. How is that done? Which person or people in the organization have that knowledge? And, what is "critical" anyway? To whom or what aspect of the organization is that information critical? Will it be critical for everyone and for what period of time will the information be of such importance? You can see the complexity of this single, simple step. Similar questions will no doubt arise at each of the other steps in the process.

Structured Approach

So, how can the private investigator approach the issue of counterintelligence? One way is to use a couple of *pro forma* workbooks for structuring the PI's thinking. One is a project sheet and the other a summary sheet. Although not a failsafe method, such an approach does provide transparency so a critical appraisal can be made of the overall approach to problem solving.

If a workbook approach was used, what might they look like? Templates for such counterintelligence assessments are shown in Tables 10.1 and 10.2. Although in an abbreviated form, these templates allow private investigators to fill in the information relevant to the assessments. This workbook approach can be used to protect a client's information, or they could be used to protect the PI's own data. Variations can be made to these templates to suit how a PI might apply it in the field. It is recommended that when computing a measure for the factors of vulnerability and risk, the descriptors and scales used in Chapter 8 of this book (Anti-Terrorist and Anti-Gang Intelligence) be used.

Table 10.1. The Private Investigator's Counterintelligence Project Sheet

Counterintelligence Project Template

Terms of References/Statement of Work

On April 01, 2013 Private Investigation Services represented by Mr. Ross Callum received the following brief from Ms. Isobel Trudeau (General Manager, Echo Oil) and Mr. R. Breedt (Risk Manager, Echo Oil):[243]

- The project's purpose, deliverables and envisaged outcome(s).
- To ascertain the origin of the recent the leakages in media reporting of mooted cooperation between Echo Oil and Foxtrot Petroleum in the exploitation of oil fields in the Blue Sea region. Recommendations should also be submitted on how to contain damage to Echo Oil's interests.
- The allocation of organizational resources such as information bases, personnel which will assist and/or should be interviewed, technology and equipment, facilities and funds.
- Mr. Breedt shall avail all necessary's Echo Oil resources to assist in the investigation. Private Investigation Services shall be remunerated as per invoiced quotation.
- The time frame for the design, execution, and conclusion of the project.
- The investigation shall be completed by September 30, 2013. Progress Reports shall be submitted at the first working day of each month. (This sheet constitutes the third such progress report and is to be handed to Mr. Breedt on July 1, 2013).
- The legal, regulatory, and procedural mandate for the project.

Echo Oil obtained government approval for exploration in the Blue Sea region. Echo Oil's executives and employers are bound by confidentiality agreements.

The Terms of Reference, summarized above, were confirmed in writing by Ms. Ramley by means of a confidential memo to Private Investigation Services (dated April 14, 2013).

Counterintelligence-Relevant Information

Information of counterintelligence-relevance to the project was determined in consultation with Mr. Breedt' and pertains to:

Item 1: Memoranda of Understanding with Foxtrot Petroleum.

Item 2: Geological Surveys of the Blue Sea Region (2011–2012)

Item 3: Minutes of Executive Meetings (2011–2013)

Appraisal of External Threats

In addition to the *Sun Newspaper,* external threat agents that could have benefited from the leakages of the information are competitor Golf Energy and the environmental activist group SeaPeace.

Appraisal of Existing CI measures in Protection of the Information

The information is stored in hard copy (archive) and in Echo Oil's IT system. Access to the archive is per controlled register and the IT system is sufficiently secured and compartmentalized. Information on the Blue Sea Project is availed on a strictly need-to-know basis. All employees dedicated to the project have signed confidentiality agreements and were screened. A review of personnel records shows that a senior geological engineer involved in the Blue Sea project, Mr. S. Corrupt, has recently been experiencing severe financial problems and substance abuse is suspected.

Recommendations on the Implementation of Additional CI Measures

It is recommended that an investigation be launched into a link between Mr. S. Corrupt and Golf Energy. For the interim Echo Oil can consider utilizing Mr. Corrupt as an unwitting platform for deceiving Golf Energy in assuming that exploration in the Blue Sea region is no longer financially feasible.

Echo Oil's further instructions are awaited.

Table 10.2.
The Private Investigator's Worksheet for Sensitive Information Protection

Counterintelligence Information Protection Template	
For the attention of:	Ms. Isobel Trudeau, General Manager, Echo Oil
Private Investigator:	Mr. Ross Callum (Private Investigation Services)
Subject:	Protection of Echo Oil's Blue Sea Project
Date:	July 4, 2013
Information Item:	Echo Oil's planned exploitation of high-yield oil fields in the Blue Sea region.
Threat Level:	High
Vulnerability:	High
Risk:	High
Recommended protective action(s):	Senior engineer, Mr. S. Corrupt, be investigated as the origin of media leaks and that he be used as disinformation 'platform' for the interim.
Implementation by:	Echo Oil and Mr. R. Callum.
Review date:	June 30, 2013.
Review Officer:	Mr. R. Breedt, Echo Oil, Risk Manager.
Project approved by:	Ms. Isobel Trudeau Date approved: April 14, 2013

KEY TERMS AND PHRASES

The key words and phrases associated with this chapter are listed below. In one or two sentences, demonstrate your understanding of each by writing a short definition or explanation.

- C-I-A of information;
- Counterespionage;
- Defensive counterintelligence;
- Offensive counterintelligence;
- HUMINT;
- OSINT;
- CYBSEC;
- TSCM; and
- COMSEC.

STUDY QUESTIONS

1. List the major categories of threat-agents and briefly describe each.
2. List the six key methods for counterintelligence and briefly describe each.

3. Discuss why it is important to use a transparent process to develop a counterintelligence information protection plan?

LEARNING ACTIVITY

Using the six-step counterintelligences process and the worksheets contained in Tables 10.1 and 10.2, apply these to some aspect of your own work. Perhaps it might be the information contained on your public website, or the information relating to a particular case you are working on. Follow each of the steps and complete the worksheet. Now, reflect on the process – was it straightforward or was it complicated, or was some aspect a bit of each? If you had to do this in the field for a client, what would you do differently? How could you tailor the worksheets to suit your needs?

Chapter 11

CLANDESTINE COMMUNICATION
METHODS

MICHAEL CHESBRO

INTRODUCTION

Two-way radio is not new to private investigators.[244] Even the 1931 legendary character Dick Tracy, a hard-boiled private detective, had a two-way wrist radio that he used to communicate with members of the police force. However, given the advances in digital communication and the widespread use of radio scanners, everyone from radio hobbyists to terrorists can listen in on these transmissions. The post-9/11 PI therefore needs to understand these devices and how he or she can use radios to their advantage.

Arguably, communications security is essential to every type of operation conducted by the private investigator, especially radio communications.[245] Not only does the investigator have a duty to safeguard the client's personal and proprietary information, but he or she needs to ensure that his or her own methods, tactics, techniques, and procedures are also safeguarded.[246]

This chapter focuses on the use of two-way radio communications by private investigators. We will discuss the importance of radio communication as well as methods of improving the overall security of communications while operating in the field. As there are several types of radio systems available to operatives, each has its own advantages and disadvantages, these will be discussed. Finally, we will look at a tactical encryption method that will allow private investigators to secure the messages they send where high-level computer-based encryption is not available or practical.

> ## Transceivers
> It should be noted that the term *radio* is used as a convenient way of describing a radio *transceiver*. That is, a transmitter and receiver in one unit – hence the name, transceiver. Transceivers can be of three types: handheld, mobile or portable, and base or desktop. All three types operate the same, the only difference is their physical size, and hence their portability (though handheld units will usually have less transmission power than the larger mobile and base units).

IMPORTANCE OF RADIO COMMUNICATIONS IN PRIVATE INVESTIGATIONS

With the ubiquity of cellular technology, smart-phones, and Internet-based video calls, many people overlook the advantages of radio communications. Radio has long been a device used for communication by the military, by law enforcement and emergency services, and by many businesses (for example, truck drivers and taxi operators). Radio has the advantage of being a communications system that is independent of commercial access to the cellular telephone system or the Internet. Radios work in areas where there are no cell-towers, and radios do not require an Internet service provider in order to communicate. Radio also allows communication with multiple parties at the same time. These, and many other advantages of radio, are why it is still a central pillar of military, government, and business communications.[247]

For the private investigator, radio communication is also an essential option. Although it may not wholly replace cell phones and Internet-based video conferencing, it is an effective way of providing control for operatives in the field. Personnel are able to coordinate activities and transmit information back to analysts and decision-makers in a timely manner. It also provides a means for checking on the wellbeing of operatives for occupational safety.[248]

TYPOLOGY OF RADIO SERVICES

To start our discussion, it is important to first understand the types of radio service that are available. Generally speaking, government agencies are assigned radio frequencies which allow them to operate their services. Businesses may apply for and be assigned radio frequencies for them to conduct their business communications. Everyone else will have to rely on one of the personal radio services established for general use.

In the United States, personal radio services include Citizens Band (CB), Family Radio Service (FRS), General Mobile Radio Service (GMRS), Multi-Use Radio Service (MURS), and the Industrial, Scientific and Medical (ISM) band. The VHF marine radio band is intended for ship-to-ship and ship-to-shore communication.[210] Many countries have similar personal radio services established.

A *band* is a range of frequencies in the radio spectrum. For instance, Australia, Canada, and the United States the 27 MHz citizen's band has *frequencies* that range from the band's low end of 26.965 MHz to a high frequency of 27.405 MHz.[250] A *frequency* is sometimes referred to as a *channel* – a specific setting on the radio "dial" to transmit and receive signals.

Finally, there is the Amateur Radio Service, also known a *ham radio,* which has the capability of providing worldwide communications. Most countries have some type of amateur radio service, and these amateur radio engineers take pride in their ability to establish communication links worldwide using a minimal amount of equipment, often much of which is home-built or field-improvised.

This chapter will mention radio services from member countries in the international Technical Cooperation Program (TCP). The TCP member countries are Australia, Britain, Canada, New Zealand, and the United States. These countries have joined together to cooperate on matters of science, technology, defense, and civil protection. The TCP countries are also the same countries that form the Five-Eyes intelligence alliance.

In Britain, there is the Private Mobile Radio (PMR446) operating in the analog mode on eight frequencies in the 446 MHz range (UHF band). Digital PMR466 operates on 16 digital voice channels. Britain also has a CB radio system operating in the 27MHz range. This radio system operates on 80 channels, 40 of which are the same as the American, Australian, and Canadian CB radio channels,[251] while the other 40 channels operate on channels between 27.60MHz and 27.99MHZ. This British CB system became a license-free service in December 2006. In New Zealand, 27 MHz band spans 26.330 MHz to 26.770 MHz with a 40 channel allocation.

Australia and New Zealand have a common 80 channel radio system operating in the 466 MHz–467 MHz range. This is a similar radio system to that in Britain (PMR446) and in the U.S. (GMRS), although the operating on different frequencies.

Canada maintains radio services that are all similar to the U.S., although there are some differences in frequency allocations. Each country has its own amateur radio service, with internationally compatible frequencies (known as *band allocations*). This international alignment allows for licensed radio operators to communicate around the world.

Specific radio frequency tables for each country's radio service can be found on the Internet, or may be obtained from the governing body for communications in each country (e.g., the Federal Communications Commission in the United States). Due to the fact that frequency allocations change from time-to-time, they have not been included. However, to ensure that a radio operator does not cause interference with other users, it is important that every radio operator be familiar with radio frequency allocations wherever he or she may be operating. It is also important from the point of view of communications security – you do not want to be operating on a frequency band where others may be listening in.

NET CONTROL STATIONS

One of the most important elements of effective radio communication is establishing a net control station. The net control station is in charge of the communications network and also serves as an information resource for operatives in the field. In law enforcement, the net control station is the police dispatcher. For the private investigator, a similar net control station is necessary in order to maintain effective communications.

The net control station logs communications, maintains maps and databases to assist field operatives, and controls communications between different operational personnel. The net control station also monitors other frequencies in order to develop a communications intelligence picture of the operational area. This is usually down via a radio scanner programmed for the key bands, or via a radio scanner that can detect radios operating within its receiving range.

For the private investigator who works in a specific area (similar to police departments working within a specific jurisdiction), his or her net control station can be permanently established in a building, and radio repeaters installed throughout the area to ensure radio coverage. In some cases, howev-

Figure 11.1. Radio net controller contacting private investigators who are conducting a rural surveillance operation (photograph courtesy of Michael Chesbro).

er, the private investigator may require a mobile net control station. In this case, a communications vehicle may be set up with radios, scanners, and computer access to the Internet (e.g., Wi-Fi and cellular telephone), as well as a complete non-voice digital communications package.

Radio Repeaters

A radio repeater is a kind of radio that receives a signal and rebroadcasts it. This is done to increase the range of incoming signals. For this reason, many radio repeaters are located on tall buildings or on hills or mountains. The additional heights increase range of the repeater based on the principle's of line-of-sight.

SCANNERS AND MONITORING COMMUNICATIONS

Radio scanning and monitoring is a worldwide hobby. Magazines such as *Monitoring Times*[252] support the radio monitoring hobby and suggest the broad popularity of this phenomenon. What the private investigator should understand from this is that hobbyists are very likely monitoring every channel in the radio spectrum, and if something sounds interesting it is almost certain that someone will be paying close attention (and perhaps even recording it).

The private investigator can use the scanner's methodology to his or her advantage in several ways. First, by monitoring the local police and emergency services frequencies, an investigator can develop an understanding of where there are problem areas in the community. Monitoring police and emergency service communications also gives the investigator firsthand information on events as they happen, which is much better than waiting to see something on the local news channel. On this point, local news agencies regularly monitor police and emergency services frequencies to get leads for their breaking news stories.

Finally, of course, the private investigator should ideally scan the frequencies for the various radio services described previously. By scanning radio communications in an area where the private investigator will be operating, he or she can develop a picture of what is happening. This type of monitoring is known as *signals intelligence*. If conducted while operating in the field, it can alert the private investigator to potential trouble – say, for instance, the local resident who phones the police because she saw "a strange man" parked in his car down the street. Such a phone call could end an important surveillance job.

COMMUNICATION PLANS

Planning is an important part of all intelligence work and communications is no different. When establishing a communications plan, it is important to plan for primary, alternate, contingency, emergency, and secure communications. This is sometimes called PACES communications. Let us examine each of these elements in turn.

The primary communications channel is where most communications take place. It is the channel monitored by everyone who is not actively engaged in communications on another frequency.

The alternate communications channel allows communication to be moved to this frequency to avoid tying up the primary channel with long communications. The alternate channel is not normally monitored by operators in the field, although the net control station should scan all of their operational frequencies. There may be more than one alternate communications channel or frequency.

The contingency communications channel is used for specific planned events where the primary and alternate communications channels won't work. For example, how will a surveillance team maintain communications if the target enters a secure area such as an airport or government building?

The emergency communications channel is used only in response to an actual emergency when it is necessary to prevent loss of life, serious injury, or catastrophic property loss. Emergency communications take precedence over all other communications.

The reference to sure communication refers to actions taken to guard against interception by people not associated with the investigation. Details of how this might be achieved are discussed later in the chapter.

The communications plan need not be any more complicated than, perhaps, a list with the PACES headings listed and next to each the frequency. A small card that could be carried by each operative might be a convenient way to distribute this plan.

UNDERSTANDING RADIO PRIVACY TONE CODES

Many radios include something called privacy codes, or CTCSS. This abbreviation stands for continuous tone-coded squelch system. It is a common, although mistaken, belief that these privacy tone codes generated by the radio keep others from hearing your radio transmissions unless they also have the same privacy tone code activated on their radio. This is not the case. What CTCSS does is keep your radio from receiving, and thus you hearing transmissions that do not have the same CTCSS code set. In effect, it simply filters the transmission of others, preventing you from hearing them, not from them hearing you. A radio with no CTCSS set will hear all transmissions, and note that a radio scanner can monitor *all* frequencies without regard for CTCSS.

DCS is an abbreviation for digital codes squelch. It is a sub-audible digital tone code that is generated by the radio and sent with the transmitted signal. In this regard, it is similar in function to the CTCSS – it blocks incoming signals that do not contain the proper radio tone code.

In most cases, investigators will not want to set either a CTCSS or DCS tone code on their radios. Doing so does nothing to secure radio communications, but does prevent you from hearing other transmissions on your frequency – which you do not want to do; you want to hear everything to keep informed. The exception to CTCSS and DCS tone code is to limit other access to a radio repeater you may be using to extend the distances operatives arc able to communicate. When sent on the intake frequency of a radio repeater, only other private investigators who are working with you will be able to activate the repeater.

The International Phonetic Alphabet is universally used by radio operators as it clarifies spelling on the air. With a weak signal or static-filled frequency, using this alphabet helps distinguish between letters. Take for example, the letters "B" and "P" which are mistaken as they can sound the same over the air. However, the words "bravo" and "papa" are less likely to be confused with each other.

RANGE OF PERSONAL RADIO SERVICES

Claims of ranges up to 50 miles (about 80 kilometers) are often promoted in the advertising and on the packaging of GMRS radios. While under ideal conditions, with unobstructed direct line-of-sight from the vantage point of a high elevation, these radios may actually transmit the ranges advertised. But in reality, these ranges are going to be significantly less.

GMRS radios operate in the ultra-high frequency (UHF) band, which is in the range of 300MHz to 3GHz, so line-of-sight is critical to effective communications. Whenever there is something between the transmitter and the radio receiver, such as buildings, trees, or land masses (i.e., hills), it can reflect or absorb the radio signals. Anything that is in the transmission path between the transmitter and receiver will reduce the effectiveness of the radio signal.

Because most field operations do not involve line-of-sight transmissions, operatives should plan for greatly reduced transmission ranges over those advertised. Under real-world conditions, a good rule-of-thumb is that actual transmission ranges are approximately one-tenth that which is advertised, with no more than a mile or two (about one to three kilometers) being reasonable for communications planning.

Short range communication is not necessarily bad. Field operatives — for example, a surveillance team — who work in fairly close proximity to each other, this will be fine. However, if distances are likely to extend beyond this, reliability will diminish rapidly.

But short operating ranges are not all negative. If your radios can only operate, say, no further than one mile (about 1.6 kilometers), there is little chance that your communications will be intercepted or overheard at greater distances. This limitation can be therefore be an advantage; however, there are better ways to ensure communications security than this.

COMMUNICATIONS SECURITY

The use of two-way radios can be monitored by anyone with a radio who can tune to the same frequency you are transmitting on. Radio scanners and broadband communications receivers are more common than one would imagine. So, a safe position to have is that all radio communications will be monitored by someone.

COMSEC
In the parlance of intelligence, *communications security* is abbreviated as COMSEC.

If the PI's work is targeted against criminals, gangs, and terrorists, it should be assumed that these targets will be monitoring all radio traffic in their area in order to exploit these communications (i.e., signals intelligence). So, whenever using radios, it is essential to include security as part of your communications plan (i.e., the *S* in PACES). To this end, we will discuss a few options available to operatives.

Option 1 – Digital Radio

Using a digital radio system as opposed to an analogue system will add a sizable level of security to PI operations. This is because digital radio systems are more difficult to monitor. Digital radios provide this increased level of protection by operating in the microwave range of the radio spectrum (around 900 MHz). Others operate in frequency bands similar to FRS radios, but use a frequency-hopping spread-spectrum technology that, as its names suggests, uses multiple frequencies so interception is very difficult.

But difficult does not mean impossible. However, it is reasonable to say monitoring this type of radio transmission is beyond the capabilities of most radio hobbyists. Digital two-way radios range in price from around $100 a pair, up to several hundred dollars per radio. Private investigators trying to establish a sound level of communications security should consider buying the better quality digital two-way radios.

Option 2 – Voice Scramblers

Some Family Radio Service (FRS) and General Mobile Radio Service (GMRS) radios have been sold with a built-in voice scrambler. This is a simple frequency inversion system that is easily unscrambled by anyone who spends a few dollars on the circuitry. The voice scrambler that comes built into these FRS and GMRS radios would provide only minimal protection from someone on the same channel or with a basic radio scanner from understanding your communications.

High-security voice scrambling is available for other types of radio systems, but in most cases, the benefits gained by using a voice scrambling system do not exceed the cost of purchasing voice scramblers. For private investigators, the use of digital communications (Option 1) and/or the use of radio codes and encryptions (which we will discuss later in this section) are more practical than attempting to set up a high-security voice scrambling system.

Option 3 – Radio Codes

Many law enforcement agencies are moving away from the use of radio codes as part of their routine communications. This is because they are finding that they need to work more and more in multiple agency task teams and work across jurisdictional lines. So, in these situations, using code words increases the potential for communications errors – for instance, does 10–51 mean an officer "needs assistance" or is he requesting a "tow-truck" – there is a big difference.

The Association of Public Communications Officers (APCO) at one time established a list of 10-codes, including those used in popular fiction – 10–4 (for acknowledgement or OK) and 10–20 (for location). The 10-code was intended for use by police agencies and it was often required to be memorized by cadets attending the police academy. As such, it is likely to be understood by, perhaps, tens of thousands of people worldwide.

However, the private investigation agency may choose to develop its own version of the 10-code. For instance, in covert operations where team members come from a single agency and regularly work together, radio codes can provide an additional degree of communications security, especially if used in conjunct with Option 1.

Option 4 – Crypto-Maps

Crypto-maps, also called, map spotting, is a method of marking reference points on maps with lettered as well as numbered dots (i.e., spots). This allows locations to be transmitted in a more secure manner over a non-secure frequency. When planning an operation in any area, personnel should mark intersections, buildings, landmarks, and reference points on their maps with matching lettered and numbered dots. This allows these locations to be referred to by a letter and number rather than a plain text location.

The same letter may be used multiple times, but if so, a unique number is assigned. For example, x-ray (X) may be used with numbers from zero through to nine, then alpha (A) is used, and again, numbers zero through to nine. So, each letter dot used will cater for up to ten locations. That means, if all the letters in the alphabet are used, you will potentially have 260 spots available for marking your map.

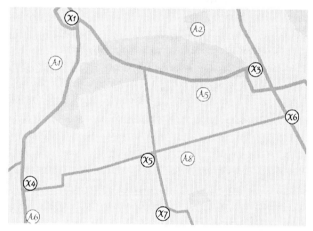

Figure 11.2. Example of a crypto-map (courtesy of Michael Chesbro).

By using map spotting an operative can state that she is approaching "x-ray-4" instead of saying she is approaching the intersection of State Street and Wilbraham Road. "Target at alpha 8" tells a listener far less than "target has entered the post office on Dwight Street." Only personnel in possession of an identically spotted map will be able to easily identify transmitted locations (see Figure 11.2).

Map spotting is particularly useful when conducting vehicle surveillance as the navigator/radio operator can keep the net control station/surveillance coordinator informed of team locations without disclosing this information to others who may be monitoring the frequency. If this option is used in conjunction with options 1 and 3, then the three form a robust communications security plan.

ETHICAL CONSIDERATIONS

Radio Licensing

In the United States, some radio services, such as amateur radio service, GMRS, and most business radio services require a license from the Federal Communications Commission (FCC) to operate lawfully. However, other services, such as CB, FRS, MURS, and ISM, are license-free. Each of the Five-Eyes countries have similar licensed radio services along with other non-licensed services.

Some PIs may be tempted to purchase and use a radio system from a different country (such as the British PMR466 radio) for use in the United States in an effort to obtain some increased degree of security and autonomy on the frequencies. It is always illegal to operate a radio on an unauthorized frequency. True, there may be far fewer people operating on these foreign frequencies in your country, but in doing so you may end up operating on a frequency assigned to a different service (say, the British PMR466 frequency may be assigned to public utilities in the United States).

Either way, it really does not increase your communications security. Foreign frequencies can be scanned as easily as any other frequency and unauthorized operation on a frequency will almost always attract more attention than will operating on an assigned, authorized frequency. For intelligence, investigation, and security work, never operate on an unauthorized frequency – doing so will only increase unwanted attention to your operations, and as such, may even result in criminal penalties.

Another example is that of marine radios. A search of the Internet will find some people advocating the use of VHF marine radios for land-based communications. This is highly illegal and will almost certainly attract the attention of the Coast Guard, and probably the Federal Communications Commission. Other illegal suggestions include modifying radios to operate outside of their intended capabilities, and increasing transmitting power by using linear amplifiers (e.g., with 27 MHz CB radios). This, too, is illegal as it can disrupt radio communication on the channel used by legitimate users, as well as adjunct channels in the same frequency band.

For private investigators who use two-way radios, it is essential that they obtain the required license. In many cases, private investigations may support criminal prosecutions, or civil litigation. It certainly does not bode well for the PI's future in an intelligence-led investigation business if the opposition's lawyers have your evidence dismissed because you used illegal means (i.e., unlicensed radio communications) to obtain it. Even if the question never comes up in court, using illegal means to conduct your business will reflect poorly on your business ethics – you risk tarnishing your standards of professional conduct. If the radio service you use requires a license, the best advice is to obtain the license. Moreover, do not modify your radios to operate outside of the frequency band licensed and only use your radio as it was designed – do not violate the law when developing your communications planning.

KEY TERMS AND PHRASES

The key words and phrases associated with this chapter are listed below. In one or two sentences, demonstrate your understanding of each by writing a short definition or explanation.

- Band;
- Communications plan;
- COMSEC;
- Frequency;
- Line-of-sight;
- Net control;
- PACES;
- Radio spectrum;
- Scanner;
- Signals intelligence; and
- UHF band.

STUDY QUESTIONS

1. Discuss the importance of radio communications security and why it is important to develop a communications plan that includes security.
2. Describe the purpose and function of a net control station, and explain how such a station would be used in a covert investigation.
3. Explain what a radio scanner is and how people who own these pose a potential risk to the covert operations of private investigators.
4. Select one of the four communications options discussed in this chapter and explain how this option might benefit a covert operative.

LEARNING ACTIVITY

1. Create a crypto-map for use in your area of operation by first obtaining at least two identical maps. One can be used by you and the other by another covert operative, or your net control station. Select the maps for areas that you will potentially work. Using the crypto-map method described, place lettered and numbered spots on at least twenty locations on each map. Remember the spots must be placed at identical locations on each map.
2. Memorize the International Phonetic Alphabet displayed in Table 11.1 and then have a friend or colleague test you.

Table 11.1. The International Phonetic Alphabet

Letter	Word	Letter	Word
A	Alpha	N	November
B	Bravo	O	Oscar
C	Charlie	P	Papa
D	Delta	Q	Quebec
E	Echo	R	Romeo
F	Foxtrot	S	Sierra
G	Golf	T	Tango
H	Hotel	U	Uniform
I	India	V	Victor
J	Juliet	W	Whiskey
K	Kilo	X	X-ray
L	Lima	Y	Yankee
M	Mike	Z	Zulu

Chapter 12

PREPARING A PROSECUTION BRIEF

HANK PRUNCKUN

INTRODUCTION

The outcome of many inquires is to provide a client with insight into an issue that is under consideration. Previous chapters have touched on a
range of inquires in this regard. However, it is also acknowledged that one
outcome that always remains is prosecuting the matter in a court of law.

But unlike fictional novels that depict courtroom drama as riveting displays
of master oratory brilliance, or cunning endgame chess moves, for the private
investigator's experience, it is likely to be limited to a single appearance to
give evidence. As simple as this sounds, the lead-up to a court appearance is
predicated by the careful preparation of a document termed a *prosecution brief.*

Although a brief may be compiled by an attorney for whom the PI is working, it may also be the private investigator who is asked to prepare the document. In either case, it is important for a PI to understand what a prosecution
brief is, and how it is prepared, especially if the PI is using intelligence methods as part of his or her investigation. This knowledge will help improve his
or her investigation, and as a consequence, provide better service to the client.
So, our examination of prosecution briefs will canvas the following:

1. A general definition of what is meant by a brief of evidence;
2. A discussion of what a private investigator needs to do to compile such
   a brief; and
3. A look at a template of a brief with some general explanatory guidelines for compiling it.

Nevertheless, this examination is in the context of an academic discussion, so
it should not be taken as legal advice.

159

BACKGROUND

Definitions

To the lay person, *prosecution* might be interpreted as the pursuit of justice in a court of law, or before a tribunal, or other judicial hearing. *Black's Law Dictionary* defines it more precisely as "a proceeding instituted and carried on by due course of law, before a competent tribunal, for the purpose of determining the guilt or innocence of a person charged with a crime."[253] Black also said that the term is also ". . . used respecting civil ligation."[254]

The term *brief* is just that – a written summary or an abbreviated account of a larger matter under consideration. It has been defined by Black as "A condensed statement or epitome of some larger document, or a series of papers, facts and circumstance, or propositions."[255]

So, a *prosecution brief* is a document that legal counsel uses as the basis to bring a matter before the courts for adjudication. But having said that, there may be many regional variations of the terms – such as, in some legal schools the term is used in conjunction with a Case brief. Here the term is used where a student provides a summary that attempts to analyze a court case so that it can be discussed in the classroom. This type of brief is not what we will be discussing – we are concerned with a summary of the investigation into the allegations – whether they are civil or criminal. This type of brief is sometimes synonymously termed a *brief of evidence*.

Purpose of Prosecution

In criminal matters, prosecution is brought about by a government authority because a person is accused of the commission of a prescribed act, or the omission of being required to do something that is defined in legislation. This actions result in either a fine being imposed or a term of incarceration, or sometimes a combination of both.

Criminal matters are prosecuted before a court by an attorney acting on behalf of the government (e.g., District Attorney, Public Prosecutor, or other titles). The accused is defended by an attorney (i.e., defense counsel).

In a civil matter, legal counsel is hired by each party to the dispute – the "prosecution is known as the *plaintiff, petitioner,* or *complainant* and the defense is known as the *defendant* or *respondent.*

Although the two types of actions might appear on the surface separate and unrelated, a civil action can be brought against a person as well as a criminal proceeding. Take, for example, the case of O.J. Simpson, where in 1995, Simpson was acquitted in a criminal trial for the alleged murders of his wife,

Nicole Brown Simpson, and friend, Ronald Goldman; but in 1997, a civil court awarded judgment against him for wrongful deaths.[256]

Brief of Evidence

A private investigator will be required to report on the progress of his or her investigation throughout the course of the inquiries. At the conclusion, some form of summary is likely to be required also.

These reports may be either formal or informal, or written or oral. But where a PI is preparing a report that might lead to prosecution (also termed *litigation* in the civil context), it will take the form of a *brief of evidence*. A brief is analogous in structure to a formal report. In other words, it is:

> . . . a structured written document in which a specific issue is examines for the purpose of conveying information, in order to report findings, to answer a request, to put forward ideas and make recommendations or offer solutions.[257]

But like most formal reports, there is a preferred style and layout for the brief to take as well as the requirements for what is contained within. At its most generic form, a brief of evidence will contain:

1. The allegation (criminal), or the claim (civil wrong), and reference to the relevant law;
2. A narrative of the facts of the case; and
3. The evidence obtained that supports the elements of the *alleged offense* or the *particulars of claim* (civil).[258]

COMPILING A BRIEF

What Is Required?

It is not possible to cover all the various forms a prosecution brief may take as these will vary from jurisdiction to jurisdiction, and will vary for bailiwicks that might entail a state/province or federal/commonwealth precinct. So, the exact form of a brief of evidence will differ. It will also differ according to whether it is addressing a criminal or civil matter. Indeed, there will usually be comprehensive court rules that specify practices and procedures that will affect the way that a private investigator goes about compiling a brief. In this regard, a PI will need to make his or her own inquiries as to the specific form. Nevertheless, in order to understand what should contribute to a prosecution brief can be discussed in generic terms.

What Is Important to Include

The form and substance of a brief has its genesis in the distinct role played by a private investigator and the lawyer managing the case. Although private investigators and lawyers have equally important roles in helping resolve a matter, the two roles are discrete.

Just as lawyers should not purport to be expert in investigative methodologies, PIs should restrain from trying to be lawyers. This is because it is the lawyer who will carry the responsibility to decide whether legal proceedings should commence. As such, it is important to include in a brief of evidence particular pieces of information that will permit the lawyer to:

- understand the allegation/claim being made;
- assesses the evidence against the allegation/claim;
- decide what charge (criminal) or relief (civil) is available against whom, and whether legal action is likely to succeed if undertaken;
- identify any additional evidence that the PI should obtain to help support legal action;
- provide appropriate disclosure/discovery in regards to the matter to the defendant's legal counsel; and
- conduct the trial in a court of law.[259]

What Should Not Be Included

Casting an eye over the six criteria for what should be included in a prosecution brief, it becomes evident that all of the information is factual-based. There is no room to include information that is not related to the case, nor is there room to include information that could be considered opinion, commentary, speculation, rumor, or gossip.

Having said that, it must be pointed out that the sources of information just discussed for exclusion, should *not* be overlooked for *intelligence purposes*. This is because these types of information generate leads, or point to areas that could be targeted for additional information collection. But, in an evidentiary-based judicial process, they are not acceptable. So, if a private investigator has used any intelligence-based approached inquiry, these aspects should remain in the PI's file; not in the lawyer's prosecution brief.

FORM OF A PROSECUTION BRIEF

Criminal Brief

A prosecution brief can be a short, simple document or it can be a voluminous set of documents depending on the matter under consideration. Take, for instance, a simple parking offense where overstaying at a curb-side park can result in a fine. At its simplest, if a parking inspector notes that a car has exceeded the specified time permitted, he or she could take a photograph of the offending vehicle. The photograph would normally include a depiction of the vehicle's physical characteristics along with its registration number, and date and time. If the parking sign was also included in the photo showing that stays in excess of, say, one hour are not permitted, then that could be the only document that might be needed to brief the prosecuting attorney. All that would be needed is for the parking inspector to sign the photographs and list his or her contact details for the court appearance. Of course, this is a somewhat simplified portrayal of a brief, but nevertheless, it could be all that is needed.

In actuality, the prosecuting agency may have a number of forms that are required to standardize all briefs of evidence that enter its offices as a means of quality control. This might include cover sheets to ensure all the investigator's details are there (yes, even parking inspectors are a class of investigators). It might include prompts to outline the relevant legislation, the alleged offender, and so on. These types of briefs may be referred to as *short form briefs* or titles depending on the jurisdiction.

Not all offenses are as simple as this example involving strict liability. Usually, they are more complicated as they require intent to be formed. These matters will require the brief to take on a larger form. These larger briefs may be referred to as *standard briefs*. But, the thrust of the document remains the same – the information that will allow a lawyer to understand and carry out the tasks outlined in the six points listed in the section on what is important to include in a brief, above.

Civil Brief

Civil briefs form the same intent as criminal briefs but rather than allegations of criminal wrong doing, they are statements of claim that outline civil wrongs. They can be simple matters and allow for a short form brief or more complicated matters that require a standard brief.

In the case of a government agency that prosecutes criminal matters, that agency will specify the form of the brief of evidence. In a civil matter, it is likely to be the attorney representing the plaintiff who will do this. He or she will be guided by the Rules of Court as these Rules will dictate what information needs to be filed in the court's registry by the attorney, as well as the specific arrangement of those filings.

Exemplar Format

Briefs can take the form of paper-based or electronic. So, the standards outlined here can be used in either way depending on the attorney's preference or the court's requirements.

- Cover sheet;
- The allegation(s) being made, or the charge(s) that are recommended to be laid in criminal matters, or the statement of claim in a civil matter;
- The PI's statement of the facts;
- The record of interview with the accused (criminal);
- A list of witnesses;
- A list of statements taken; and
- A list of exhibits.

The cover sheet contains the essential details of the case so that anyone viewing the document (which could range from a few sheets of paper held together with a staple, to a bound folder, or a set of bound folders). It facilities a quick and easy way to understand what is contained within.

The allegation, or statement of claim, may appear on a separate page for clarity with an extract of the section of the legislation to which it refers.

The various lists are just what they purport – alphabetical or chronological lists of people who can attend court and give an account of their observations regarding some aspect of the matter subject to the legal proceeding; or pieces of evidence collected that demonstrate aspects of the case being asserted.

The record of interview is a typed version of what was said between the investigator and the accused person in a criminal matter. It is usually in "I said," "he said" format, verbatim.

These elements of a brief should be self-evident. However, the statement of facts needs some clarification. The statement of facts is a document that sets out "the story" in a chronology way. It describes facts of the alleged offense, but in doing so, this chronology needs to set out the facts that comprise the elements of the offense, not of the investigation. This chronology therefore needs to be based in fact, and should be written in an objective way that avoids emotional or journalistic language. Where there are witness statements or exhibits that offer corroboration, these should be cross-referenced appropriately within the document.

Is some jurisdictions, there is a requirement to produce a *certificate of disclosure* to the defendant's attorney. This outlines what evidence the prosecution has, what will alleged in court, and what the prosecution will not call on as evidence. In civil cases, *discovery* is applied for through the court process but serves the same purpose. If this applies in your jurisdiction, then an added element to the prosecution brief will be *disclosure*.

KEY WORDS AND PHRASES

The key words and phrases associated with this chapter are listed below. In one or two sentences, demonstrate your understanding of each by writing a short definition or explanation.

- Brief of evidence;
- Complainant;
- Cover sheet;
- Defendant;
- Disclosure;
- Petitioner;
- Plaintiff;
- Prosecution;
- Record of interview;
- Respondent;
- Short form briefs;
- Standard briefs; and
- Statement of facts.

STUDY QUESTIONS

1. List the components that are typical of a brief of evidence.
2. Explain why the form a prosecution brief may take differs from jurisdiction to jurisdiction.
3. Discuss the pieces of information that are important to include in a brief.

LEARNING ACTIVITY

Based on what you understand about intelligence work, explain why it is important not to include intelligence information, intelligence methods, or investigative methods in a prosecution brief. Would your explanation apply to both criminal briefs and civil briefs? Why?

Chapter 13

LEGAL ISSUES FOR INTELLIGENCE-LED PRIVATE INVESTIGATORS

RICK SARRE

INTRODUCTION

Each day in the countries of the Five-Eyes Intelligence Alliance – Australia, Britain, Canada, New Zealand, and the United States – there are investigations being undertaken across a wide spectrum of commercial and other activities. A number of legal questions arise out of their practices. What laws apply to empower private investigators? What laws are in place to limit the authority of these personnel, and more specifically, what legal authorities are in place that might impact on the use of intelligence by private operatives? These investigations may occur on both private property and in public areas. Does that make a difference? Very little has been published to address these questions directly. This chapter goes some distance in filling that legal void.

LAWS THAT EMPOWER PRIVATE INVESTIGATORS

Background

Given the rapid expansion of the private security commercial sector, one might assume that careful attention would have been paid to the legal framework within which the activities of security personnel take place. Unfortunately, this has not been the case. The legal rights and powers of private security providers are determined by little more than a piecemeal array of common law principles, practical assumptions, and *ad hoc* legislation that was designed principally for private citizens and especially those who own property.

The powers and immunities of private investigators are thus unclear, inconsistent, change from jurisdiction to jurisdiction, and differ markedly from those of the public police even though they may be carrying out many of the same investigation tasks as police, and in the same locales.[260]

Given the rapid expansion of the presence of private investigators in security activities, it is surprising that so little attention has been paid to the legal framework under which they work. One of key reasons is the vast array of settings in which security personnel operate. The sheer panoply of options related to private security work (guards, CCTV monitors, transit police, cash-in-transit personnel) militates against any attempt to regulate security personnel other than on an *ad hoc* basis.[261]

True, there has been legislation passed in all Five-Eyes jurisdictions that deal with the registration, licensing, identification, and training of investigation agents. However, the main aim of this legislation is to require licences for these personnel, and to check those who wish to enter their industry against certain criteria and training standards. It typically does not deal with powers *per se* at all.

The paucity of law guiding this field of endeavour is confusing for private security personnel and the public alike. There are few legal decisions and precedents emerging from the courts. Hence, it is difficult to find, let alone describe, a satisfactory body of law on the subject.

In contrast, public police have coercive and intrusive powers. There are thus distinct differences between the powers of public police and private agents. For example, public police are given statutory immunity from civil suit in circumstances where their beliefs and acts are "reasonable." Private investigators are afforded no such luxury. Indeed, private operatives remain vulnerable to, and constantly run the risk of, being sued in the torts of assault, false imprisonment, intentional infliction of mental distress, defamation, nuisance, and trespass to land and to the person. This is not to say that police do not run these risks, but because they have legal immunities at their disposal by virtue of their empowerment legislation, they are far less likely to find themselves on the losing end of a civil suit brought by an aggrieved person who feels that his or her rights have been violated.

Moreover, public police may act to prevent the commission of an offense before it actually happens (acting upon a suspicion). This concession is not granted to private investigators (or anyone else for that matter). Public police powers, duties, rights, responsibilities and immunities have been so often debated in the courts that there is now a large and continually expanding body of law on these issues. The same cannot be said for private security law.

In short, the public police have considerable powers to arrest, search, and interrogate. By contrast, the law relating to the activities of private investigators, who may engage in many of the same tasks, remains largely untested. Few matters come before the courts for judgment because they are most likely settled out of court to keep publicity and costs to a minimum.

For the purposes of this chapter, two potential areas of legal interest for private investigators have been chosen. The first is the use of surveillance technology, and the second is the process of inquiry. These issues have been chosen because they are activities in which both public police and private investigators are regularly called upon to act. In both of these examples, the law applicable to police is reasonably clear; the rules relating to private investigators, in contrast, are a hotchpotch.

LAWS THAT LIMIT THE PRIVATE INVESTIGATOR'S AUTHORITY

Covert Surveillance

Covert surveillance has become commonplace around the world. According to corporate surveys in Australia, for example, more than half of Australia's largest companies undertake video surveillance of employees and of visitors to their premises.[262]

In all modern democracies, insurance firms, and their contracted investigators, regularly covertly film and photograph suspected perpetrators of insurance fraud. During passive surveillance of personal injury claimants, it is not unknown for investigators to place heavy items near a person's house, and wait with a video camera to film the person as he or she attempts to move them.[263] The common law does not prohibit such filming, but the tapes may not be admissible as legal evidence if the person under surveillance can prove to a court that there are public policy reasons for not allowing filming of this type. There may also be difficulties, certainly ethically if not legally, if the placing of the object aggravates the injury.

An argument could be made that a store's changing and fitting rooms should be under camera surveillance for a legitimate commercial interest, that is, as a deterrent to theft. But since the potential for innocent persons to be embarrassed is great, as is the potential for inappropriate conduct by security employees, cameras in these locations are unlikely to be treated favorably by the courts. Arguably, filming which intrudes upon intimate or private space (such as toilets, showers, or change rooms) will most likely be deemed unconscionable conduct in the absence of specific and informed permission. In that event, there may be a remedy (in the torts of trespass to person, trespass to land, nuisance, or defamation) available to any person adversely affected by such conduct in circumstances where the elements of the particular tort have been established. Conversely, where there may have been an affront to dignity that was merely consequential upon a legitimate and legislatively protected interest (for example, the right to have theft or cheating exposed under a clearly authorized policy of police "integrity testing"), there is, arguably, little or no likelihood of a legal remedy for an aggrieved person who may have been caught out.

The criminal law, too, may provide some assistance to those confronted by covert monitoring, but only in circumstances where other offenses (such as stalking or criminal trespass) have been committed. There may even be charges arising from the general purpose of the activity, for example, if there was an element of indecency about the intent of the person installing the camera, as illustrated in *Carger v The Police*.[264] In this case, Mr. Carger was convicted of being on premises for an illegal purpose (to place a spy camera in his housemates' bathroom) and of behaving in an indecent manner, contrary to section 23 of the *Summary Offences Act 1953* (South Australia). He was fined A$250 and required to carry out 40 hours of community service.

Listening Devices

All Five-Eyes jurisdictions have rules regulating the use of listening devices. These statutes typically make it an offense to listen to or record a private conversation using a listening device.[265] Broadly speaking, it is illegal to install a listening device without an appropriate law enforcement warrant, which can only be obtained from a court in special circumstances. Without the appropriate warrant, the court may exclude any evidence recorded, on the basis that it was illegally obtained, so its collection may have been in vain.

By way of example, in South Australia, it is an offense under the *Listening and Surveillance Devices Act 1972* to listen to or record a conversation via a listening device without prior consent, even if the person using the device is a party to the conversation. Indeed, it is an offense to publish what was said or even a summary of the substance of the recording. An exception is where the listening device is used in the "public interest" or for the protection of the "lawful interests" of a party to the conversation. There is also a defense in section 7(1) of the Act for recording a conversation to which a person is not a party if it is reasonably necessary to do so; for example, where there is an imminent threat of violence.

Telephone Interceptions

Telephone interceptions happen on a daily basis in all Five-Eyes jurisdictions. In Australia, they are authorized under legislation where the relevant party seeks a warrant.[266] Today, the most common categories of offenses listed in warrants are drug-related (mainly trafficking), bribery, corruption, and murder.

Telephonic eavesdropping is regulated by the Australian *Telecommunications (Interception and Access) Act 1979.* The Act (section 6) defines "interception of a communication passing over a telecommunications system" as consisting of "listening to or recording, by any means, such a communication in its passage over that telecommunications system without the knowledge of the person making the communication." Section 7(2)(b) makes it illegal, except with a warrant, to intercept (including by scanner) a communication passing over a telecommunication system without the knowledge of the person making the call. A warrant can be obtained through a judge or a member of the Administrative Appeals Tribunal designated by the responsible Minister of the Crown. It is an offense to tape telephone conversations without a warrant unless both parties are aware of the recording and give permission. It is also illegal to use or possess equipment for the purpose of intercepting a telecommunication.

To what extent can private investigators engage in these types of interceptions? There is some scope for private investigators to use listening devices where they are acting to support police or a recognized crime fighting authority, such as the Australian Crime Commission. Generally speaking, an applicant for such authority must be able to show reasonable grounds to support the need for the listening device (such as the belief that a serious offense has been or is likely to be committed). If the warrant is granted, there will be conditions attached in relation to the placement, timing, and retrieval of the listening device.

It is an offense to deal with (use or copy) information that has been obtained by an unlawful interception or a suspected unlawful interception.[267] The criminal penalty for interception or dealing with information is imprisonment for up to two years. There is provision in the Act for an aggrieved person to claim damages in a civil court, including punitive damages, against any person who has breached the Act. In *R v Smith,*[268] a private investigator installed an illegal interception device on the telephone service of one of his client's former employees. The client and the investigator were found to have conspired to intercept a telecommunication contrary to the *Crimes Act 1914* (Commonwealth) and were each sentenced to two years imprisonment.

It is a moot point whether holding up a tape recorder to a telephone is an "interception" for the purposes of the Act. In *The Queen v Giacco,*[269] the South Australian Supreme Court held that such an act did not constitute "passing over a telecommunications system" required by section 7(1). That did not mean, however, that the act of recording by a handheld tape recorder is legal.

While the use of a tape recorder may escape the specific prohibition of the Act, it may nevertheless be caught by the listening devices and surveillance legislation of the states and territories. As it happened, the court found that, on the facts in *Giacco,* there was no breach of the *Listening Devices Act 1972* (South Australia) (as it then was) and therefore the anomaly was not addressed formally by the Supreme Court. However, legal commentator Sally Walker[270] cites the judgment in *AIFME '97 Pty Ltd v Norley Pty Ltd*[271] as authority for the proposition that state and territory listening devices legislation *can* apply to fill the gap in the national legislation if the recording of the telephone conversation is by the use of a recorder not attached to the telephone itself.

Internet Surveillance

Is the *Telecommunications (Interception and Access) Act 1979* (Commonwealth) capable of applying to the inappropriate interception of material communicated via the internet?[272] That question is partially addressed in the *Telecommunications (Interception and Access) Amendment Act 2006* (Commonwealth),[273] which allows the Australian Security Intelligence Organisation (ASIO), if there is a threat of terrorism, to intercept email, SMS text messages and voicemails between individuals.[274] Significantly, the Act gives ASIO access to information collected by other law enforcement agencies, too.[275] This is in accordance with a general initiative arising out of a meeting of the Standing Committee of Attorneys-General in 2002, to foster a national set of mutually recognized powers including, amongst other things, electronic surveillance.[276]

LEGAL ISSUES REGARDING INTELLIGENCE
BY PRIVATE OPERATIVES

Access to Private Information

For the purposes of assessing the capacity of governments to protect an individual's privacy, it is important to examine the issue of access to information databases. Government agencies regularly access public and private datasets containing information on citizens. Few would doubt that this is appropriate in defense of a nation or in the fight against fraud. The law is crafted to ensure that the activities carried out do not unnecessarily invade individual privacy.

Laws passed by governments have enabled some restrictions to be placed upon the collection, retrieval, and cross-matching of data. The following discussion highlights the rules, and reveals some loopholes in those laws.

Access to Government-Held Information by the Private Sector

Some scholars have been pointing out for over a decade that private investigators are virtually united in the view that they should be allowed greater, albeit controlled, access to government-held information.[277] Governments do not agree, probably because of the abundance of past evidence that inquiry agents (and those who instruct them) are prone to break the rules and make unauthorized enquiries of government database operators.[278] For example, in 1992, the Independent Commission Against Corruption found evidence of widespread fraud in relation to the sale of government-held data and information, which led to police officers involved in this scam being prosecuted.[279]

Severe penalties generally apply for those illegally seeking access to data and engaging in data sharing. The offenses include (in the Australian context, for example) seeking inappropriate access to computer data,[280] corrupting or bribing an official to provide data,[281] and obtaining information by false pretenses.[282] Clients of private investigators who request them to access data in breach of the *Crimes Act 1914* (Commonwealth) are liable to suffer the same penalties as the investigator.

In Australia, an inquiry agent who receives information from an agency in breach of the legislation may be directed by the Commissioner to destroy or hand over the information, or to pay compensation or costs.[283] However, a determination by the Commissioner is not binding unless legal action is taken in the Federal Court to enforce it. Determinations may also be subject to review by the Administrative Appeals Tribunal.

One final piece of legislation that regulates the public's access to government-held information is found in the *Telecommunications Act 1997* (Commonwealth) Part 13, which, on the one hand, prohibits disclosures of information by carriers and carriage server providers (amongst others) acquired by virtue of their business. However, on the other hand, all states and territories have freedom of information legislation that allows, under some circumstances, private access to government-held files.[284] For the most part, however, the legislation is highly restrictive and personal data is usually exempted from the list of accessible information.

Access to Non-Government Information by the Private Sector

The invasion of the territory of individual privacy in the twenty-first century is more likely to result from the technology possessed by private entities who exchange information between themselves than by governments. For decades, companies have been collecting detailed information about consumers, to allow them to track and interact with customers, suppliers, and markets. The management of that data was often haphazard, and selling of information was rife.

The activities of collection, stockpiling, and sales of information were all largely unregulated, unless it involved credit references, which attracted some legislative attention in the 1970s. Yet a survey in 1997 indicated that 70 percent of companies in Australia supported the introduction of privacy legislation that would cover the corporate sector. [285] The national government finally acted. Four years in the making, [286] the *Privacy Amendment (Private Sector) Act 2000* (Commonwealth) was passed by the Australian parliament on December 6, 2000. [287] Interestingly, the legislation had been introduced into parliament in December 1999, just two weeks after the media giant Publishing and Broadcasting Limited announced that it was joining with the U.S. company Acxiom to create a warehouse of information on up to 15 million Australians.[288] The effect of this Act is to apply the provisions of the 1988 privacy legislation to the private sector. The Act came into effect on December 21, 2001.

It is now illegal for companies (including investigative agencies to whom the legislation applies) [289] to collect or transfer sensitive personal information without an individual's permission. [290] Companies to which the legislation applies now need to be careful to ask clients only the basic information they need to carry on business, and they must tell customers how any information will be used, and to whom it will be disclosed. People must be given the choice to opt out of mailing lists when they provide personal data for business transactions. And the sale or disclosure of personal information collected by, or for, political parties is banned.

The legislation gives the Federal Privacy Commissioner the power to investigate privacy breaches by private sector bodies, order compensation to aggrieved persons, and seek injunctions through the Federal Court. The Act sets out detailed guidelines in relation to the manner of collection, storage, and use of personal information by private companies and organizations. The Act incorporates the National Principles for the Fair Handling of Personal Information, developed by the Privacy Commissioner after consulting with business and consumer groups. They are similar to the Information Privacy Principles but have been tailored towards the activities of private businesses and individuals, as opposed to governments. The *Privacy Amendment (Private Sector) Act 2000* (Commonwealth) allows, however, information to be shared with agencies involved in law enforcement and crime prevention. [291]

Computer Hacking

"Hacking" into computer systems (where interceptions are premeditated and designed to be fraudulent) is a criminal offense under the *Criminal Code Act 1995* (Commonwealth), which outlaws unauthorized access to computer systems using the telecommunications network.[292] A conviction attracts significant criminal penalties.[293] Security issues arising out of cyber-aggression have also been discussed academically.[294]

Australian Security Intelligence Organisation operatives are given specific immunity under the *Australian Security Intelligence Organisation Amendment Act 1999* (Commonwealth) from any laws that outlaw hacking into personal computers. Private investigators are afforded no such luxury.

DISCUSSION

State and federal parliaments have filled the gaps with a raft of legislation designed to dampen the enthusiasm of sleuths and would-be sleuths. Until recently, optical surveillance devices were not included in listening devices legislation, but five state and territory jurisdictions, along with the national parliament, have now included surveillance (and tracking) devices in their legislation. There is, nonetheless, a woeful and confusing lack of uniformity in the law. New South Wales is the only jurisdiction to have targeted workplace surveillance specifically, but other jurisdictions seem set to follow.

The national prohibition on telephonic eavesdropping is less convoluted, although the lack of clear direction regarding email interception and authorized access into information systems does need federal legislative attention. Evidence gathered in contravention of the law (or gathered in grossly unfair circumstances) may not be admitted as evidence in later civil or criminal proceedings. The rules of evidence that allow a judge to rule certain matters inadmissible provide something of a disincentive for overzealous security personnel.

Surveillance by access to private information is also subject to regulation at the federal level. The legislative rules that have applied since 1988 to the government sector have now been extended to the private sector, although the new regime is replete with exemptions and does not apply to a significant proportion of Australian businesses. Nor does it apply to information collected prior to the commencement of the Act.

The Information Privacy Principles are a new addition to the privacy framework in Australia. They apply to limit the amount of electronic scrutiny and data storage that security personnel can engage in. But there are still some concerns, especially around credit referencing.

The rules regulating electronic surveillance, therefore, are many and varied. They operate at state and federal level. They are a mixture of legislation and common law. Many differ from state to state. They often have not addressed or even contemplated new technologies. A nationally operating private security firm will need to be vigilant in order to be sure that its surveillance and data-gathering practices are not falling foul of the law in any jurisdiction in which it operates.

When exceptional authority is bestowed upon those who administer and enforce the law, it requires legislative action through parliamentary debate. For that reason, the rules regulating public policing are set out prospectively to authorize the taking of particular action, and also retrospectively to show interested forums, such as the courts and parliaments, that the action was justified in the circumstances.[295]

Private investigators and all other private security operatives are now undertaking many of the same policing roles as police officers, but the laws that apply to empower and restrict them are not in the same league, and there is an argument that they should be better articulated by parliaments. Broadly-based legislation giving specific powers to all government licensed agents, however, does not exist in Australia. Australian parliaments have, for the most part, simply set up government licensing regimes. They have not specifically set out powers and immunities.

True, there is *ad hoc* legislation that applies to some situations. But this legislation applies to all people including security personnel and is thus not specific to them. In other words, parliaments have avoided broadly-based legislation that covers the powers and immunities of private security officers more generally. One can sympathize – it is a difficult task to specify private police powers across the board, given the many forms and varieties of private operatives that exist and the multitude of activities in which they may be engaged.[296] In addition, many private security firms are, or are becoming, national and transnational corporations, and thus any general attempt to set legislated rules which transcend national and international boundaries would be difficult to do, let alone to implement and enforce.

CONCLUSION

As law enforcement moves more and more into private hands, the traditional legal powers that apply to inquiry agents are becoming out-dated. The powers and immunities of private investigators are often unclear and inconsistent, dependent upon fine distinctions, and differ from jurisdiction-to-jurisdiction. One would be forgiven for expressing some despair. It could be argued that it is imperative that the legislatures of countries with advanced economies act to provide some greater certainty regarding these matters as a matter of priority.

Table 13.1. The Private Investigator's Checklist of Legal Issues

Legal Issues Check List		
Issue	*Impact*	*Mitigation Strategy*
Legal authority to conduct investigations	Inappropriate actions that may lead to legal action	Improved training
Privacy concerns	Potential legal suits	Greater recognition of privacy rights
Civil liberties infringements	Defiance of rights if not done properly	Education
Specific statutory constraints	Investigators are required to keep within legal boundaries	Legal advice that informs codes of conduct

KEY WORDS AND PHRASES

The key words and phrases associated with this chapter are listed below. In one or two sentences, demonstrate your understanding of each by writing a short definition or explanation.

- Computer hacking;
- Covert surveillance;
- Cybercrime;
- Freedom of information;
- Immunity from prosecution;
- Information privacy principles
- Jurisdictional limits;
- Privacy rights;
- Trespass to person; and
- Warrants.

STUDY QUESTIONS

1. Research the laws that govern private investigations in your jurisdiction and describe the aspects of these laws (statutes and common law) as they relate to empowering private operatives. In your view, are they adequate?
2. Describe the laws in your jurisdiction that limit the authority of private investigators (if any). Do you think there should there be more limitations?

3. Describe the legal authorities that exist in your jurisdiction that might impact on the way private investigators use intelligence, e.g., privacy, civil liberties, and statutory constraints. Discuss whether you think these are clear enough, easily accessible, and understood?

LEARNING ACTIVITY

Private investigators, even those who use intelligence to lead their investigations, have no special powers of inquiry. There have been moves by some associations that represent these operatives to be granted government legislated powers to be able to gain access to information resources that are not currently available.[297] Given this situation, outline what training investigators should undergo in order to justify the exercise of greater powers. In an idea world, what safeguards (e.g., audit and oversight) arrangements might a government require to ensure PIs would comply with such expanded powers?

Chapter 14

ETHICAL ISSUES FOR INTELLIGENCE-LED PRIVATE INVESTIGATORS

Mark S. Bradley

INTRODUCTION

The role of the private investigator and the methods they use have long received considerable public attention, scrutiny, and criticism.[298] Arguably, one of the most prevailing perceptions is that private investigation is a "black art" that more often than not, transgresses established laws and regulations, and invariably disregards ethical considerations as well as self-regulating codes of conduct in order to get a result.[299] This view is so pervasive that in PI fiction novels that there is a genre known as "hardboiled" where private investigators have, through their experiences, become hard and callous.[300]

> "Dashiell Hammett's Centennial Op cleans up Personville in *Red Harvest,* a microcosm of a failed city, and ironically has to escape before he becomes any more like the killers whom he has set in motion."[301]

Perhaps to some extent this perception is fuelled by the proliferation of films, television shows, and books which often showcase the less than ethical things the private investigator may do when investigating a case. Unfortunately, a number of recent high-profile scandals, including the Hewlett-

179

Packard "pretexting" case[302] where it was alleged that private investigators for Hewlett-Packard surreptitiously obtained private telephone records of journalists, and more recently, the News International telephone "hacking" scandal,[303] have done nothing to disprove these perceptions.

BACKGROUND

In the United Kingdom, the Leveson Inquiry in the culture, practice, and ethics of the press was established by the U.K. Government in 2011 to investigate the relationships between the media and private investigators and the alleged tactics they employed to hack the mobile telephones of celebrities and victims of crime.[304] The inquiry lead to the collapse of a national newspaper owned by News International, the launch of several police investigations and the arrests of private investigators, police officers, and several journalists – including the newspaper's editor.[305]

In some states/provinces of countries, the private investigation industry remains unregulated (or lightly regulated), relying only on the voluntary codes of ethical conduct to guide investigation standards. There are, however, many established laws in place which clearly define the boundaries within which the private investigator is able to lawfully operate, such as the United Kingdom's *Regulation of Investigatory Powers Act 2000*. This statute regulates the powers of public bodies to carry out surveillance and investigation and also covers the interception of communications.

There is a growing need for the private investigation industry to act responsibly when undertaking assignments for clients. While understandably clients expect results, and will not always give consideration or care as to how the supporting evidence is obtained, it is essential that private investigators undertake their responsibilities within responsible, practical, and ethical limits; else they run the risk of not only dulling they reputations, they chance going to jail.

While it can be accepted that there have been great strides in ensuring that proper accountability mechanisms have been put in place for police, within the private sector, private investigators have far less direct control over their activities and as a consequence they are less accountable to the public at large. This lack of accountability leaves the door open to allegations of abuse of positions and a strengthening debate for greater regulation of the industry.

There are a range of reasons why it is essential that investigations are conducted professionally and in accordance with recognized laws, norms, and principles, whether they are complex cases, or just routine inquiries. At the heart of these reasons is honesty, trust, and integrity – all of which the civil and criminal systems of justice are founded.

> "The only thing necessary for the triumph of evil is for good men to do nothing."
> Sir Edmond Burke, eighteenth-century English statesman

In order to remain within the law and abide by recognized ethical standards, it requires private investigators to work differently in order to obtain the intelligence or evidence ethically. In this chapter, we will explore the ethical issues that all private investigators need to be aware of, and also to adhere to if they are to demonstrate integrity when dealing with clients. In doing so, we will discuss the need for transparency, accountability, confidentiality, objectivity, respect, and the importance of operating within the law. But first, there is a need to understand the reasons why these issues are important.

RATIONALE

The private investigator must never lose sight of the fact that at some future date, an investigation he or she conducted may come under intense scrutiny by external parties. These inquiries may demand that all documentation held by him or her to be handed over to a court or tribunal.

It is therefore essential that from the outset of any investigation, every effort should be made for it to be conducted ethically. Moreover, every decision and action needs to be duly considered, justified, and recorded. It is important to remember that while conducting an investigation, what may seem like an inconsequential action or decision at the time could have important consequences at some later stage.

It is now common place for private investigators to be required to justify in courts, tribunals, and government inquiries the details of every aspect of their work from the start to its conclusion – just as their law enforcement counterparts have to do. To this end, it is suggested that *policy files* should be maintained by the private investigator.

A policy file is a record of all the important decisions he or she has made. The policy file contains the important issues decided on during an inquiry. The policy file therefore allows the private investigator to record the reasons why he or she has decided to do certain things, or not do certain things. This often serves to protect the private investigator from subsequent criticism at court or public inquiries.

Probably the most important aspect of the management of any investigation is the systematic recording of the private investigator's decisions. The recording of why various lines of inquiry were pursued or why they were not pursued is important, and the detailed recording of decisions and the reasons for making each decision is encouraged.

The best way to facilitate this is to use the policy file to record key decisions. However, the private investigator needs to be mindful that it is the definitive record upon which he or she will rely. So, this means thinking ahead to a point if they are subsequently asked to account for their integrity and their decisions at some future date.

So, from the start of the assignment it is important for the investigator to have been well briefed by the client. Clear and unambiguous terms of reference should be agreed to and countersigned by the client and the private investigator with an explicit understanding by all concerned of the boundaries and the limitations of the investigation, including the ethical standards that will be followed.

ETHICAL STANDARDS

Transparency

In order to set the issue of ethics in context, we need to understand a few concepts that govern the private investigator's attitude and behavior, stating with the concept of transparency. The term *transparency* refers to holding both the investigator and his or her sources accountable for their actions. By making the PI personally accountable, there is less opportunity for there to be any abuses of processes and contraventions of the law. A failure to be transparent in conducting an investigation can, and often does, lead to a propensity to act corruptly or illegally. Transparency is vitally important in the context of private investigation work as it generally allows for free an unfettered access by courts and regulators to source information and product material obtained and held by private investigators.

Accountability

Accountability refers to being held to account, and answerable for the actions undertaken by both private investigators and those acting on their instructions during the course of an inquiry. There is the assumption that private investigators should always remain accountable for the decisions and actions they make, and for the integrity of all material they obtain during the course of their investigations.

Confidentiality

In both status law and common law, members of the public have varying rights to privacy. These laws also include provisions about the information obtained about them and how it must not be improperly used or divulged. Generally speaking, whatever information the private investigator sees, hears, or learns about their target that is confidential in nature, must be kept within the terms of the investigation unless legal oversight requires otherwise (e.g., a court order, subpoena, etc.). It is important that private investigators ensure that they have systems in place to ensure the integrity and confidentiality of the information they obtain. Furthermore, there should be strong ethical consideration given by the private investigator regarding the circumstances by which unauthorized, sensitive, and confidential material comes into their possession.

Objectivity

It is important that any investigation undertaken by the private investigator is conducted in an objective, independent, and third-party manner. The private investigator should ensure that his or her investigation is balanced and fair, and all relevant and available facts are investigated. It is essential that the PI remembers that his or her primary objective is to uncover the truth and not to try and build a case against a particular person or organization. Objectivity is often regarded as the principle or standard that puts aside emotions, preconceived ideas, and prejudices as the operative pieces together all of the evidence.[306]

Respect

It is important that the private investigator respects the human rights and fundamental freedoms of all individuals during the course of his or her investigations. Similarly, the PI should respect the rule of law and ensure that he or she is, at all times, responsible for his or her own acts and omissions.

Operating within the Law

The private investigator does not have police powers, nor is he or she exempted from legal constraints relating to investigations or investigative techniques. Invariably the PI has the same powers as those afforded to civilians. As such, the private investigator needs to be conscious of operating within the law. This is particularly relevant when engaging in covert investigations requiring technical surveillance measures, or when handing sensitive material "leaked" by third parties. News reports document many high-profile cases that have highlighted the vulnerabilities of private investigators, and the consequences of their actions, when not conforming with the rule of law.

Reporting a Crime

This is an issue that can create an ethical and moral dilemma for the private investigator. There is no consistency internationally regarding the legal obligations to report a crime; for example, while in some states of the United States, there is the offense of "misprision" for failing to report a felony, others states do not have this offense. There are requirements in the United Kingdom to report matters linked to terrorism and money laundering, but generally there is no requirement to invoke some form of civil duty and report a crime.

As a consequence, and in the absence of any form of client confidentiality laws, the issue of reporting a criminal offense uncovered by the private investigator may come down to his or her own personal moral standards. In failing to report a crime, the private investigator must be confident that he or she is not in any way aiding or abetting the commission, or continued commission, of an offense. Moreover, the private investigator must ensure that by being involved in a case on behalf of a client he or she has not somehow been inadvertently drawn into an offense already under commission.

Dashiell Hammett's code of professional conduct, which was derived from his mentor at the Pinkerton Detective Agency – Jimmy Wright of Baltimore – was: "Don't' cheat your client. Stay anonymous. Avoid undue physical risk. Be objective. Don't become emotionally involved with a client. And never violate your integrity."[307]

ETHICAL CASE PREPARATION

We can see from our previous discussion of the contextual issues of private intelligence and investigation that the ultimate goal should be to obtain the highest quality evidence for clients in order to establish the truth about the matter under investigation. In order to achieve this goal, it is important that investigators do not go beyond the exercising of recognized ethical norms and standards in order to achieve these outcomes.

When setting out on an investigation, it is reasonable for a PI to form a view in his or her mind as to what they are seeking to achieve, and in some instances, to actually hold some preconceived ideas of what the final submission of evidence may actually look like. But, the primary task of the private investigator should never be lost – to discover the truth and subsequently present the facts to the client or even before a court or inquiry.

It is worth underscoring that it is not the purpose to prosecute at all costs, but the discovery of what the truth is. If that means establishing a person's innocence, then that *must* be done. History has recorded numerous cases where evidence was either ignored, discarded, not collected, or otherwise used or interpreted inappropriately, and hence, failed to establish the truth of the mat-

Figure 14.1. Mrs. Lindy Chamberlain-Creighton (center, in front of the microphones) and Dr. Michael Chamberlain (directly behind her) with their son, Aiden Chamberlain (left of his father in an open-collar shirt), in Darwin, June 12, 2012. The group addressed the world's media after hearing the findings of the Northern Territory's Coroner, Elizabeth Bolton, whose findings finally cleared their names regarding the death of their daughter/sister, Azaria in 1980 (photograph courtesy of Hank Prunckun).

ter under investigation. Take for instance the wrongful conviction of Lindy and Michael Chamberlain in 1980 of the death of their infant daughter Azaria. It took more than thirty years and a series of the most sensational legal cases to finally clear the family's name (see Figure 14.1).[308]

So, as the investigation unfolds, the PI will gradually piece together evidence to support the allegation or hypothesis. The PI will build a case based upon facts which might consist of accounts by witnesses, surveillance material, and information from informants, or even evidence from forensic analysis of exhibits obtained during the course of the investigation. As the investigation develops, it is likely that the original perceptions formed about the case may alter several times. It is also likely that conflicting evidence may emerge which may contradict the perceived version of events.

It may be that as the investigation unfolds information may come to light that negates or disproves original hypotheses about issue under investigation. At this point, it may be convenient to disregard these pieces of conflicting evidence and rely only upon facts that tend to support the allegation of hypothesis. This might be because these conflicting pieces of evidence are considered not worth pursuing further as it does not fall within the known facts about the investigation. But for whatever the reason, it is unacceptable to conceal or fail to consider these conflicting issues further.

Nevertheless, when it comes to the preparation of a report for the client, it could well be the case that there are genuine reasons for not disclosing to the client, or indeed to the public, certain information. For example, it might be prudent not to disclose sources of information, or operational methods or techniques to protect individuals or commercial tradecraft. If this is the case, there must be transparent and accountable systems in place to ensure that this is done in compliance with the law, and in such a way that the integrity of the entire investigation will not be compromised at some later date.

An effective way of addressing this is for the private investigator to maintain a policy file. This folder records the PI's reasoning surrounding his or her actions and decisions with regard to all aspects of an investigation.[309] In this way, should the private investigator be challenged at some later date, say, in a court, he or she will have a contemporaneous record of their decision making process.

In the case of documentation prepared for court, the policy file is essential that the private investigator makes every effort to disclose all the material obtained, even if it contradicts what the investigator has been commissioned to investigate. Full and comprehensive records should be retained by the PI of all material obtained during the course of the investigation, and what was subsequently handed to the client at the conclusion of the case.

In the case where the evidence obtained for a client is to be heard in a court of law or before a tribunal, it is essential that the private investigator is open and transparent with the appointed prosecutor or the defense lawyer. Even when advice and guidance from a lawyer regarding investigation tactics are not readily available, the PI must always bear in mind that every decision he or she makes, and every tactic he or she employs to obtain evidence will undoubtedly be scrutinized, and perhaps challenged before a judge.

SOME GUIDING PRINCIPLES

Experience shows that there are a number of principles that if employed can guide an investigations along the ethical path. If these are principles are adhered to, they help ensure a trouble-free investigation.

Principle One – Sticking to the Facts

The first principle is not jumping to conclusions. Foremost is the doctrine of remaining open-minded about the case and to avoid focusing upon preconceived ideas. Under no circumstances should the private investigator make assumptions about what the outcome as this tends to lead the PI to undertake the task by only seeking evidence that tends to support that theory. This can be quite difficult particularly where a client is strong-willed or holds a firm view that his or her interpretation of events is right.

The private investigator should be prepared to accept conflicting evidence which at first inspection does not support his or her theory and also be prepared to challenge earlier perceptions and theories that he or she may have held about a case. They should never be afraid to explore this new evidence even if it brings them into conflict with their client.

Few private investigators will have the luxury of working with a team. Those that are part of such a team have to be prepared to take advantage of the combined views and opinions of those around him or her while those who work alone need to be disciplined in their approach.

Whether the private investigator is working as part of a team or working alone there are basic guidelines they need to follow at the commencement of any investigation. Stated as questions to be considered:

- what do I know about this case?;
- what don't I know about this case?;
- what do I need to know about this case?; and finally,
- what are the lawful and ethical options available to me in order to find out?

Principle Two – Remaining Objective

Privately investigated matters are usually more complicated to investigate as they do not always fall into the stereotypical "police crime scene" scenario. In many cases, the investigation has to be started cold; there may be no "victim" in the sense of a violent crime, and very often there are no witnesses that can be immediately identified to assist the investigation.

As a consequence, the private investigator may ultimately have to commence an investigation by deciding what their most important lines of inquiry are likely to be. As such, the use of logic is key to remaining objective. This is important principle that should remain at the fore of the PI's mind throughout the investigation.

As part of the logic of the decision-making process, it is important that the PI's initial assessment is broken down into three key areas.

- account;
- clarification; and
- challenge.

In order to establish the facts of the matter being investigated, the private investigator will naturally seek information from witnesses, suspects, and "victims." These accounts, usually is statement form, provide an account of what they observed with their senses – their knowledge of, or involvement in, the issue being investigated.

When examining other sources of information, these accounts will need to be interpreted by the PI in relation to the other facts. For example, the private investigator may infer that the investigative target entered an arrangement to supply prohibited chemicals to a criminal gang because of specific information provided to him or her by, say, a neighbor who observed the men meeting.

The degree of difficulty involved in inferring an account from a particular source depends largely upon the nature and credibility of that source, and if there are any legal or procedural considerations relating to how the material must be dealt with. So, common sense dictates that the more information private investigators have about the matter under investigation, the easier it will be to draw inferences about the contribution that a particular source is able make to the inquiry.

Having obtained an account from the source, private investigators should then start to clarify any inconsistencies or ambiguities that the account contains. This may involve testing it against other material already gathered or facts already verified by the private investigator.

Once again, experience shows that even sources of information which at first glance appear to be of unquestionable reliability can be wrong; and information that appears to indicate one thing can later be found to support a totally different interpretation of events.

If we are to follow an ethically sound model of investigation, private investigators should, therefore, continually challenge both the meaning and the reliability of any information they gather.

It is good working practice that PIs should treat all information as possibly being incorrect, and regard all sources of information as having the potential to mislead the investigation. This is best summed up by the ABC mnemonic:

- Assume nothing;
- Believe nothing; and
- Challenge everything.

Every account should be checked for inconsistency or conflict with other information the private investigator has obtained. The main reason why investigators make errors, and are most likely to be misled, is because they have not paid sufficient attention to detail, relying on "gut instinct" and making *prima facie* assumptions about circumstances, or the veracity of evidence. Most importantly, information likely to be admitted as evidence in a legal proceeding should never be accepted without question – because the legal counsel for the other party will not and you will be cross-examined on this information. Private investigators should constantly search to corroborate the key pieces of information.

Principle Three – Surveillance for Intended Purposes

Post the 9/11 terrorist attacks, as well as those perpetrated on London, Madrid, Bali, and Mumbai, we are all living in an increasingly surveillance-conscious world where the majority of us have come to accept that this is a routine occurrence in our day-to-day life. This surveillance takes many guises – from the monitoring of shopping patterns and trends through our store loyalty cards through to the remote observation of our journeys made in our vehicles country wide through the use of various automated number plate recognition systems.

Within the United Kingdom, closed circuit television has become a routine fact of life post the July 7, 2005 bombings, not only in the community's busy city streets, but also the systems that feed into these venues – the public transport systems that service shopping malls, airports, and the business districts. Our cell phones can be tracked and our locations pinpointed with alarming accuracy whenever we make or receive a call or a text message.

Society remains divided with regards to the ethics of such pervasive surveillance. Many individuals regard the increase in surveillance as being but a small price to pay to guarantee our safety. In many cases, these raw data are never used until an incident occurs, then they are analyzed. If surveillance is to be used to society's good, then those who employ surveillance need to be mindful of how precious a person's privacy is and not to risk jeopardizing the usefulness of surveillance by using the images for any purpose other than those intended.

Principle Four – Right to Privacy, Proportionality, and Necessity

Surveillance could be regarded as the core business of private investigation. Nevertheless, the investigator should be ever mindful of not breaching privacy laws and the human rights of individuals they are perusing.

Each of the Five-Eyes countries have legislation that covers these matters. By way of example, we will look at the qualified rights within Europe. This entails a person's right to respect for their private and family life, home, and correspondence, as provided for by Article 8 of the *European Convention of Human Rights*. This is not unlike the U.S. Constitution that contains what is collectively known as the Bill of Rights – that is, the first ten amendments of the Constitution. Although Australia does not have a bill of rights enshrined in legislation, these same rights are captured in common law privileges. New Zealand has the *New Zealand Bill of Rights Act, 1990* and Canada has *Canadian Bill of Rights,* S.C. 1960, c. 44.

The *Human Rights Act* was enacted within the U.K. in November 1998. The European Convention on Human Rights places consideration of an individual's rights to privacy and fair trial at the very heart of law enforcement operations. It is Article 8 of this convention that is most likely to be engaged when public authorities seek to obtain private information about a person by means of covert surveillance.

In it, Article 8 guarantees the right to respect for private and family life. The infringement of someone's right to privacy should be justifiable on the grounds of proportionality and necessity. The degree of intrusion proposed should be proportionate to the seriousness of the crime being investigated and should take account of the character and standing of the suspect. The technique adopted should also be a necessary means of obtaining the desired result.

Whether it is the *Human Rights Act* or the various amendments of the U.S. Constitution (i.e., the Bill of Rights), or any other similar statute the principles in the other five-eyes countries, they affect the manner in which an investigation is undertaken by providing a set of standards which must be met in order to permit interference in the rights of privacy of an individual. For a profession such as private investigators to inquire into the affairs of a citizen, they must be able to show that their activities have observed the rule of law, had legitimate aims, and are proportionate.

As far as this applies to the proportionality of actions undertaken by investigators, there is also a recognized proportionality test that can be applied when assessing his or her actions. In European law, there are generally acknowledged to be four stages to a proportionality test, namely:

- there must be a legitimate aim for a measure – the investigator is operating within the law;
- the measure must be suitable to achieve the aim (potentially with a requirement of evidence to show it will have that effect);
- the measure must be necessary to achieve the aim, and that there cannot be any less onerous way of doing it – for example, is the investigator using a sledge hammer to crack a nut?; and
- the measure must be reasonable, considering the competing interests of different groups at hand.

When dealing with a human rights concern (Article 8, or other), it may be helpful for the private investigator to use the mnemonic JAPAN when considering his or her actions. For investigators to ask themselves whether their investigative actions are *justified, appropriate, proportionate, accountable,* and *necessary* helps them maintain an ethical investigation and one which, if all the elements are answered in the affirmative, will invariably prevent the investigator from breaching the spirit of the law.

- Justification (legality) – that there were reasonable grounds to suspect some knowledge or involvement relevant to the case commissioned by the client;
- Appropriate – that the proper procedures have been followed, recorded, and all actions were authorized under law;
- Proportionality – that the nature of the interference or investigation is proportional to the matter being investigated in its seriousness;
- Accountability – all the options were considered and all the relevant factors have been recorded; and
- Necessity – that the methods used are necessary for the purpose of the inquiry.

WORKING WITH INFORMANTS

Informants may be considered to be an important source of information for some private investigation work. History, however, shows that there are many potential pitfalls to consider when deciding whether to work with informants. Police forces have, over the years, realized just how problematic informants can be, and internationally authorities have strictly regulated their use and control by police and other investigatory agencies.

> ## "You don't have to take out a search warrant to look for trouble."[310]

Private investigators do not have to adhere to any code of conduct or restricted working practices when dealing with informants; however, they can, and are likely to, suffer consequences if they fail to manage them ethically. Let us look as some of the key issues relating to informant usage:

- informants are very often difficult to control and manage;
- they have the potential to become an embarrassment to the private investigator and his or her client;
- their credibility may be questionable in court or before a tribunal;
- history has shown that in many cases, informant's personal problems often interfere with investigations and the presentation of cases. It is important that the PI conducts a background check on the informant to establish how his or her lifestyle and personal history might be viewed by the "reasonable man";
- informants of the opposite gender can take full advantage and become a temptation;
- be mindful of the fact that informants often violate the law themselves. Be suspicious as to where they are obtaining their information from, particularly if the information is in documentary or electronic format. Be mindful that the informant may have broken the law him/herself in order to actually obtain that information that he or she is about to hand to you. Question the informant about his or her sources of intelligence, and remember that invariably ignorance of the fact is no defense;
- informants may not be reliable especially if they lead unregulated lifestyles;
- informants might be able to be bought by a higher bidder;
- some informants lie, or exaggerate the truth, or tell the PI what he or she might want to hear, rather than the facts; and
- informants bring you information, but they can also take your information to their sources. This is an issue for why the PI should understand counterintelligence theory and practice.

The motives of an informant for giving information to the private investigator are, for the most part, self-serving. This means that the PI should be conscience that the information he or she obtain might be exaggerated or completely false. Some common informant motives include these:

- Fear – concern for his or her own well-being or that of his or her family. Informants motivated by fear must be handled cautiously to avoid potential coercion problems;
- Protection – a desire for protection from the law or from other criminal elements can motivate criminals to become informants. The PI should be careful not to overpromise and always to stay within the law;
- Vanity – a desire to be looked upon in a favorable light;
- Revenge – motivated to help the private investigator in order to get even with someone for any of a number of reasons;
- Repentance – will attempt to redeem him- or herself, or sooth a guilty conscience by helping the investigator;
- Money – willing to obtain and provide information for money;
- Competition – an attempt to eliminate competition of another criminal element; and
- Conscience – for conscience sake, they desire to stop some act from being committed or help reduce crime in general.

To conclude, the private investigator should not automatically assume that an informant's information is accurate; he or she should always seek to corroborate that information from other sources and treat whatever an informant states with some degree of skepticism.

KEY TERMS AND PHRASES

The key words and phrases associated with this chapter are listed below. In one or two sentences, demonstrate your understanding of each by writing a short definition or explanation.

- Accountability;
- Confidentiality;
- Objectivity;
- Policy file;
- Respect;
- The mnemonic ABC;
- The mnemonic JAPAN; and
- Transparency.

STUDY QUESTIONS

1. List the four guiding principles suggested for ethical private investigation work?
2. Discuss the thinking behind the mnemonic ABC?
3. Discuss the reasons why a PI would consider using the principles contained in the mnemonic JAPAN?
4. Select one of the eight reasons suggested why an informant might be motivated to provide information, and explain why this factor could compromise an investigation.

LEARNING ACTIVITY

Search the news stories in your state/province over the past five years for an example of where the private investigator has been accused of some unethical or illegal conduct. From the news account, discuss whether using the principles enshrined in the mnemonic JAPAN might have overcome the trouble the PI found him or herself in.

NOTES

1. Ross Douthat, "It's Still a Post-9/11 World," in *New York Times,* September 5, 2011, New York Edition, A19.
2. Rick Sarre and Tim Prenzler, *The Law of Private Security in Australia,* second edition (Pyrmont, NSW: Thomson Reuters, 2009).
3. Jerry Ratcliffe, *Intelligence-Led Policing* (Devon, UK: Willan Publishing, 2008), 6.
4. Terry L. Schroeder, *Intelligence Specialist 3 & 2, vol. 1* (Washington, DC: Naval Education and Training Program Development Center, 1983), 2–1.
5. Christopher Andrew, Richard Aldrich, and Wesley Wark, *Secret Intelligence: A Reader* (London: Routledge, 2009), 1.
6. Some explanation is needed here. The long-form name is United Kingdom of Great Britain and Northern Ireland and is known simply as the United Kingdom (which is abbreviated UK). The UK comprised four countries – England, Scotland, Wales, and Northern Ireland, whereas Great Britain comprises the same countries but not Northern Ireland. For short, Great Britain is referred to as Britain. However, some people confuse England with Britain and also with the United Kingdom, and in doing so use the three names synonymously. Although England is a country within this international arrangement, it is not synonymous with either Great Britain or the United Kingdom.
7. An alliance that began in 1947 under what is known as the UKUSA Agreement. This was an agreement that brought together signals intelligence agencies of Australia, Britain, Canada, New Zealand, and the United States to monitor cytological targets around the world. James Bamford, *The Puzzle Palace: A Report on NSA, America's Most Secret Agency* (Boston: Houghton-Mifflin, 1982), 309.
8. *Operations officer* is the term currently used for what was the tradition title of *case officer.*
9. T. J. Waters, *Class 11: Insider the CIA's First Post-9-11 Spy Class* (New York: Dutton, 2006).
10. Richard Eells and Peter Nehemkis, *Corporate Intelligence and Espionage,* 185.
11. Heinz Duthel, *Rupert Murdoch: The Politico Media Complex Mogul* (Charleston, SC: CreateSpace, 2011), 348.
12. David Henderson, *Field Intelligence: Its Principles and Practices* (Melbourne: Government Printer, 1904).
13. Patrick F. Walsh, *Intelligence and Intelligence Analysis* (New York: Routledge, 2011).

14. Christopher Andrew, *Defend the Realm: The Authorized History of MI5* (New York: Alfred A. Knopf, 2009), 3, 808.

15. Heinz Duthel, *Rupert Murdoch,* 349.

16. Heinz Duthel, *Rupert Murdoch,* 349.

17. Born Samuel Dashiell Hammett on May 27, 1894, Maryland. Died January 10, 1961 (aged 66) and buried in Arlington National Cemetery. Dashiell Hammett, *Complete Works* (New York: The Library of America, 1999), 940 & 959.

18. Steven Marcus, "Notes on the Texts," in Dashiell Hammett, *Complete Works,* 960–967.

19. Dashiell Hammett, as cited in Kirby McCauley, Marin H. Greenberg, and Ed Gorman, (Eds.), *Nightmare Town: Stories* (New York: Alfred A. Knopf, 1999), ix.

20. Simon Chesterman and Angelina Fisher (Eds.), *Private Security, Public Order: The Outsourcing of Public Services and Its Limits* (Oxford: Oxford University Press, 2009).

21. John E. Farley, *Sociology* (Englewood Cliffs, NJ: Prentice-Hall, 1990), 87–88.

22. See for instance the second book of the *Holy Bible* (and/or the Hebrew *Tanakh*), Exodus, chapter 20, versus 1–17. Although the Muslim religious text – the *Holy Quran* – does not contain this Decalogue in one chapter, scholars point out that there are similar passages throughout the book. Ejaz Naqvi, *The Quran: With or Against the Bible? A Topic-by Topic Review for the Investigative Mind* (Bloomington, IN: iUniverse, 2012).

23. Dashiell Hammett, "One Hour," in *Nightmare Town: Stories,* Kirby McCauley, Martin H. Greenberg, and Ed Gorman (Eds.) (New York: Alfred A. Knopf, 1999), 253.

24. Henry Campbell Black, *Black's Law Dictionary,* Fourth Edition (St. Paul, MN: West Publishing, 1951), 536.

25. New South Wales Government, *Commercial Agents and Private Inquiry Agents Act, 2004* (Sydney: New South Wales, 2004).

26. Note that there is the widely used casual term for private investigator is *gumshoe,* but we have avoided using informal expression in this book. William Morris, editor, *The American Heritage Dictionary of the England Language* (Boston: American Heritage Publisher and Houghton-Mifflin, 1971), 587; and, Josiah Thompson, *Gumshoe: Reflections in a Private Eye* (London: Macmillan, 1988).

27. Heinz Duthel, *Rupert Murdoch,* 349.

28. For example, see true story of private investigator Keith Schafferius, who is a child retrieval expert. Keith Schafferius and Grantlee Kieza, *The Retriever* (Sydney: HarperCollins Publishers, 2010).

29. Dashiell Hammett, *The Maltese Falcon* (New York: The Modern Library, 1934).

30. Allan Pinkerton, *The Spy of the Rebellion: Being a True History of the Spy System of the United States Army During the Late Rebellion* (Hartford, CT: M. A. Winter & Hatch, 1883).

31. Tony Ulasewicz with Stuart A. McKeever, *The President's Private Eye* (Westport, CT: MACSAM Publishing Co., 1990).

32. For more details on this issue, see this book's *Preface.*

33. David and St. John are the first names of his two sons. He combined them to form this particular pseudonym.

34. For example, take the recent release of former CIA operative Robert Baer's book, *Blow the House Down* (New York: Crown, 2006); the National Security Council's former Deputy Director for Political-Military Affairs, Lieutenant Colonel Oliver North's books, including *The Jericho Sanction* (Nashville, TN: Bradman and Holman Publishers, 2003 – with co-author Joe Musser); and, former Deputy Assistant Secretary of State for Intelligence, Richard A. Clarke's book *The Scorpion's Gate* (New York: G. P. Putnam's Sons, 2005), to mention just a few.
35. Although scholars such as Prunckun use the term *business intelligence,* others use a variety of terms; for instance, *competitor intelligence, competitive intelligence, corporate intelligence.* I have used business intelligence in this chapter as it is a more encompassing term than the others. See Hank Prunckun, *Scientific Methods of Inquiry for Intelligence Analysis* (Lanham, MD: Scarecrow Press, 2010), 14.
36. For instance, James E. Ackroyd, *The Investigator: A Practical Guide to Private Detection* (London: Frederick Muller, 1974); Gene Blackwell, *The Private Investigator* (Los Angeles: Security World Publishing, 1979); and, Anthony Manley, *The Elements of Private Investigation: An Introduction to the Law, Techniques, and Procedures* (Boca, Raton, FL: CRC Press, 2009).
37. Patrick F. Walsh, "Intelligence and National Security Issues in Policing," in Philip Birch and Victoria Herrington (Eds.), *Policing in Practice* (Sydney: Palgrave Macmillan, 2011), 109.
38. See, Burch, James. "A Domestic Intelligence Agency for the United States? A Comparative Analysis of Domestic Intelligence Agencies and Their Implications for Homeland Security." *Homeland Security Affairs,* vol. 3, no. 2 (June 2007), available at: http://www.hsaj.org/?article=3.2.2 (accessed July 30, 2012).
39. Patrick F. Walsh, "Intelligence and National Security Issues in Policing," 110.
40. Patrick F. Walsh, "Intelligence and National Security Issues in Policing," 110.
41. SIGINT, or signals intelligence, is a generic term given to the process of collecting intelligence from intercepted electromagnetic waves, or signals. SIGINT includes the interception of radio messages (COMINT), radio signals from military equipment (TELINT), and signals from radar (ELINT). The U.S. National Security Agency (NSA), the Australian Defence Signals Directorate (DSD), the British Government Communications Headquarters (GCHQ), the Canadian Communications Security Establishment (CSEC), and the New Zealand Government Communications Security Bureau (GCSB) are the Five-Eyes intelligence agencies responsible for SIGINT related work.
42. Patrick F. Walsh, "Intelligence and National Security Issues in Policing," 110.
43. Patrick F. Walsh, *Intelligence and Intelligence Analysis* (New York: Routledge, 2011), 17.
44. John Grieve, "Developments in UK Criminal Intelligence," in Jerry Ratcliffe (Ed.), *Strategic Thinking in Criminal Intelligence,* Second Edition (Sydney: Federation Press, 2009), 30–46.
45. See for example, Peter Gill and Mark Phythian, *Intelligence in an Insecure World* (Oxford: Polity Press, 2006), 3; Jerry Ratcliffe, *Intelligence Led Policing,* 105.
46. For a discussion of oversight mechanisms for intelligence collection in national security and policing agencies of Five Eyes intelligence alliance see, Patrick F. Walsh, *Intelligence and Intelligence Analysis,* 227.

47. Patrick F. Walsh, "Intelligence and National Security Issues in Policing," 116.
48. There is an increasing volume on all aspects of analytical and intelligence failure in the literature, particularly since 9/11. See for example, Richard Betts, "Analysis, War, and Decision: Why Intelligence Failures are Inevitable." *World Politics,* 31, no. 1, (1978): 61–89; Amy Zegart, *Spying Blind* (Princeton: Princeton University, 2007).
49. Competing hypotheses can be used with many different problems in national security and policing intelligence contexts. It can be used when it is likely that other explanations for events or potential developments in the future could be possible, and helps the analyst reduce their natural tendency to satisfy themselves by going with the first answer that comes to them. Red cell analysis is trying to get into the mind of an adversary, particularly their behavior and decision-making. For an excellent explanation of these and other structured analytical techniques and tools see, Richards Heuer and Randy Pherson, *Structured Analytical Techniques* (Washington, DC: CQ Press, 2010).
50. Patrick F. Walsh, "Intelligence and National Security Issues in Policing," 121.
51. Hot spots are specific locations or areas where crime is concentrated. The general theory of analyzing hot spots is that they are areas where the same offenders are committing most of the crimes.
52. Justine J. Dintino and Fredrick T. Martens, *Police Intelligence Systems in Crime Control: Managing a Delicate Balance in a Liberal Democracy* (Springfield, IL: Charles C Thomas, 1983), 6.
53. Donald O. Schultz and Loran A. Norton, *Police Operational Intelligence,* revised third printing (Springfield, IL: Charles C Thomas, 1973), 35–38.
54. For an interesting discussion on what to consider with regard to client-based intelligence tasks, see, Jonathan Nicholl, "Task Definition," in Jerry Ratcliffe (Ed.), *Strategic Thinking in Criminal Intelligence,* second edition (Sydney: Federation Press, 2009), 66–85.
55. Lexis Nexus is a global provider of legal, government, corporation information to professionals in the law, corporations and academics (www.lexisnexis.com), and Stratfor is a provider of strategic intelligence on global business, economic, security and military affairs (www stratfor.com).
56. Oliver Higgins, "Intelligence Collection," in Jerry Ratcliffe (Ed.), *Strategic Thinking in Criminal Intelligence,* second edition (Sydney: Federation Press, 2009), 89–90.
57. Jon Rees and Dan Atkinson, "News of the World Fallout Sees Takeovers Stall on Fears Investigators Break Hacking Law," *Daily Mail* (UK) (August 28, 2011) http://www.dailymail.co.uk/home/index.html (accessed July 11, 2012).
58. Inductive reasoning involves moving from specific cases to general conclusions where deductive reasoning is the reverse: Moving from general cases to specific conclusions. Both kinds are used by intelligence analysts, though inductive reasoning is more employed given there are usually a number of information gaps that cannot be filled during the intelligence process.
59. For instance, see Ronald M. Hankin, *Navigating the Legal Minefields of Private Investigation* (Flushing, NY: Looseleaf Law Publications, 2008), and Rick Sarre and Tim Prenzler, *The Law of Private Security in Australia,* 2nd edition (Sydney: Thomson Reuters, 2009).

60. Garry Maher, *Investigating Made Simple: A Guide to the Principles and Practices of Complaint and Incident Investigation* (Noosaville, Queensland: Acumen Learning, 2007), 27.

61. The Australian School of Security and Investigations, http://www.trainingschool.com.au/certificate3.html (accessed July 4, 2012).

62. Kevin Macnish, "Stalkers, Private Investigators and the Reason Behind PI Licenses" *Pursuit Magazine,* http://pursuitmag.com/stalkers-private-investigators-and-the-reason-behind-pi-licenses/ (accessed July 4, 2012).

63. Helen Arfvidsson, *My Generation Case Study Employment and Education Theme the Positive Potential of Informal Learning* (Göteborg: Goteborgs Stad, Stadskansliet, 2009), 1.

64. Hank Prunckun, *Handbook of Scientific Methods of Inquiry for Intelligence Analysis* (Lanham, MD: Scarecrow Press, 2010), 3–4.

65. Sotirios Sarantakos, *Social Research* (South Melbourne: Macmillan Education, 1995), 52.

66. Bruce Berg, *Qualitative Research Methods for the Social Sciences* (Boston: Allyn and Bacon, 2001), 251.

67. Hank Prunckun, *Handbook of Scientific Methods of Inquiry for Intelligence Analysis,* 20.

68. See note 5 in Chapter 5 for details on the use of the term *threat* in this context.

69. For a detailed discussion of a range of analytical approaches to intelligence-led investigation, see Hank Prunckun, *Handbook of Scientific Methods of Inquiry for Intelligence Analysis,* 135–159.

70. For a more detailed account of the steps involved in analysis of competing hypotheses see Richards J. Heuer, Jr., "Analysis of Competing Hypotheses," in *Psychology of Intelligence Analysis* (Washington, DC: Central Intelligence Agency, 1999), 95–109.

71. Judy Lambert, Jane Elix, and Bianca Priest, *Values Mapping: A Flexible Tool for Building Sustainability Partnerships,* http://www.communitysolutions.com.au/pdf/ValuesMappingPaperFinal.pdf (accessed July 11, 2012).

72. Australian Institute of Private Detectives, *National Code of Practice for Investigators and Mercantile Agents,* http://www.aipd.com.au/pdf/COP_Adopted220908.pdf (accessed July 11, 2012).

73. Philip C. Kendall and Gary L. Fischler, "Behavioral and Adjustment Correlates of Problem Solving: Validational Analyses of Interpersonal Cognitive Problem-Solving Measures" in *Child Development,* Vol. 55, No. 3 (June 1984), 879–892.

74. The term *open-source intelligence* is often abbreviated as OSINT.

75. Ken Mark MacBean, "The Enterprise Agent," *PI Magazine,* Nov./Dec. 2010, 45.

76. Robert David Steele, *On Intelligence Spies and Secrecy in an Open World* (Oakton, VA: OSS International Press, 2001).

77. Peter Gill, Peter and Mark Phythian, *Intelligence in an Insecure World* (Cambridge: Polity Press, 2006).

78. Julian Richards, *The Art and Science of Intelligence Analysis* (Oxford: Oxford University Press, 2010).

79. Named after the English mathematician, George Boole, who invented this system of logic.

80. Accessed, October 30, 2012.
81. Hank Prunckun, *Handbook of Scientific Methods of Inquiry for Intelligence Analysis* (Lanham, MD: Scarecrow Press, 2010), 35.
82. Denis Campbell, *Egypt Unshackled: Using Social Media to @#:) the System* (London: Cambria Books, 2011).
83. Chuck Chambers, *The Private Investigator's Handbook* (New York: Penguin, 2005).
84. Search conducted October 31, 2012.
85. Richard Eells and Peter Nehemkis, *Corporate Intelligence and Espionage: A Blue Print for Executive Decision Making* (New York: Macmillan, 1984), 4.
86. Sun Tzu, The Art of War, translated by Samuel B. Griffith (London: Oxford University Press, 1963), 129.
87. Patrick F. Walsh, *Intelligence and Intelligence Analysis* (New York: Routledge, 2011).
88. Other terms for a *target-of-interest* can include: *person-of-interest, organization-* or *business-of-interest, problem-of-interest,* and *issue-of-interest.* All of these can be targets for profiling.
89. Note that the term *threat* is used in a way that differs from the way it is used in Chapter 8 (Anti-Terrorist and Anti-Gang Intelligence). Here we are using the term to mean *risk, danger,* or *hazard.* This is because SWOT analyses are used so extensively in business that the terms SWOT is universal and would cause confusion if used differently.
90. Source: Hank Prunckun, *Handbook of Scientific Methods of Inquiry for Intelligence Analysis* (Lanham, MD: Scarecrow Press, 2010), 137.
91. Based on the book by the same name: Frank W. Abagnale with Stan Redding, *Catch Me if You Can: The True Story of a Real Fake* (New York: Grosset & Dunlap, 1980).
92. Hank Prunckun, *Counterintelligence Theory and Practice* (Lanham, MD: Rowman & Littlefield, 2012), 114.
93. For example, see chapter one in Hank Prunckun, *Counterintelligence Theory and Practice,* 1–16.
94. Michael Chesbro, *Save Your Identify: ID Theft Awareness, Prevention, and Recovery* (Boulder, CO: Paladin Press, 2004), 4.
95. Hank Prunckun, *Counterintelligence Theory and Practice,* 134–135.
96. Gene Blackwell, *The Private Investigator* (Los Angeles: Security World Publishing, 1979).
97. Lisa A. Kramer and Richards J. Heuer Jr., "America's Increased Vulnerability to Insider Espionage," *International Journal of Intelligence and Counterintelligence,* (2007): 20: 50–64.
98. W. Steve Albrecht, Chad Albrecht, and Conan C. Albrecht, "Current Trends in Fraud and its Detection," *Information Security Journal: A Global Perspective,* (2008): 17:1, 3.
99. Lisa A. Kramer and Richards J. Heuer Jr., "Technological, Social, and Economic Trends That Are Increasing U.S. Vulnerability to Insider Espionage" (Monterey, CA: Defense Personnel Security Research Center, 2005).
100. Lisa A. Kramer and Richards J. Heuer Jr., "Technological, Social, and Economic Trends That Are Increasing U.S. Vulnerability to Insider Espionage."

101. Peter Maass and Megha Rajagopalan, "Does Cybercrime Really Cost $1 Trillion?" *ProPublica,* August 1, 2012, http://www.propublica.org/article/does-cyber-crime-really-cost-1-trillion (accessed November 1, 2012).

102. Federal Bureau of Investigation, "Financial Crimes Report to the Public Fiscal Years 2010–2011," http://www.fbi.gov/stats-services/publications/financial-crimes-report-2010-2011 (accessed November 1, 2012).

103. Federal Bureau of Investigation, "Economic Espionage."

104. Hank Prunckun, *Handbook of Scientific Methods of Inquiry for Intelligence Analysis* (Lanham, MD: Scarecrow Press, 2010), 73–75.

105. In the first instance, see Hank Prunckun, *Handbook of Scientific Methods of Inquiry for Intelligence Analysis* (Lanham, MD: Scarecrow Press, 2010).

106. PricewaterhouseCoopers, *PwC Global Economic Crime Survey 2011,* http://www.pwc.com/en_GX/gx/economic-crime-survey/assets/GECS_GLOBAL_REPORT.pdf (accessed November 1, 2012).

107. Scott H. Belshaw, "Private Investigation Programs as an Emerging Trend in Criminal Justice Education? A Case Study of Texas," *Journal of Criminal Justice Education,* (2012), 1–19.

108. Bureau of Labor Statistics, U.S. Department of Labor, "Job Outlook," *Occupational Outlook Handbook,* http://www.bls.gov/ooh/protective-service/private-detectives-and-investigators.htm (accessed October 16, 2012).

109. Integrity Research Associates, *Defining Political Research,* http://www.integrity-research.com/cms/2012/06/11/defining-political-intelligence-%E2%80%93-part-1/ (accessed August 16, 2012).

110. Jean-Paul Brodeur, "High Policing and Low Policing: Remarks about the Policing of Political Activities," *Social Problems Vol. 30 No. 5 Thematic issue on Justice,* June, 1983, 507–520.

111. Barnes, Trevor, "Special Branch and the First Labour Government," *The Historical Journal,* 22, 4, 1979, 941–951.

112. Richard Hall, *The Secret State: Australia's Spy Industry* (Stanmore, New South Wales: Cassell Australia Ltd, 1978).

113. Nelson Blackstock, *COINTELPRO – The FBI's Secret War on Political Freedom* (New York: Vintage Books, 1975).

114. John Drabble, "To Ensure Domestic tranquillity: The FBI, COINTELPRO – White Hate and Political Discourse, 1964–1971," *Journal of American Studies Vol. 38,* Issue 2, August, 2004, 297–328.

115. Roth Zarchary, *Political Intelligence: Wall Street Pays Handsomely for Washington Inside Dope,* March 19, 2012, *Yahoo News,* http://news.yahoo.com/blogs/ticket/political-intelligence-wall-street-pays-handsomely-washington-inside-154326575.html (accessed August 16, 2012).

116. Jason Teven, "An Examination of Perceived Credibility of the 2008 Presidential Candidates Relationship with Believability, Likeability and Deceptiveness," *Human Communication,* Vol. 11, No. 4, 2008, 385.

117. Ben Packham, "Labor Dirt Unit Critics Seize on Claims of in Julia Gilard's Office," *The Australian,* June 14, 2012.

118. Jessica Marszalek, "LNP Dirt File Dumps a Lose-Lose on Leader," *AAP Newswire,* October 12, 2011.

119. Jessica Marszalek, "LNP Dirt File Dumps a Lose-Lose on Leader."
120. The Inquisitor, "Democrats Dig Up Dirt on Mitt Romney's Potential Veeps," http://www.inquisitr.com/297463/democrats-dig-up-dirt-on-mitt-romneys-potential-veeps/ (accessed August 28, 2012).
121. G. Gordon Liddy, *Will: The Autobiography of G. Gordon Liddy* (London: Severn House, 1981).
122. Ironically, even experienced operatives can go wrong if they lose their ethical compass – take for example the case of G. Gordon Liddy, who was a former FBI agent, and E. Howard Hunt, who was a former CIA officer. They were key agents in the 1972 failed political intelligence operation known as Watergate, and both were convicted by the courts and sentenced to serve time in prison for their part in the illegal operation.
123. Tony Ulasewicz with Stuart A. McKeever, *The President's Private Eye: The Journey of Detective Tony U. From NYPD to the Nixon White House* (Westport, CT: MACSAM Publishing Co, 1990), 240.
124. Tony Ulasewicz with Stuart A. McKeever, *The President's Private Eye,* 240.
125. Hank Prunckun, *Handbook of Scientific Methods of Inquiry for Intelligence Analysis* (Lanham, MD: Scarecrow Press, 2010), 152–155.
126. The company's former trading name was Holdingham Group Limited, see http://wck2.companieshouse.gov.uk/6126b0cd71092169668ce6271ce474d6/com pdetails (accessed September 14, 2012).
127. Melissa Sweet, "Turning Journalists into Spooks," *Crikey,* July 31, 2008, http://www.crikey.com.au/2008/07/31/turning-journalists-into-spooks/ (accessed August 28, 2012).
128. A Coskun Samli and Jacobs Laurence, "Counteracting Global Industrial Espionage: A Damage Control Strategy," *Business and Society Review,* 108:1, 2003, 95–113.
129. George Friedman, *The Next Decade: Where We've Been. . .and Where We're Going* (New York: Doubleday, 2011).
130. Andrew Folwer, The Most Dangerous Man in the World: The Explosive True Story of Julian Assange and the Lies, Cover-ups and Conspiracies He Exposed (New York: Skyhorse, 2011).
131. Adam Weinstein, "WikiLeaks Goes Inside Corporate America's Wannabe CIA," http://m.motherjones.com/politics/2012/02/wikileaks-strafor-leak-corporate-intelligence, February 27, 2012 (accessed August 31, 2012).
132. Chris Spannos, "An Unethical Record – Stratfor and the New York Times," August 24, 2012, http://www.nytexaminer.com/2012/08/an-unethical-record-stratfor-the-new-york-times/ (accessed August 31, 2012).
133. See Chapter 8 for a discussion about conducting threat assessments. Although Chapter 9 discusses this in relation to terrorists and gangs, the threat assessment methodology can also be applied to political motivated groups.
134. Parmy Olson, *We Are Anonymous: Inside the Hacker World of LulzSec, Anonymous, and the Global Cyber Insurgency* (New York: Little, Brown and Company, 2012).
135. Time Magazine (Eds.), *What is Occupy?: Inside the Global Movement* (New York: Time Books, 2011).

136. Exclusive Analysis Ltd., http://www.exclusive-analysis.com/index.html (accessed September 14, 2012).

137. Darker Net, http://darkernet.wordpress.com/2012/08/07/intelligence-gathering-firm-expands-into-infiltration-of-protest-groups/ (accessed August 28, 2012).

138. Philip Doring, "The Watchdog's Kennel in Clandestine Croyden, " in *The Age,* January 7, 2012, http://www.theage.com.au/national/the-watchdogs-kennel-in-clandestine-croydon-20120106-1poox.html (accessed September 14, 2012).

139. National Open Source Intelligence Centre, http://www.nosic.com.au/ (accessed September 14, 2012).

140. Margot Webb, *Coping with Street Gangs* (New York: Rosen Publishing Group, 1990).

141. United Nations Office of Drugs and Crime, *World Drug Report 2012* (New York: United Nations, 2012), 63.

142. Louise I. Shelly, "The Unholy Trinity: Transnational Crime, Corruption, and Terrorism," *Brown Journal of International Affairs,* vol. XI, issue 2, 2005, 101–111.

143. David L. Cater, *Law Enforcement Intelligence: A Guide for State, Local, and Tribal Law Enforcement Agencies,* second edition (Washington, DC: U.S. Department of Justice, Office of the Community Oriented Policing Services, 2009), 21.

144. National Gang Intelligence Center and National Gang Targeting, Enforcement & Coordination Center, *National Gang Report 2009* (Washington, DC: National Drug Intelligence Center, 2009), iii.

145. Robert J. Bunker and John P. Sullivan, "Integrating Feral Cities and Third Phase Cartels/Third Generation Gangs Research: The Rise of Criminal (Narco) City Networks and BlackFor," *Small Wars and Insurgencies,* vol. 22, no. 5, 2011, 764–786.

146. They could also be applied to investigating threats posed by fanatical cults, their members or their leaders if these threat-agents share the same underlining factors.

147. This chapter is based on the analytical methods discussed in Chapter 11 ("Analytic Techniques for Counterterrorism," pp. 162–181) of the author' book: Hank Prunckun, *Scientific Methods of Inquiry for Intelligence Research* (Lanham, MD: Scarecrow Press, 2010).

148. U.S. Department of Defense, *Joint Publication 1-02, Department of Defense Dictionary of Military and Associated Terms* (Washington DC: Department of Defense, October 18, 2008), 132.

149. Walter Laqueur, *The New Terrorism: Fanaticism and the Arms of Mass Destruction* (New York: Oxford University Press, 1999).

150. In this sense, political can also mean having a radical or extreme view of a particular religious doctrine.

151. Paul Wilkinson, *Daily Telegraph* (London), September 1, 1992, cited in Fred R. Shapiro (Ed.), *The Yale Book of Quotations* (New Haven, CT: Yale University Press, 2006), 825.

152. Federal Bureau of Investigation, *Gangs,* http:// http://www.fbi.gov/about-us/investigate/vc_majorthefts/gangs (accessed 19 September 2012).

153. See discussion of Black Swans in Nassim Nicholas Taleb, *The Black Swan: The Impact of the Highly Improbable* (Penguin Books: London, 2010). Note that Black Swans can also be improbable events that are positive or fortuitous in nature – they do not need to be considered solely as incidents that are negative.

154. For a refresher on the four types of data used in intelligence analysis, see Hank Prunckun, *Scientific Methods of Inquiry for Intelligence Research.*

155. Carl Hammer, *Tide of Terror: America, Islamic Extremism, and the War on Terror* (Boulder, CO: Paladin Press, 2003).

156. Dr. Victoria Herrington, personal communication, May 3, 2009.

157. Moisés Naím, *Illicit: How Smugglers, Traffickers, and Copycats are Hijacking the Global Economy* (New York: Anchor Books, 2005), 5.

158. Moisés Naím, *Illicit,* 12–37.

159. Nils Gilman et al. (Eds.), *Deviant Globalization: Black Market Economy in the 21st Century* (New York: Continuum Books, 2011), 1.

160. Dashiell Hammett, "The Assistant Murderer," in Dashiell Hammett, *Nightmare Town: Stories,* Kirby McCauley, Martin H. Greenberg and Ed Gorman (New York: Alfred A. Knopf, 1999), 129–161.

161. Louise I. Shelley, "The Unholy Trinity: Transnational Crime, Corruption, and Terrorism," *Brown Journal of World Affairs,* 11, no. 2, (2004): 101.

162. John R. Wagley, "RL33335: Transnational Organized Crime: Principal Threats and U.S. Responses," *Congressional Research Service Report for Congress,* (Washington, DC: Library of Congress, 2006), 6.

163. Dipak K. Gupta, "Exploring the Roots of Terrorism," in *The Roots of Terrorism: Myths, Realities and Ways Forward,* Tore Bjørgo (Ed.) (London: Routledge, 2005), 28.

164. Daniel Byman, *Deadly Connections: States That Sponsor Terrorism* (Cambridge: Cambridge University Press, 2005), 1–2.

165. Loretta Napoleoni, *Terror Incorporated: Tracing the Dollars Behind the Terror Networks,* (New York: Seven Stories Press, 2005), 31–48.

166. Louise I. Shelley, *The Unholy Trinity,* 101.

167. Louise I. Shelley, *The Unholy Trinity,* 101.

168. Michael Freeman, "The Sources of Terrorist Financing: Theory and Typology," *Studies in Conflict and Terrorism,* 34 no.6, (2011).

169. Daniel Byman, *Deadly Connections,* 1–2.

170. The World Bank and the International Monetary Fund, *Comprehensive Reference Guide to Anti-Money Laundering and Terrorist Financing* (Washington, DC: The World Bank and the International Monetary Fund, 2006), 1.

171. Thomas J. Biersteker and Sue E. Eckert, "Introduction," in *Countering the Financing of Terrorism,* Thomas J. Biersteker and Sue E. Eckert (Eds.) (London: Routledge, 2008), 1.

172. John T. Picarelli and Louise I. Shelley, "Organized Crime and Terrorism," in *Terrorism Financing and State Responses: A Comparative Perspective,* Jeanne K. Giraldo and Harold A. Trinkunas, (Eds.) (Stanford, CA: Stanford University Press, 2008), 40–41.

173. See, John T. Picarelli and Louise I. Shelley, *Organized Crime and Terrorism,* 46–47.

174. Al Valdez, "The Origins of Southern Californian Latino Gangs," in *Maras: Gang Violence and Security in Central America,* Thomas Bruneau (Ed.) (Austin, TX: University of Texas Press, 2012), 40.

175. Loretta Napoleoni, *Terror Incorporated: Tracing the Dollars Behind the Terror Networks* (New York: Seven Stories Press, 2005), 41–42.

176. Gretchen Peters, *Seeds of Terror: How Heroin Is Bankrolling the Taliban and al Qaeda* (New York: Thomas Dunne Books, 2009), 130.

177. Michael Freeman, "The Sources of Terrorist Financing: Theory and Typology," *Studies in Conflict and Terrorism,* 34, no. 6, (2011).

178. Scott Stewart. "Terrorism Tradecraft," *Security Weekly* (Austin, TX: Stratfor Global Intelligence, 2012).

179. Michael Freeman, *The Sources of Terrorist Financing,* 462.

180. Based on data provided by Thomas J. Biersteker and Sue E. Eckert, "Introduction," 7.

181. John Mueller and Mark G. Stewart, *Terror, Security, and Money: Balancing the Risks, Benefits, and Costs of Homeland Security* (Oxford: Oxford University Press, 2011), 3.

182. Chris Dishman, "Terrorism, Crime, and Transformation," *Studies in Conflict and Terrorism,* 24, no.1, (2001); Louise I. Shelley, and John T. Picarelli, "Methods and Motives: Exploring links between Transnational Organized Crime and International Terrorism," *Global Crime,* 9, no. 2, (2005).

183. Max G. Mainwaring, *Gray Area Phenomena: Confronting the New World Disorder – Studies in Global Security Series* (Boulder, CO: Westview Press, 1993).

184. Tamara Makarenko, "The Crime-Terror Continuum: Tracing the Interplay Between Transnational Organized Crime and Terrorism," *Global Crime,* 6, no. 1, (2004): 131–133.

185. This model was developed by Tamara Makarenko, *The Crime-Terror Continuum,* 131.

186. Tamara Makarenko, *The Crime-Terror Continuum,* 131–140.

187. Ryan Clarke, *D-Company: A Study of the Crime-Terror Nexus in South Asia* (New York: Routledge, 2011), 116; John Rollins and Liana Sun Wyler, "R41004: International Terrorism and Transnational Crime: Security Threats, U.S. Policy, and Considerations for Congress," *Congressional Research Service Report for Congress,* (2010), 15; Ajey Lele, "A Shift from Crime to Terrorism: Assessing D-Company," *South Asian Journal of Conflict and Terrorism,* 1 (2005), 44; Ryan Clarke and Stuart Lee, "The PIRA, D-Company, and the Crime–Terror Nexus," *Terrorism and Political Violence,* 20, no. 3, 385; HIS Jane's, "Bad Company – South Asia's Regional Criminal Organisation," *Jane's Intelligence Review,* (2009).

188. Moisés Naím, "Mafia States: Organized Crime Takes Office," *Foreign Affairs,* 91, no. 3, (2012): 100–111.

189. Moisés Naím, *Mafia States,* 101.

190. Moisés Naím, *Mafia States,* 101.

191. Tamara Makarenko, *The Crime-Terror Continuum,* 138.

192. John Rollins and Liana Sun Wyler, "R41004: International Terrorism and Transnational Crime: Security Threats, U.S. Policy, and Considerations for Congress," 14–16.

193. Phil Williams, "Terrorist Financing and Organized Crime: Nexus, Appropriation, or Transformation," in *Countering the Financing of Terrorism,* Thomas J. Biersteker and Sue E. Eckert (Eds.) (London: Routledge, 2008), 145–146.

194. Phil Williams, "Warning Indicators and Terrorist Finances," in *Terrorism Financing and State Responses: A Comparative Perspective,* Jeanne K. Giraldo and Harold A. Trinkunas (Eds.) (Stanford, CA: Stanford University Press, 2008), 82.

195. Phil Williams, *Warning Indicators and Terrorist Finances,* 82.

196. Phil Williams, *Warning Indicators and Terrorist Finances,* 84.

197. Dashiell Hammett, "The Assistant Murderer," 130.

198. Roy Godson, "Counterintelligence: An Introduction" in Roy Godson (Ed.), *Intelligence Requirements for the 1980s: Counterintelligence,* Volume 3 (Washington DC: National Strategic Information Center Inc., 1980), 1.

199. Newton S. Miler, "What Is Counterintelligence – Discussants," in Roy Godson (Ed.), *Intelligence Requirements for the 1980s,* 40.

200. John A. Nolan, "Confusing Counterintelligence with Security Can Wreck Your Afternoon," in *Competitive Intelligence Review,* vol. 8, no. 3 (1997): 55.

201. Alain Francq, "The Use of Counterintelligence, Security, and Countermeasures," in Craig S. Fleisher and David L. Blenkhorn (Eds.), *Managing Frontiers in Competitive Intelligence,* (Westport, CT: Greenwood Publishing Group, 2001), 71 and 85.

202. Alain Francq, "The Use of Counterintelligence, Security, and Countermeasures," 71; and John A. Nolan, "Confusing Counterintelligence with Security Can Wreck Your Afternoon," 53.

203. Alain Francq, "The Use of Counterintelligence, Security, and Countermeasures," 75.

204. Roy Godson. *Dirty Tricks or Trump Cards – U.S. Covert Action and Counterintelligence.* (New Brunswick, NJ: Transaction Publishers, 2001), 2.

205. Roy Godson. *Dirty Tricks or Trump Cards.*

206. Stan A. Taylor, "Definitions and Theories of Counterintelligence," in Loch K. Johnson (ed.), *Strategic intelligence – Counterintelligence and Counterterrorism: Defending the Nation Against Hostile Forces,* Volume 4 (Westport, CT: Praeger Securities International, 2007).

207. Frederick L. Wettering, "Counterintelligence: The Broken Triad," in *International Journal of Intelligence and Counterintelligence,* vol. 13, no. 3 (2000).

208. Hank Prunckun, "A Grounded Theory of Counterintelligence," in *American Intelligence Journal,* vol. 29, no. 2: 6–13. See also Chapter 3 in Hank Prunckun, *Counterintelligence Theory and Practice* (Lanham, MD: Scarecrow Press, 2012).

209. Hank Prunckun, *Counterintelligence Theory and Practice.*

210. Hank Prunckun, *Counterintelligence Theory and Practice.*

211. Cognizance is taken of the fact that the C-I-A acronym is a term that originated and is widely used within information technology sciences. The term is equally useful within the discipline of intelligence studies.

212. Kenneth E. DeGraffenreid, *The Cox Report: The Unanimous and Bipartisan Report of the House Select Committee on U.S. National Security and Military Commercial Concerns with the People's Republic of China* (Washington, DC: Regnery Publishing, 1999).

213. *Industrial Espionage News,* http://www.tscmvideo.com/news/industrial-esionage-news.html (accessed June 25, 2008), 7–10.

214. James Kitfield. "Spies of All Stripes Have Discovered That There is Life After the Cold War – The Espionage Sequel," in *Air Force,* vol. 90, no. 3 (2007): 2.

215. As quoted by Michel E. Kabay, *Industrial Espionage* (Vermont. Norwich University, 2008), 7–8.

216. Federal Bureau of Investigation, *Federal Bureau of Investigation (FBI) Strategic Plan: 2004–2009* (Washington, DC: Federal Bureau of Investigation, 2004), 17.

217. National Gang Intelligence Center, Federal Bureau of Investigation, *2011 National Gang Threat Assessment* (Washington, DC: Federal Bureau of Investigation, 2011).

218. The *al-Qaeda Training Manual,* http://www.justice.gov/ag/manualpart1_1.pdf (accessed July 26, 2012).

219. See, for example, M. Harry, *The Muckraker's Manual: Handbook for Investigative Reporters,* second edition (Port Townsend, WA: Loompanics Unlimited, 1984).

220. United States of America. *Report to the President of the United States on the Intelligence Capabilities of the United States Regarding Weapons of Mass Destruction* (Washington DC: The Commission on the Intelligence Capabilities of the United States Regarding Weapons of Mass Destruction, 2005), 381.

221. See *WikiLeaks* at http://wikileaks.org/About.html (last accessed August 14, 2012).

222. Christopher Kush, *The One-Hour Activist: The 15 Most Powerful Actions You Can Take to Fight for the Issues and Candidates You Care About* (San Francisco: Jossey-Bass, 2004).

223. United States of America. *Counterintelligence in the 21st Century: Not Just a Government Problem* (California: Address by J.F Brenner to the Armed Forces Communications and Electronics Association (AFCEA) Counterintelligence Conference, December 4, 2007), 14.

224. Mark Ciampa, *Security Awareness – Applying Practical Security in Your World,* Third Edition (Boston: Course Cengage Learning, 2010), 6.

225. Office of the Director of *National Intelligence, National Intelligence Strategy of the United States of America.* 16–17 (Washington, D.C.: Office of the Director of National Intelligence, October 25, 2005).

226. Stan A. Taylor, "Definitions and Theories of Counterintelligence," 6.

227. United States of America. *Commission on Weapons of Mass Destruction,* 545.

228. Some cyber security practitioners use the term *social engineering,* but as Prunckun points out, this is incorrect – it is simply a pretext. Says he, "Social engineering is a slang term that commonly refers to an individual act of manipulation (usually for fraudulent purposes) to gain access to IT systems. This is vastly different from its true meaning, which is large-scale societal planning. The use of the term *social engineering* in this context is incorrect. The technique is nothing more than a ruse, subterfuge, or pretext. In fact, *pretext* is the term most used by private investigators – PIs rely heavily on this technique as a means of gaining information about their targets." Hank Prunckun, *Handbook of Scientific Methods of Inquiry for Intelligence Analysis* (Lanham, MD: Scarecrow Press, 2010), 91.

229. Stan A. Taylor, "Definitions and Theories of Counterintelligence," 5–6; Fredrick L. Wettering, "Counterintelligence: The Broken Triad," 270–274.

230. Frederick L. Wettering, "Counterintelligence: The Broken Triad," 271.

231. "Bungling Spy Who Left Secret Files on Train Faces the Sack," *Daily Mail Reporter,* June 13, 2008, http://www.dailymail.co.uk/news/article-1025810/ Bungling-spy-left-secret-files-train-faces-sack.html (accessed 25 July 2012).

232. Gary T. Marx, "Some Concepts that May be Useful in Understanding the Myriad Forms and Contexts of Surveillance," in Len V. Scott and Peter Jackson, (Eds.), *Understanding Intelligence in the Twenty-First-Century – Journeys in the Shadows* (London: Routledge, 2004), 78–98.

233. Peter Gill and Mark Phythian, *Intelligence in an Insecure World* (Cambridge: Polity Press, 2006), 29–30 and 95–101.

234. Frederick L. Wettering, "Counterintelligence: The Broken Triad," 281.

235. Frederick L. Wettering, "Counterintelligence: The Broken Triad," 281–284.

236. These different descriptors of human intelligence sources are not mutually exclusive. Under certain conditions a HUMINT source can, for example, be typified simultaneously as a mole, a defector, and a double agent.

237. Alain Francq, "The Use of Counterintelligence, Security, and Countermeasures," 75.

238. Depending on the jurisdiction within which the investigation is conducted, legislation could prescribe the reporting of such incidents to authorities.

239. In contrast, some scholars within intelligence studies remain adamant that the positive intelligence cycle also explains statutory counterintelligence. The intelligence cycle is, however, not at all an accurate reflection of the counterintelligence process (in statutory intelligence services). There is in fact a fierce debate within intelligence studies of whether the traditional cycle explains positive intelligence – left alone counterintelligence. For an overview of this debate see, Petrus C. Duvenage and Mike Hough, "The Conceptual Structuring of the Intelligence and the Counterintelligence Processes: Enduring Holy Grails or Crumbling Axioms – Quo Vadis?," in *Strategic Review for Southern Africa,* vol. 33, no. 1, (2011), 29–77.

240. Bill DeGenaro, "A Case for Business Counterintelligence," in *Competitive Intelligence Magazine,* vol. 8, no. 5 (2005); and Marie-Luce Muller, *Creating Intelligence – Competitive Intelligence Series,* volume 4 (Randburg, South Africa: Knowledge Resources Pty Ltd, 2002), 4–5 and 8.

241. Recall from the discussion in chapter eight that *vulnerability* is the sum of *attractiveness, ease of attack,* and *impact.*

242. *Risk* is the sum of *likelihood* and *consequence.*

243. The Terms of Reference are critical in assisting the private investigator in aligning his or her actions with the client's needs from the outset. They are also essential in ensuring the transparency (and legality) of investigations.

244. The functionality two-way radio provides has been espoused for decades, as an example, see William T. Patterson, *Private Investigation Training Manual* (Boulder, CO: Paladin Press, 1978), 117.

245. See Chapter 9 (Defensive Counterintelligence: Communications Security) in Hank Prunckun, *Counterintelligence Theory and Practice* (Lanham, MD: Rowman & Littlefield, 2012).

246. It could be argued that the methods, tactics, techniques, and procedures used by PIs are generally known and documented in various text books; so too are the illusions employed by magicians. But no professional magician would reveal their illusions; nor should the private investigator.

247. For instance, former CIA case officer (i.e., operations officer) Robert Baer refers to his use of two-way radios at various points in his book in relation to national security intelligence. See Robert Baer, *See No Evil: The True Story of a Ground Soldier in the CIA's War on Terrorism* (New York: Crown, 2002). For a history of the radio equipment that has been used by agents, resistance, partisans, and special forces, from pre-World War Two until the 1980s, see Louis Meulstee and Rudolf F. Staritz with Jan Bury, Erling Langemyr, Tor Marthinsen, Pete McCollum and Antero Tanninen, *Wireless for the Warrior: A Technical History of Radio Communications Equipment in Clandestine and Special Forces Operations,* Volume 4 (Dorset, England: Wimborne, 2004).

248. Michael Chesbro, *Communications for Survival and Self-Reliance* (Boulder, CO: Paladin Press, 2003).

249. The U.S. *Telecommunications Act of 1996* exempts recreational boaters from the requirement for a ship radio station license; so many boat builders/suppliers do not install these devices. So, if you are involved in recreational boating, you may wish to consider adding a VHF marine radio as this is a key piece of safety equipment.

250. The 27 MHz CB band is also known as the 11 meter band as this is the wave length of the frequency.

251. The frequencies from 26.965 MHz to 27.405 MHz are divided into 40 channels that are generally separated by a 10 KHz spacing.

252. See, http://www.monitoringtimes.com (accessed July 4, 2012).

253. Henry Campbell Black, *Black's Law Dictionary,* Fourth Edition (St Paul, MN: West Publishing, 1951), 1,385.

254. Henry Campbell Black, *Black's Law Dictionary,* 1,385.

255. Henry Campbell Black, *Black's Law Dictionary,* 240.

256. Vincent Bugliosi, *Outrage: The Five Reasons Why O.J. Simpson Got Away with Murder* (New York: W. W. Norton, 2008).

257. Charles Sturt University, *Business and Report Writing Skills* (Sydney: Charles Sturt University, 2008), 43.

258. Karen Twigg (Ed.), *Guidelines on Brief Preparation* (Canberra: Commonwealth Director of Public Prosecutions, 2003).

259. These points are adapted from those put forward by Karen Twigg (Ed.), *Guidelines on Brief Preparation,* 2.

260. The legal powers, rights and immunities of private investigators are located generally across four legal fields: the criminal law; the law of property; the law of contract (both in terms of contracts of employment, and the contracts that apply to paying customers); and employment law. These legal fields are dealt with in Rick Sarre and Tim Prenzler, *The Law of Private Security in Australia,* Second Edition (Sydney: Thomson Reuters, 2009), Chapter 3.

261. Rick Sarre, "Private Security in Australia: Some Legal Musings," *Journal of the Australasian Law Teachers Association,* 3(1/2), 45–54, 2010.

262. J. Catanzariti, "Staff Monitors Urged to Watch Legal Issues," *Weekend Australian,* September, 1998, 12–13.

263. S. Hardy and Tim Prenzler, "Legal Control of Private Investigators and Associated Private Agents: Profile and Issues," *Australian Journal of Law and Society,* 16(1), 2002, 1–20.

264. [2004] SASC 388.

265. See for example, J. Eisenberg, "Hear Today, Gone Tomorrow – Listening Devices Revisited," *Communications Law Bulletin,* 1993, no. 13, 12.

266. Note the introduction in December 2004 of the *Telecommunications (Interception) Amendment (Stored Communications) Act* (Commonwealth), which amended the *Telecommunications (Interception and Access) Act 1979* (Commonwealth) to provide that stored communications (such as emails) can now be accessible by persons with lawful access to the equipment (such as the Australian Federal Police) without the need to obtain a separate warrant.

267. Section 63. See *Kizon v Palmer* (1998) 100 A Crim Rep 86 at 92–101 per Northrop and Branson JJ.

268. (1991) 52 A Crim Rep 447.

269. (1997) 68 SASR 484 at 491 per Cox J, with whom Millhouse and Perry JJ agreed.

270. Walker, S *Media Law: Commentary and Materials,* Pyrmont, NSW: LBC, 2000, p. 894.

271. Supreme Court of New South Wales, unreported, August 8, 1997.

272. See G. Greenleaf, "'Interception' on the internet – The Risk for ISPs," *Privacy Law and Policy Reporter,* 3, 93, 1996; R. Magnusson, "Privacy, Surveillance and Interceptions in Australia's Changing Telecommunications Environment," *Federal Law Review,* 27, 33, 1999.

273. First introduced September 19, 2003.

274. See A. Wilson, "Federal Privacy Concerns Over New email Law" August 30, 2004. See Australian Broadcasting Corporation *Lateline* April 14, 2008, "Row Developing Over Federal Government Plan to Allow Companies to Intercept Emails in Order to Tackle Cyber-Terrorism."

275. For example, they will be able to receive and use intercepted information obtained by other law enforcement agencies, to acquire and use assumed identities, and to access financial transaction reports.

276. Press release, Minister for Justice and Customs, Senator Chris Ellison, July 29, 2002, "A New Standard Gauge for Law Enforcement."

277. Tim Prenzler and Michael King, "The Role of Private Investigators and Commercial Agents in Law Enforcement," *Trends and Issues in Crime and Criminal Justice,* 234, Canberra: Australian Institute of Criminology, 2002, 6.

278. Tim Prenzler, "The Privatization of Policing," in Rick Sarre and John Tomaino (Eds.), *Key Issues in Criminal Justice* (Adelaide: Australian Humanities Press, 2004), 286–288.

279. Tim Prenzler and Rick Sarre, "The Policing Complex," in Adam Graycar and Peter Grabosky (Eds.), *The Cambridge Handbook of Australian Criminology* (Melbourne: Cambridge University Press, 2002), 69.

280. *Crimes Act 1914* section 76B.

281. *Crimes Act 1914* section 73.

282. *Privacy Act 1988* section 18T, Invasion of Privacy Act 1971 (Queensland) section 10.

283. S. Hardy and Tim Prenzler, "Legal Control of Private Investigators and Associated Private Agents: Profile and Issues," *Australian Journal of Law and Society,* 16(1), 2002, 1–20.

284. FOI Act 1989 (Australian Capital Territory), FOI Act 1989 (New South Wales, FOI Act 1992 (Queensland), FOI Act 1991 (South Australia), FOI Act 1991 (Tasmania), FOI Act 1982 (Victoria), FOI Act 1992 (Western Australia), FOI Act 1982 (Commonwealth).

285. S. Woolley, "The 'Yes' case for Privacy" *The Australian,* March 5, 1998, 11.

286. First mooted by the House of Representatives Standing Committee on Legal and Constitutional Affairs, "In Confidence: A Report on the Inquiry into the Protection of Confidential Personal and Commercial Information held by the National Government paragraphs 10.6–10.8 (Canberra: Australian Government Publishing Service, June 1995).

287. Constitutional power was provided by the interstate trade power, and the telegraph and telephone power, since all information is transferred by telephonic means.

288. Editorial, *The Australian,* December 1, 1999, 12. See comments from the Acxiom CEO, Mr Andrew Robb in "The Chance to Get Exactly What You Want," *The Australian,* December 4, 1999, 23. Concerns were nevertheless expressed by the Financial Services Consumer Policy Centre. See Paul McIntyre, "Privacy Laws a Template for Trust?" *The Australian, Media,* December 20, 2001, 4,

289. The legislation covers all health businesses and any businesses that turn over more than A$3 million a year, which is around 60,000 businesses. This accounts for only about 3 percent of the two million businesses currently operating in Australia, but it does represent around 70 percent of all business activity.

290. The legislation is not retrospective, so there can be continued trading in existing lists. Individuals can still check information on pre-existing lists, and correct it, where that information is used after December 21, 2001. The Act does not impinge upon legitimate journalistic activities.

291. Michael King and Tim Prenzler, "Private Inquiry Agents: Ethical Challenges and Accountability," *Security Journal,* 16(3), 2003, 7–18.

292. In October 2003, a 17-year-old was arrested for hacking offenses in Brisbane, Queensland after the Australian High Tech Crime Centre received a complaint from an Australian Internet service provider. "Computer Hacker of Prominent Internet Service Provider to Face Court," *FindLaw,* October 30, 2003.

293. F. Bavinton, "The Relationship between Computer Hacking and the Law," unpublished MA (Research) thesis, University of Melbourne, 1998.

294. S. L. Miceli; S. A. Santana; and B. S. Fisher, "Cyber-Aggression: Safety and Security, Issues for Women Worldwide," *Security Journal,* 14(2), 2001, 11–28.

295. Richard Ericson, *Reproducing Order: A Study of Police Patrol Work* (1982), 15.

296. An attempt in Canada to bring some uniformity to the law (in this case, the law of trespass on private land) failed in the mid-1980s. See Philip Stenning, "Governance and Accountability in a Plural Policing Environment – The Story So Far," *Policing: A Journal of Policy and Practice,* 3(1), 2009, 22–33, 2009, p 28.

297. Security Professionals Task Force, *Results and Analysis of a Survey Conducted by the Interim Security Professionals' Taskforce to Identify the Views of Security Professionals in Australia Regarding the State and Future of Their Profession* (Canberra: Australian Government Attorney-General's Department, April 2008).

298. By way of example, see Heinz Duthel, *Rupert Murdoch: The Politico Media Complex Mogul* (Seattle, WA: CreateSpace, 2011), 346.

299. One of many examples reported in the world's press includes Brookes Barnes, "Pellicano and Lawyer Convicted in Wiretapping," *New York Times,* August 30, 2008, C1, New York Edition. See also the summary of "dubious business practice and outright corporate crimes" in Richard Eells and Peter Nehemkis, *Corporate Intelligence and Espionage: A Blueprint for Executive Decision Making* (New York: Macmillan, 1984), 138–139, as well as Jacques Bergier, *Secret Armies – The Growth of Corporate and Industrial Espionage* (New York: Bobbs-Merrill, 1975).

300. See for instance, Lewis D. Moore, *Cracking the Hard-Boiled Detective: A Critical History from the 1920s to Present* (Jefferson, NC: McFarland & Company, 2006).

301. Lewis D. Moore, *Cracking the Hard-Boiled Detective,* 25.

302. Matt Richtel, "Hewlett-Packard Settles 'Pretexting' Suit," *New York Times,* February 14, 2008, Business Section.

303. "Murdoch Aide Arrested in Phone Hack," *The Times of India,* March 14, 2012, 1; and, Ashis Ray, "Murdoch Aide, Hubby Held in Hacking Case," *The Times of India,* March 14, 2012, 15.

304. "The Prime Minister announced the setting up of the *Inquiry under the Inquiries Act 2005* in July [2011], following the exposure of alleged criminal activity, 'phone hacking,' at the News of the World. He announced the Inquiry to the House on 13 July 2011." http://www.levesoninquiry.org.uk/faqs/ (accessed August 23, 2012).

305. The Right Honourable Lord Justice Leveson, *An Inquiry into the Culture, Practices and Ethics of the Press,* Volumes I through IV (London: The Stationery Office, 2012).

306. Objectivity as an ideal was argued by Water Lippmann – see for instance, Peter Novick, *That Noble Dream: The 'Objectivity Question' and the American Historical Profession* (New York: Cambridge University Press, 1999), 162.

307. William F. Nolan, "Introduction," in Dashiell Hammett, *Nightmare Town Stories* (New York: Alfred A. Knopf, 1999), xiii.

308. The tragic death of Azaria was the result of a dingo attack and was the subject of the Hollywood motion picture starring Meryl Streep and Sam Neill – *Evil Angels* (Hollywood, CA.: Warner Bros., 1988).

309. This can be either a hardcopy file or an electronic record. In fact, notes that are made by hand in the filed can later be electronically scanned and saved to a policy file on a computer. Other options are possible depending on the work style and electronic devices available to the private investigator.

310. Anonymous, cited in Evan Esar, *20,000 Quips and Quotes* (Lyndhurst, NJ: Barnes and Noble, 1995), 709.

INDEX

A

Abagnale, Frank W., 70
ABC mnemonic, 189
agent. *See* private investigator
air marshal, 7
al-Qaeda Training Manual, 135
anti-gang intelligence. *See* anti-terrorist and
    anti-gang intelligence
anti-terrorist and anti-gang intelligence,
    97–111
    anti-terrorism defined, 98
    ease of attack, 108, 109, 110, 208n241
    gang defined, 99
    threat
        agents, 21, 27, 32, 97, 98, 101–102,
            103, 106, 107, 109, 111, 133,
            134–136, 137, 140, 142,
            203n146
        analysis, 100–102
        assessment, 103–106
        community, 102–103, 105
        identification, 102–103
        profile, 103
    two-phase investigation, 99–100
    vulnerability analysis, 106–110
ASIO. *See* Australian Security Intelligence
    Organisation
Australia, 5, 10, 17, 20, 21, 32, 35, 40, 86, 87,
    88, 90, 93, 122, 138, 147, 148, 167, 170,
    171, 172, 173, 174, 175, 176, 190, 195n7,
    197n41, 210n266, 211n289, 211n292
Australian Institute of Private Detectives, 40
Australian Security Intelligence
    Organisation, 20, 86, 172, 175

B

Bali, 3, 122, 189
black hole syndrome, 124
black swans, 106, 204n153
brief of evidence, 161
    See also prosecutions brief
Britain, 5, 17, 21, 22, 32, 35, 40, 86, 87, 122,
    147, 148, 167, 190, 195n6, 195n7,
    197n41
business intelligence, 19, 90, 91, 132, 140,
    197n35

C

Canada, 5, 17, 21, 32, 35, 40, 86, 87, 122,
    147, 148, 167, 190, 195n7, 212n296
car jackings, 99
Central Intelligence Agency, 6, 19, 24,
    202n122
Chamberlin case
    coroner's court hearing, 185
    wrongful conviction, 185–186, 212n308
Chapin, Dwight, 89
China. *See* People's Republic of China
C-I-A of information, 133–134
CIA. *See* Central Intelligence Agency
civil unrest, 98
    See also anti-terrorist and anti-gang
        intelligence
clandestine communication methods
    band defined, 147
    channel defined, 147
    communication plans, 150–151, 153
    communications security, 153–156
    crypto-maps, 155–156

Soviet Union, 20, 21, 115
special branch, 86
strategic intelligence, 25, 198n55
structured analytics
    counterintelligence, 141–143
    techniques/approach, 24, 28, 39, 198n49
    thinking, 6, 60
Sun Tzu, 59
surface web. *See* open-source information
surveillance countermeasures, 77
SWOT analysis, 28, 38, 61, 64–65, 67–68,
    200n89
    analytic matrix, 65
    explanation of threat, 200n89
Sydney Opera House, 108

T

tactical intelligence, 25, 30
    worksheet, 30
target profile
    background, 59–60
    context, 61
    example of, 65–68
    group-of-interest, 63
    initial considerations, 62
    intelligence gaps, 61, 64, 65
    parts of, 62–65
    person-of-interest, 61
    support to investigations, 60–61
    target-of-interest, 62, 63, 94, 200n88
target-of-interest, other terms used for,
    200n88
    See also target profile
technical surveillance countermeasures, 12,
    137, 184
template. *See* worksheet
terrorism
    forms of, 100
    narco-terrorism, 119–121
    pre-globalization, 115–116
    state-sponsorship, 115–116, 117, 120, 127
    use of crime, 122–123
thematic analysis, 50
threat, explanation of, 200n89
threat-agents, 21, 27, 32, 97, 98, 101–102,
    103, 106, 107, 109, 111, 133, 134–136,
    137, 140, 142, 203n146

    See also anti-terrorist and anti-gang
        intelligence
threat analysis, 100–102
    formula, 101–102
threat identification, 102–103
threat profile, 103, 104
training
    learning plan, 43
    lifelong learning, 42
    skills, 32–43
    value mapping, 40–41, 95
TSCM. *See* technical surveillance
    countermeasures

U

UK. *See* United Kingdom
UKUSA Agreement, 195n7
Ulasewicz, Anthony "Tony," 12
United Kingdom, 195n6
    See also Britain
United States, 5, 7, 17, 20, 21, 30, 32, 35, 40,
    56, 74, 86, 87, 88, 92, 119, 132, 137,
    147, 148, 156, 167, 184, 195n7
universe of information, 47–49
    digital domain, 47
    explicit knowledge, 48
    hard copy domain, 47
    tactic knowledge, 48
unknown variables. *See* black swans
USA. *See* United States

V

vulnerability analysis, 106–110
    formula, 107–108
vulnerability defined, 106

W

Watergate, 16, 88, 202n122
Wikileaks, 92, 136
worksheet
    counterintelligence, 142
    investigative intelligence, 30
    sensitive information protection, 143
    See also personal learning plan

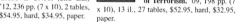